# NATIVE ALIENATION

CHARLOTTE COTÉ
AND COLL THRUSH
*Series Editors*

Charles A. Sepulveda

# NATIVE ALIENATION

*Spiritual Conquest
and the Violence
of California Missions*

UNIVERSITY OF WASHINGTON PRESS   SEATTLE

*Native Alienation* was made possible in part by the University of Washington Press Authors Fund.

Copyright © 2024 by the University of Washington Press

Design by Mindy Basinger Hill / Composed in Garamond Premier Pro

All rights reserved. No part of this publication may be reproduced or transmitted in any form or by any means, electronic or mechanical, including photocopy, recording, or any information storage or retrieval system, without permission in writing from the publisher.

UNIVERSITY OF WASHINGTON PRESS  *uwapress.uw.edu*

LIBRARY OF CONGRESS CATALOGING-IN-PUBLICATION DATA

*Names*: Sepulveda, Charles A., author.
*Title*: Native alienation : spiritual conquest and the violence of California missions / Charles A. Sepulveda.
*Other titles*: Spiritual conquest and the violence of California missions
*Description*: Seattle : University of Washington Press, [2024] | Series: Indigenous confluences | Includes bibliographical references and index.
*Identifiers*: LCCN 2024019721 | ISBN 9780295753263 (hardcover) | ISBN 9780295753270 (paperback) | ISBN 9780295753287 (ebook)
*Subjects*: LCSH: Indians of North America—Missions—California. | Catholic Church—Missions—California. | Missions—California. | California—Church history.
*Classification*: LCC E78.E15 S46 2024 | DDC 266/.2794—dc23/eng/20240904
LC record available at https://lccn.loc.gov/2024019721

♾ This paper meets the requirements of ANSI/NISO Z39.48-1992 (Permanence of Paper).

# CONTENTS

Acknowledgments  *vii*

PREFACE  Yaraarkomokreme' 'Eyoohiikmo Honuukvetmo  *xi*

INTRODUCTION  A Spiritual Conquest  *1*

ONE  Slavery and Disavowal: Native Alienation  *23*

TWO  Hallucinations of the Spanish Imaginary:
Mission Revival Architecture  *51*

THREE  Apocalyptic Colonialism: Environmental Devastation
of Wanáw Waníicha/Kahoo' Paxaayt/Santa Ana River  *77*

FOUR  Canonization Fodder: Resisting the Canonization
of Junípero Serra  *95*

FIVE  Ramona Redeemed? The Politics of Recognition
and Rematriation  *121*

CONCLUSION  The Afterlife of Native Alienation  *141*

Notes  *149*

Bibliography  *165*

Index  *179*

# ACKNOWLEDGMENTS

I began working on *Native Alienation* at the University of California, Riverside (UCR). The Ethnic Studies Department pushed me to think deeply about the histories of slavery and genocide. Through my studies, I began to see how the California missions were slave regimes, but it took me years to find a way to explain how that could be when Indians were not bought and sold by the priests. Through my interdisciplinary studies at UCR I found the way. I am grateful for my training at UCR and the faculty and students I studied with, including Lucha Arévalo, Maile Arvin, Pickels Camacho, Ren-yo Hwang, Jodi Kim, Anthony Macias, Jennifer Náhera, Robert Perez, Loubna Qutami, Michelle Raheja, Arifa Raza, Marlen Rios, Dylan Rodríguez, J. Sebastian, Brian Stephens, Cliff Trafzer, Luis Trujillo, Kēhaulani Vaughn, and Alex Villalpando, among many others. I give special thanks to Robert Perez for his guidance and mentorship through the PhD.

I began my first tenure-track position in the Ethnic and Women's Studies Department at Cal Poly Pomona. I am grateful for the time I spent with my colleagues there, and I thank Sandy Kewanhaptewa-Dixon, José Aguilar-Hernández, Anita Jain, Jocelyn Pacleb, Alvaro Huerta, Gilbert Cadena, Marcos Pineda, and Erica Ben for their support.

I am thankful for the support from the Ethnic Studies Division at the University of Utah and the School for Social and Cultural Transformation. The faculty and staff have been generous with their encouragement, including Lourdes Alberto, Elizabeth Archuleta, Maile Arvin, Andrea Baldwin, Matt Basso, T. Melanie Bean, Jaimie Crumley, David De Micheli, Edmund Fong, Lezlie Frye, Annie Fukushima, Sarita Gaytán, Claudia Geist, Alborz Ghandehari, Erin Graham, Kim Hackford-Peer, Kimberly Jew, Baodong Liu, María Morales, Ed Muñoz, Wanda Pillow, Susie Porter, Angela Robinson, William Smith, Armando Solorzano, Kathryn Stockton, Thomas Swensen, and Myra Washington. I am also thankful for the Department of Education, Culture, and Society at the University of Utah, including Cynthia Benally, José Gutiérrez, Leticia Alvarez Gutiérrez, Alexander Hyres, Frankie Laanan, Frank Margolis, William Smith, Wenyang Sun, Kēhaulani Vaughn, and Veronica Valdez.

*viii* ACKNOWLEDGMENTS

I want to thank my colleagues and relatives with whom I have served on land conservancy boards. At the Acjachemen Tongva Land Conservancy: Tina Calderon, Wallace Cleaves, Angela Mooney D'Arcy, Dustin Murphy, and Joyce Stanfield Perry. At the Tongva Taraxat Paxaavxa Land Conservancy: Wallace Cleaves, Kimberly Morales-Johnson, Tony Lassos, Casandra Lopez, L. Frank Manriquez, AnMarie Mendoza, Samantha Morales-Johnson, Ian Schiffer, and Jay Lamars. Thank you for working with me on land return and rematriation. I also must thank Angela Mooney D'Arcy and the Sacred Places Institute for Indigenous Peoples for your support and the Land Rematriation Fellowship.

Funding for the research in this book includes the Ford Foundation Postdoctoral Fellowship, the Eugene Cota-Robles Fellowship, and the Graduate Assistance in Areas of National Need Fellowship in Native American Studies. My manuscript was selected to be part of the Northwestern University Council for Race and Ethnic Studies Summer Book Manuscript Workshop, and I want to thank all those who gave me critical feedback, including Geraldo Cadava, Ji-Yeon Yuh, Shannon Speed, Courtney Berger, and Lourdes Alberto.

Thank you to the University of Washington Press for publishing my book. Special thanks to Editorial Director Larin McLaughlin and the editors of the Indigenous Confluences Series, Charlotte Coté and Coll Thrush.

Others I would like to thank are, in no particular order, Michael Lerma, Adrian Lerma, Alfred Flores, MyLinh Nguyen, Susie Parras, Erik Bayona, Lorene Sisquoc, Craig Torres, Mary Ann Irwin, Cindi Alvitre, Keith Camacho, Matias Belardes, Domingo Belardes, Wyatt Belardes, Josh Little, Brandon Duran, Jacque Nuñez, Mark Mendez, Joe Parker, Charlene Ryan, Kelly Stewart, Theresa Stewart-Ambo, Elizabeth Cameron, 'Inoke Hafoka, Daniel Hernandez, William Madrigal, Deborah Miranda, Jessa Calderon, Beyaja Notah, Cheyenne Reynoso, Megan Awwad, Rebecca Robles, Kiri Sailiata, Karalee Vaughn, Kai'a and Kawai Duro, and Marie, Stella, and Millie Davis.

I am thankful for my parents, Carolyn Thorsen and Charles Sepulveda, for always believing in me; to my stepparents Jim Thorsen and Gail Sepulveda; and to my extended family, including my cousins/brothers Matthew Davis and Tyler Davis.

And finally, thank you to my partner, Kēhaulani Vaughn, for her dedication, inspiration, patience, and love throughout the years, helping me make this book a reality.

I dedicate this book to my daughter, Kāheawai Neshuun Sepulveda, and our ancestors, whom we sing into our world every night.

# PREFACE

## Yaraarkomokreme' 'Eyoohiikmo Honuukvetmo

With two priests and ten soldiers, the Spanish established Mission San Gabriel Arcángel on September 8, 1771, at its first site, the village of Isankanga, also known as Whittier Narrows, California. With the assistance of the local Taraaxam (Indian people), they constructed a church and housing using the same native plants the Taraaxam use in making their kikiiy (houses). The materials used included shi'iiy (tule) and shaxaat (willow). The strangers to Tovaangar ("the earth," or Taraaxam homelands, the Los Angeles Basin and southern Channel Islands) were initially viewed as kuuyam (guests) by the Taraaxam, who offered gifts of food and shelter. Franciscan priest Francisco Palóu wrote in 1773 about the founding of San Gabriel: "Their friendship was such that on the day when the fathers moved to the mission the [Taraaxam] wished to carry their cots, and decorated them with many wild flowers from the fields. With the aid of so many workers these dwellings were finished in a few days, and a good stockade was also made for defense, and some corrals for the cattle and horses."[1] The Taraaxam welcomed the Spanish to their lands despite their differences and gave their labor to help make their guests comfortable, as all good hosts do.

A month after the mission was founded, it was reinforced with more soldiers, and relations between the Taraaxam and the Spanish rapidly deteriorated. The kuuyam failed to see the humanity of the Taraaxam, viewing themselves as superior. On October 19, 1771, Chichiinavro'am (Spanish people) rapidly became violent, and a soldier raped a Taxaat woman. The woman's husband was the tomyaar, or chief of the local village. He hurriedly assembled a group of nanaawme'ar (fighters) to execute justice against the predator. They came upon two soldiers on horseback, identified the offender, and the tomyaar directed his chuu'ar (arrow) at him. The attack was so sudden that the soldier did not have time to buckle his layered leather jacket, which could save his life from an attack. Nonetheless, he deflected the chuu'ar with his shield, avoiding the death the sovereign Taraaxam condemned him to.[2]

The two soldiers, according to California mission president and Franciscan priest Junípero Serra, left the mission that morning with one going "out to gather the herd of cattle . . . and [it] seems more likely to get [rape] himself a woman." After surviving the attack, the "soldier, along with some others, killed the principal Chief of the gentiles."[3] With a shot from his musket, the soldier killed the tomyaar, who fell to the ground dead where he stood. The gunshot, with its booming echo across the field and the immediate death of the tomyaar, shocked the Taraaxam. In the distance, more Chichiinavro'am soldiers rushed to the battle, and the Taraaxam fled, expecting a volley of shots to cut them down. Palóu explains that when the shot was heard at the mission, "the corporal came running with the rest of the soldiers" and found that they had just killed the Indian and "ordered his head cut off. Fixing it on a pole he placed it in public view to frighten the rest." The tomyaar's head on a post, according to Junípero Serra, was a "sign of triumph" by the soldiers.[4] A few days after the death of the tomyaar, additional soldiers arrived at the mission, making another attempt for justice, including now for the tomyaar, nearly impossible with the soldiers' weaponry, meant for war and not justice. The Spanish thought they had restored peace when they sent threatening soldiers to the Taraaxam village "to let the Indian know that they had no fear of them, and also to tell them to be quiet, for they had not come to make war on them unless they gave reason for it, and that they had already seen that the Spaniards had treated them well as long as they did no damage."[5] The Spanish considered this threat of violence as peace, and there would be no consequence for the soldier who had raped the Indian woman and killed the tomyaar.

According to Palóu, "After some days had passed the Indians came to the mission to beg for the head of their chief, which, through the supplications of the fathers, had already been removed from the pole, and they gave it to them. But, although they made no further attack, they did not frequent the mission until little by little fear left them."[6] Relations moving forward would be forever troubled by this initial violence and resistance. The Chichiinavro'am had the opportunity to be kuuyam but instead viewed themselves, their culture, and their authority as superior while viewing the Taraaxam as lacking humanity and as ideal flesh for sexual violence and spiritual possession. The Taraaxam resistance slowed Spanish progression in Southern California. The work of the missionaries, according to Franciscan scholar Zephyrin Engelhardt, "was seriously endangered; and their efforts for the spiritual and temporal well-being of the natives."[7] Mission San Buenaventura was planned to be the third mission founded by the Fernandeños in Southern California, directly after Mission San Gabriel. Still, it wasn't established until 1782, more than ten years later, because of the violence at San Gabriel and the Franciscans' difficulty in baptizing more Taraaxam.

The Taraaxam sought justice in other ways, and their spiritual people used medicine against the founders of San Gabriel. "Shortly afterwards the two ministers of the mission of San Gabriel fell ill and were compelled to return to [Baja] California. In consequence, the reverend father president [Junípero Serra] appointed in their places the two who were waiting there."[8] The founding of Mission San Buenaventura was delayed; however, the missionaries and soldiers at Mission San Gabriel would continue to inflict violence justified by a logic of possessing Native bodies, souls, and lands. Simultaneous Taraaxam resistance would be persistent, sometimes with nanaawme'ar but more often through refusal.

The sexual violence at Mission San Gabriel continued after this incident. Junípero Serra criticized Capitán Pedro Fages in his *representación* of May 21, 1773. Serra held Fages responsible for the actions of the soldiers, which prevented the priests' work of spiritually possessing the Indians. He wrote that six or more soldiers would leave the mission each morning and go to the Taraaxam rancherias looking for women. He stated, "the dexterity they possess in catching with the lasso a cow or a mule; and in the same manner they lassoed Indian women, in order to gratify their unbridled lust; and occasionally when the Indian men sought to defend the women, the soldiers killed several with musket balls." The Taraaxam boys, Serra writes, were not "safe from the lewdness of the soldiers" and were also raped by the men.[9] Serra states that one of the priests who departed Mission San Gabriel left because he was sick from the sexual violence being committed by the soldiers.

In the first year of San Gabriel, nothing, according to Serra, was accomplished other than violence against the Taraaxam. The priests had baptized only four children, two of whom were orphans. Serra wrote, "This mission

*xiv* PREFACE

gives me the greatest cause for anxiety; the secular arm down there was guilty of the most heinous crimes, killing the men to take their wives." These unimaginable scenes of subjection, particularly the rapes of women and boys, were not viewed by the Spanish judicial system or the priests as injuries individual Indians could experience.[10] Indian women, due to their race, gender, and religion, were viewed by the Spanish soldiers as sexually violable. Despite centuries of experience with evangelization and attempting to convert Indians in the Americas, "the Franciscans apparently never developed an effective policy to prevent the wholesale sexual exploitation of the native peoples whom they were supposedly helping," explained Luiseño-Cahuilla scholar Edward D. Castillo. He further clarified, "the problem was inherent in an 'evangelization' program that, in the final analysis, relied on military force to secure native acquiescence to Franciscan authority."[11] According to Serra's statements, he was primarily concerned about sexual violence because it was affecting the success of God's material and spiritual conquest and not because of the harm to Indian people and communities.[12] According to Serra, Taraaxam resisted missionization because of the gratuitous sexual violence and murders by the mission patrollers, causing some Taraaxam to become physically hostile toward the priests. Likewise, the military leaders in California were concerned that the violence against Indian women would cause the Indians to "learn to kill soldiers," as Governor Felipe de Neve y Padilla put it, and make conquest more difficult.[13]

Historian Antonia Castañeda explains that California Indian cultures were far different from the Spanish empire's violent conquest. Within California Indian social norms, rape "rarely, if ever, occurred."[14] The Spanish military's sexual violence against them worked against the interests of the colonial project. Yet Native bodies were, and continue to be, viewed similarly to their lands—as violable and possessable. Thus, conquest is gendered and sexualized violence, genocide, and land dispossession, all facilitated in California through spiritual domination, enslavement, and alienation from Native land and heritage.

Most reports about the missions during their time, particularly from priests such as Junípero Serra, list accomplishments, requests, and possessions. For example, Serra reported the number of Mission San Gabriel livestock: cattle, sheep, goats, pigs, horses, and mules. Along with the reported number of animals, Serra documented the number of neophytes (Indian converts to Christianity). He reported that between San Gabriel's founding and December 1774, they had "baptized 148 Indians . . . the Mission is composed of 19 new Christian Indian families with 154 persons, all of whom live at the Mission in their little huts of poles."[15] Although Indians were not viewed as chattel by the mission slave regime, their fungible, accumulable bodies were counted in enumeration lists alongside the cattle possessed by the mission. They were viewed as little more than domesticable animals who could expand the spiritual empire of church and state through their labor, violable flesh, and souls.

This book discusses the violence of conquest (that demands dispossession and the social death of the enslaved), including the environmental devastation, the legacy of romanticizing Indian death at the missions and its disavowal of slavery, and California Indian resistance. The history I tell is more than events; it is the processes of forming structures of possession—a continuum and an incomplete project that includes past, present, and future violations and gratuitous terrorism to land, bodies, souls, and collective ontologies. I do not write about violence to perform a spectacle of human or ecological suffering but to advance the analytical field of knowledge about California Indian histories and move beyond any discursive impulse toward benevolent missionary conquest and its erasure. I write to better understand the afterlife of conquest and Native California's spiritual possession.

With few exceptions, most scholarship on California's history lacks the stories of individual California Indians. A notable example centering individuals is an article by John Macias, who used the California mission records to write about Mission San Gabriel's history of violent racialization and what I call Native alienation. Martin Rizzo-Martinez's care for individuals colonized by Mission Santa Cruz makes *We Are Not Animals* a critical addition to the field. Moreover, I must highlight the importance of the Early California Population Project Database (ECPP) and historian Steven Hackel, who was instrumental in its creation. The work of all those involved in creating the ECPP has made this book possible. Yet too often the Indians at the missions have been nameless, faceless people from a generalized area against whom violence, or often benevolence, was inflicted. The erasure of Indigenous people's individuality and their detribalization within history results from

Painting by Ferdinand Deppe depicting Mission San Gabriel as it looked in 1828, 1900–1910, detail 2. California Historical Society, California Historical Society Collection, 1860–1960.

the colonial mission of Native alienation. The archival materials that historians rely on were created by those who documented what was important to conquest. My book includes individuals when possible, but I too rely on the colonial archive. Yet my telling of history is a genealogical meditation with a different purpose than that of traditional historians. Within the ECPP, I have found the baptismal records of some of my ancestors, including those from the village of Yaanga, also known as Yabit, and today as downtown Los Angeles.

My fifth great-grandmother, María Dolores, was born around 1767 in the village of Yaanga, approximately ten miles from the current site of Mission San Gabriel.[16] She was born four years before the founding of the mission by the Spanish. María Dolores married a settler (*poblador*), José Carlos Rosas, who was listed in the 1790 census as Indio from Rosario, Sinaloa, Mexico. Two of his brothers, José Maximo and José Marcelin, also married Indian neophytes, María Antonia from the village of Jajamobit and María Vejar from Cahupet in 1785 and 1796, respectively.[17] Rosas's father, Basillio,

PREFACE  *xvii*

is listed as *coyote* on the 1790 census—meaning he was mixed with an approximation of one-quarter Spanish ancestry and three-quarters Indian (of unknown tribal origin), and his mother, María Manuela Calistra Hernández, was *mulata*—approximately half Black and half Spanish. María Dolores and José Carlos Rosas married on July 4, 1784, at Mission San Gabriel, three years after he settled on her people's lands.[18] He was approximately twenty-six years old, and she was seventeen. She was baptized as a Christian on the same day as their wedding, and the priests named her María Dolores. The available archival documents do not include a Native name for her. Her parents' names are not listed either; the mission documents state that her parents were gentiles (nonbaptized Indians) from Yabit. The archive does not explain why they married, nor why she converted to Christianity. As I write in chapter 4, Spanish governance incentivized settlers to marry neophyte women.

José Carlos Rosas and María Dolores had nine children, including a daughter Severiana Josefa (b. 1787), whose baptismal record listed her as *razón*—meaning non-Indigenous, and short for *gente de razón*, "people of reason." Her sister, Serafina Antonia, born September 2, 1785, is listed as *mestiza* on her baptismal record. The same priest, Miguel Sánchez, recorded both baptisms. Several of María Dolores and José Carlos's children are listed as razón, including José Domingo, baptized at Mission San Juan Capistrano in 1801; the documents state he had an origin of "MISSION (1/2)." Baby José Domingo would sadly survive for only nine days before he was buried at the mission cemetery in San Juan Capistrano. His father, José Carlos, is listed in the burial record as a soldier of the San Diego Presidio.[19]

Daughter Serafina Antonia married José Antonio Romero in 1801 at Mission San Juan Capistrano, where he served as a soldier.[20] Both were recorded as razón—the priest viewed them as possessing whiteness despite her mother being listed on the marriage document as *india*. Romero and his parents were listed as being from the Los Angeles pueblo. Still, their ethnicity is not listed, and his ethnicity as razón does not provide evidence of his racial origins. I could not find a baptismal record for him or records for his parents other than on the marriage document. José Antonio Romero and Serafina Antonia Rosas had nine children. Six were baptized at Mission San Gabriel, and three were baptized at Mission San Juan Capistrano by seven different

*xviii*  PREFACE

priests. All were reported to be razón, including María Dorotea, baptized at San Gabriel in 1815.[21] She married Julián Antonio Chávez, and together, they owned land in Yaanga, in an area known today as Chavez Ravine.

The racial politics of Spanish California and, later, Mexican California are complex and messy. The genealogy can be challenging to trace, and the race recorded in the documentation is unreliable, changes, and tells us little about lived racialized realities. The opposite of *gente de razón* is *gente sin razón*—"without reason." *Sin razón* are the nonbaptized, the pagan, the non-Christian of any tradition, the Indian, the gentile, and the Indigenous from anywhere. The binary of razón and sin razón (Christian and non-Christian) flattens race despite a complex racial caste system. Indians and Blacks could become razón through baptism, making their racial identities difficult to trace since the primary documentation of people's lives in colonial California was the mission records, which leave out gentiles, who were at the bottom of the racial hierarchy. Nonbaptized Indians were considered "without reason" or humanity by the colonizers. The project of missionization as the driver of colonization in California functioned through the binary of Christian/non-Christian, working to alienate people from their non-Christian heritage and making people of color, including Indigenous, Black, and Afro-Indigenous peoples, complicit in the spiritual possession of land, bodies, and souls. It was a "spiritual conquest," as Serra called it, functioning through Native alienation to devour the souls of California Indians, ending the former worlds of individuals like María Dolores.

Today, the widely used definition for American Indian and Native American is the US government's legal designation: one must be a member of the 574 federally recognized tribes. American Indians can also include people who may qualify for citizenship but, for whatever reason, are not enrolled. American Indian is a political, not racial, identity. The widely used definition originates from an Anglo-American historical perspective. María Dolores and her descendants may not qualify as American Indian according to this limited definition. Today's Taraaxam tribal nations from Tovaangar, variously named Gabrieleño, Gabrielino, Tongva, Kizh, Shiishongna, and Shoshone, are unrecognized by the US government in a nation-to-nation relationship.[22] The descendants of María Dolores and other Taraaxam are not considered American Indian through the widely used definition, despite the gratuitous terror and trauma their ancestors experienced—this is Native alienation. No amount of genealogical or DNA evidence can change who is and who is not American Indian according to the Anglo-American political classification based on federal recognition.[23] This widely used definition erases the long history of racialization, including the gratuitous terror of enslavement, genocide, and sexual violence the Taraaxam are survivors of. The descendants of the Taraaxam are Indian, even if unrecognized by the latest colonial nation in a long history of colonialism.

The story of María Dolores and José Carlos Rosas only exists for my family through the archive. The alienation has been almost complete. Some cultural knowledge and materials, such as beautifully woven baskets, were passed down, but their stories have been erased. The stories of my grandmother's family on her maternal side are limited to a listing of church events and dates. And yet I feel fortunate to know their names, a little about their racial backgrounds, and that María Dolores was Yaavet. I can only imagine the gratuitous terror throughout the time she and José Carlos lived. Sometimes, the existing stories are sickening, such as the one I began with. But these stories need to be known. The people who lived the stories or lived during the same time also add to the significance of how we can emotionally connect to our kinship through a genealogical meditation on history and become speakers for the dead, telling their stories that colonialism has erased. We can never return to the worlds our ancestors inhabited, but we can learn from the past to create a better future.

The women and boys the predators went after with lassos could have included María Dolores and her relatives, even if their stories no longer exist and their descendants are not recognized as American Indians by the US government. This book is my attempt to better understand the lived experience of ancestors such as María Dolores, the changing world California Indians live in, the mission system built to possess their lands, bodies, and souls, and the afterlife of conquest founded on Native alienation.

Yaraarkomokreme' 'Eyoohiikmo Honuukvetmo

*We Remember Our Ancestors*

# NATIVE ALIENATION

# INTRODUCTION

## A Spiritual Conquest

California Indian histories after the beginning of colonialism abound with examples of refusal and resistance. They also demonstrate copious accommodation, integration, assimilation, separation, and other creative forms of survival. Refusal and resistance are as perpetual as colonialism; they will continue until Native peoples are free and have their land back. Despite California Indians' long history in California and their abundant forms of resistance after colonialism, historians and anthropologists have often separated California Indian history from California and global histories.[1] In doing so, they undermine tribal sovereignty and disregard the creativity of tribal communities, past, present, and future, to remain in relationality with a responsibility to the land. California Indians have primarily written the few texts connecting California history with present-day California Indian nations. These texts, including the one you are reading, comprise a long history of generative and restorative refusal.

Books such as *We Are the Land* by Damon B. Akins and William J. Bauer Jr., Rupert and Jeannette Costo's *Missions of California*, Cutcha Risling Baldy's *We Are Dancing for You*, and Deborah A. Miranda's *Bad Indians* are a few examples of California Indian writings in refusal of the non-Indian story of the vanished Native. These texts also correct the misinformation that California Indians were docile and easily conquered, which disregards California Indians' continuous and creative forms of resistance—from rebellions intent on killing all the Spanish priests and soldiers at the missions to regenerating cultural knowledge, including ways to rematriate and restore land and cultures devastated by colonialism. California Indians embody resistance as the survivors of genocide(s). Not only are their refusals often disregarded in the histories of California, but the gratuitous terror of conquest has too often been mischaracterized or disavowed. This book aims to add to the grammar of California history through theory and the archive to better understand resistance, ongoing dispossession, and Native alienation integral to the colonial project in California.

## 2 INTRODUCTION

Mission priest Gerónimo Boscana included early examples of refusal in what would later become a classic work on Acjachemem culture, titled *Chinigchinich*. Most historians and anthropologists who have studied this primary text have glossed over the resistance it reports. For example, in 1817, at Mission San Juan Capistrano, Boscana writes, "an Indian 35 years of age, who . . . was well instructed [in Catholicism], became afflicted with a dangerous disease, and died." Despite his knowledge of Christianity and being accompanied by priests, the neophyte refused the last rites. He would not confess and receive the sacrament of Communion—the Eucharist or body and blood of Christ. Boscana wrote, "No persuasion on the part of his friends, or exhortations of the priests, could prevail upon him to confess, and partake of the holy sacrament; at the bare proposal, he became frantic, and uttered expressions, which were contemptuous and blasphemous." Boscana visited the Indian before he died to "give him that consolation, which the promise of our holy religion impart to the penitent soul." Boscana's efforts were "all in vain," though, as the Acjachemem refused to be alienated from his ancestors' heritage as he was dying. Boscana's words were "ineffectual" and "spurned with disgust." The Indian "manifested such extreme grief and displeasure."[2]

Boscana describes what happened next in chilling detail: the Indian's "limbs were extended—the froth came from his mouth—his eyes rolled back into his head, presenting a true picture . . . of one condemned to the torments of hell; and three persons were insufficient to confine him." According to Boscana, someone in the room exclaimed, "Why do you not confess?" The Indian convert knowingly replied in anger, "Because I will not. If I have been deceived whilst living, I do not wish to die in delusion!" This was his last refusal—"his last words; for soon after, he expired."[3] His last rite/right was to refuse the colonial and spiritual conversion of Native land and life.

Father Gerónimo Boscana's example features the final refusal of one Indian at Mission San Juan Capistrano in 1817—refusing the holy sacrament and, with it, the work of the Franciscans in California to convert him to Christianity and fully possess his soul. He would not confess and take the sacrament, arguing that the missionaries had deceived him while he was alive and that he would not die in delusion. His refusal and pointed analysis targeted the Franciscans' spiritual conquest of his body, soul, and land. Scholars and Native peoples know Boscana's writings for his detailed description of Acjachemem lifeways, ceremonies, and creation stories. Despite his interest in Native origins and cultures, Boscana, as a priest, was deliberate in his responsibility to eradicate the same Indigenous ways of life that he documented. Boscana dominated and possessed Native bodies and souls for church and state. His writing reveals his and the colonizer's racialized views of Indians, comparing them to "a species of ape" with a "corrupt natural disposition." He also states that California Indians "do not manifest the least industry or ingenuity," and they do not tell the truth unless it is to injure another.[4]

Boscana's missionary work in California meant saving Indians from their inherent nature by bringing salvation through baptism. According to the missionaries, the Native who refused Christian hegemony was a blasphemous fugitive living outside society, vulnerable to punishment and premature death. *Native Alienation* argues that the logic organizing California Indian defense from colonialism is beyond isolated events, such as the individual Acjachemem who refused to confess his sins on his deathbed. The refusals and resistance of California Indians are in defense of their lives, their identities, their spirits, their lands, their genders, their sexualities, and their being—all of which the colonizer has sought to alienate, eliminate, expel, replace, and possess. Native refusals to colonial violence are continuous.

As a religion, Catholicism often portrays its involvement in colonialism as fundamentally benevolent. For example, Catholic priest and historian Father Francis Guest wrote in 1985, "as far as they [Franciscans] were concerned, the primary reason for the colonization of Alta California by the Spanish government was the evangelization of the Indians."[5] Their goal of evangelizing the Native is depicted as benevolent both by the church and by many professional and amateur historians. Missionary colonial violence against the Indians is often explained temporally as the standard treatment of all those who disobeyed. For example, historian James A. Sandos explains that colonial missionary violence was the same as any father disciplining his child.[6] The priests, accordingly, have been written about by many scholars as benevolent surrogate fathers, teaching and disciplining. The priests' punishment of the Indians was, therefore, not extreme, abhorrent, or an anomaly. As Father Guest explains, "these methods of punishing recalcitrant Indians

## 4  INTRODUCTION

had been common throughout New Spain for over two hundred years. . . . Franciscans . . . were following a precedent sanctioned by long-established custom and the example of thousands of missionaries."[7] According to this logic, Native resistance to Christianity and the fathers required spiritual punishment—not violent retribution. It was routine for the missionaries to chastise the Indians using shackles, stocks, and whipping to persuade their submission to the dominion of God.

San (Saint) Junípero Serra, the founder and president of the California mission system, wrote unemotionally about corporal punishment: "when it appeared to us that punishment was deserved, they were flogged, or put into the stocks, according to the gravity of their offense."[8] If Indians fled from the mission, the missionaries were obliged to send soldiers to return them to the missions and punish them so that the priests could continue providing them with spiritual teachings. Historian and Franciscan priest Zephyrin Engelhardt explained that once an Indian had become the possession of the missionaries, they were not permitted to return to a "wild and immoral life; because they bore the *indelible mark* of a Christian upon the soul which it was not allowed to desecrate."[9] Engelhardt's explanation reveals how the missionaries viewed baptized Indians as spiritual possessions bearing an "indelible mark" that could not be forgotten or removed. According to the missionaries, once the Indians were baptized, their freedom and sovereignty were extinguished.

The church no longer has the authority to physically harm its congregation (though many children remain vulnerable to priests' sexual violence). Despite the end of their physical punishments, there remain instances in which priests use their position of authority to both coerce their congregants and spiritually chastise recusants. Today, the penitent confessionary freely accepts spiritual punishment as an atonement for their sins. For example, after confession, the penitent must give penance—a punishment that makes amends for their sins. Penance can be as simple as saying prayers, such as the Our Father or Hail Mary prayers, a certain number of times. Confession was the sacrament Boscana offered to the dying Indian at Mission San Juan Capistrano in 1817 to complete the process of possessing his soul.

Priests also spiritually chastise through exorcism—a spiritual expulsion of demons from an individual or affected area. The Catechism of the Catholic

Church states, "When the Church asks publicly and authoritatively in the name of Jesus Christ that a person or object be protected against the power of the Evil One and withdrawn from his dominion, it is called exorcism. . . . Exorcism is directed at the expulsion of demons or to the liberation from demonic possession through the spiritual authority which Jesus entrusted to his Church."[10] From the description Father Boscana provided, the priest may have deliberated whether the Indian at San Juan Capistrano was demonically possessed—"one condemned to the torments of hell"—and if the priest should perform an exorcism.

Catholic priests have increasingly performed exorcisms in the United States in the wake of social unrest as a spiritual chastisement of resistance to state authority and periodic violent confrontations with police.[11] For example, an exorcism was performed in Portland, Oregon, on October 17, 2020, after months of peaceful Black Lives Matter protests in the city that included sporadic violence. Archbishop Alexander K. Sample led 225 congregation members to a city park, where he offered a rosary for peace and conducted the exorcism. Quoted in the Catholic journal *Crux*, Archbishop Sample candidly stated, "There is no better time than in the wake of civil unrest and the eve of the elections to come together in prayer."[12] The gathering for the exorcism took place six days after what had been called an "Indigenous Peoples' Day of Rage" in Portland, resulting in the toppling of Abraham Lincoln and Theodore Roosevelt statues.[13] Activists had scrawled "Land Back" and "Dakota 38" on the base of the Lincoln statue—a Native demand for the rematriation of land and remembrance of Native and American history that disrupts the multiculturalist discourse of Lincoln as the Great Emancipator.

Abraham Lincoln is responsible for the largest mass execution in the history of the United States, when thirty-eight Dakota were hanged in 1862 after being found guilty for their involvement in what is known as the Minnesota Uprising. Theodore Roosevelt gave several speeches that promoted racial genocide, including in 1886, when he declared: "I don't go as far as to think that the only good Indian is the dead Indian, but I believe nine out of every ten are."[14] The art added to the presidents' statues and their toppling was a response to the memorialization and glorification of anti-Indian violence and the continued military and settler occupations of Native lands. Archbishop Sample's exorcism was a direct response to Indigenous demands for land back.

*6* INTRODUCTION

On the same day as the Portland exorcism, the archbishop of San Francisco exorcised demons at San Rafael, California, after the statue of San Junípero Serra at San Rafael Mission, less than thirty minutes north of San Francisco, was toppled on October 12, Indigenous Peoples' Day, nationally celebrated as Columbus Day. Activists poured red paint on the statue and then used ropes to pull it down, breaking it at the ankles and leaving only the feet on the statue's base. San Francisco Archbishop Salvatore Cordileone, who performed the exorcism, explained, "We pray that God might purify this place of evil spirits, that he might purify the hearts of those who perpetrated blasphemy."[15] Cordileone's exorcism was nonconsensual. The activists who organized the statue's toppling did not ask for their politics to be exorcised—which, rather than demonic possession, is what the archbishop was responding to. However, his exorcism was not a metaphor; it was a spiritual chastisement in response to blasphemy and anti-Christian actions by the activists, whom Cordileone understood as possessed by evil.

Kānaka Maoli scholar Maile Arvin writes about what she calls the settler-colonial logic of possession through whiteness. She explains that this logic is anti-Indigenous, anti-immigrant, and anti-Black. Arvin offers the "logic of possession" in contrast to Patrick Wolfe's "logic of elimination."[16] She argues that possession expresses "the permanent partial state of the Indigenous subject being inhabited (being known and produced) by a settler society." Arvin describes possession as based on racial constructs: a "whitening" of Polynesians and similar processes through the discourse of mestizaje in Latin America that not only whitens but engulfs "the human and natural resources of a place for the purposes of white settlers."[17] Settler colonialism, according to Arvin, dispossesses Native peoples and invariably possesses their land and consumes what settlers find valuable from Indigenous people's cultures and spirituality, creating knowledge about them through white supremacy. Robert Nichols contends that dispossession is the theft of Native land and the simultaneous creation of possessable and consumable property. He also argues that dispossession in the context of slavery is theft of the body and self-ownership. Adding to Nichols's critical theorization, this book argues that conquest and the dispossession of Indigenous land not only transforms "nonproprietary relations into proprietary ones" and transfers "control and title of this (newly formed) property" but transmutes a place possessed with spirit into one possessed as property. The religious and secular transformation of place *with* spirit into place *without* alienates human–land relations toward a mechanistic view wherein the land is regarded as a resource and not as kin.[18] Furthermore, the mission subjected Indians to the theft of their bodies and souls. No longer, according to the Christian faith, would neophytes' souls be with their wicked ancestors after death; their souls were perpetually bound through baptism to be saved and delivered unto God—a logic of spiritual possession.

Building from Arvin, I propose that possession was enacted through a "spiritual conquest," as Junípero Serra called it in 1770. The spiritual conquest enforces a spiritual authority and, with it, the attempted spiritual possession of Native bodies, souls, and their land: what I call a logic of spiritual possession, enacted through Native alienation. In California the logic of conquest transformed Native land and life into spiritual possessions. The Spanish viewed the Indigenous people of California as fungible, enacting replacement through their own Native bodies possessed by European worldviews—they were not only replaceable but disposable. The Indians held captive and forced to labor at the missions were possessed by demonic white supremacy inextricable from land dispossession. Church and state viewed Indian (non-Christian) agency as evil criminality. Neophytes were rendered incapable of consent or of acting as adults with the freedom to make decisions for their future, but simultaneously they were held criminally liable and capable of agency.[19] For instance, the Indian fugitive was in violation of stealing themself, their labor, and their soul. Their crime was punishable with lashes, stockade, and imprisonment. They were not stealing property that could be bought and sold but possessions with spiritual significance and value for God. The Franciscan order had renounced property and did not possess Indians as such. In his analysis of the Franciscans, Giorgio Agamben writes that they viewed life, land, and bodies as "property but only as common use."[20] Land and bodies were for the work of God, used in common, and not property in a market. The Franciscan nonpropertied commons that created use of land and bodies meant the dispossession of the self for the Indigenous peoples of California and slavery without monetized property. The commons, in the Franciscan worldview, required the dispossession of Native land as a sacred relationship with responsibility and reciprocity—a Native alienation.

## 8 INTRODUCTION

For Father Guest, the Franciscans' primary reason for colonizing California was evangelization, and through baptism, the Indians were dispossessed of their precolonial bodily and spiritual freedoms. Father Guest bases his argument on the written records of the Franciscan missionaries who worked lovingly to harvest the souls of the Indians. Junípero Serra wrote in a letter to Father Juan Andrés in 1769 from San Diego: "Let them [priests] not think they come for any other purpose than to bear hardships for the love of God and the salvation of souls." In another letter to Father Andrés in 1770, Serra described the colonization of California as a spiritual conquest: "to stir up the world to undertake the spiritual conquest of this New World, and give to God, before very long, thousands of souls."[21] As Father Guest and San Serra argue, conquest can be understood as organized through a logic of spiritual possession enacted through Native alienation—the taking of Native bodies, souls, and their land for God. Serra clarifies that conquest was not secular without spiritual intent and rationalization. Indian death (their disposability), if it came after baptism, was celebrated as a harvest of souls for God.

Archbishop Salvatore Cordileone's exorcism in 2020 was an attempt to dispossess activists of their agency in determining whether a statue of Serra should memorialize conquest and, in turn, continue the spiritual possession of land and people. He characterized the activists as a "small, violent mob" and stated, "This kind of behavior has no place in any civilized society." The activists' actions can be described as a generational refusal—a continuum—as their numbers (approximately sixty people) included members of the Coast Miwok whose ancestors had been enslaved and possessed by the mission. Cordileone argued that the toppling of Serra statues was an attack on the Catholic faith, "not only on public property, but now on our own property."[22] In his statement, Cordileone underscores the logic of spiritual possession that views Native peoples as already dispossessed and simultaneously asserts a spiritual possession over Indigenous peoples and their lands; they are now "ours." As a process of acquiring lands and resources, colonialism has almost always included theological rationalizations, from the Doctrine of Discovery to Manifest Destiny. These justifications include a secular possession of the land and signify a divine spiritual possession. For some, these are long-gone eras; however, the Doctrine of Discovery remains US law and was cited by US Supreme Court Justice Ruth Bader Ginsburg as recently as 2005, signifying the continued spiritual possession of land, even if applied through secular legal reasoning.

Cordileone asserts that Junípero Serra was a "great man who sacrificed to protect the rights of the oppressed." According to Cordileone, those who vilify Serra are misinformed: "Father Serra and his fellow Franciscans renounced all worldly pursuits to give their lives to serving the native peoples and so protected them from the abuses of their fellow Spaniards."[23] Cordileone's assertion of a benevolent Franciscan mission contrasts how many California Indians understand their histories. Dean Hoaglin, one of the Coast Miwok of Marin who attended the gathering that toppled the statue at San Rafael, stated: "Our people were forcibly put here. They did not ask to come here to this mission. They were enslaved here."[24] These contrasting perspectives are shaped by Native experiences of dispossession and the colonizers' possession of Native peoples and their lands rationalized through faith. In the story told by Cordileone and others, though, the Indians' consent and agency outside of colonial law ended once they were baptized—they were the sole/soul possession of the mission.

My use of *possession* to explain conquest is slippery, as double entendre takes advantage of the dual meaning of *possession*: (1) the state of having, owning, or controlling something; and (2) the state of being controlled by a demon or spirit.[25] Conquest, as a logic of spiritual possession, functions through an ideology of ownership and control over land transformed into property (dispossession from the non-Christian) and the possession of Native souls with the intent of transforming and alienating Indigenous kinship and spirituality based on place. Possession also structures the colonial view of Native refusals and resistance as acts of evil and blasphemy. Possession indicates the various ways in which Indigenous peoples are inhabited and possessed by white supremacy. My use of *possession* reveals that conquest is not merely part of an incorporeal past but is an ongoing project that haunts the Native present and future.[26] California Indian resistance has long been a response to conquest as a spiritual project.

White supremacy, as an apparatus of racialized human dominance, was formed through conquest.[27] Reginald Horsman argues that the white race was articulated into being as a "separate, innately superior people" destined to bring "good government, commercial prosperity, and Christianity to the

San Rafael demonstrators topple Junípero Serra statue on Indigenous Peoples' Day, 2020. Photo by Douglas Zimmerman, *Marin Independent Journal*.

American continents and to the world."[28] The tangled history of racial formation has deep roots as a spiritually guided project that viewed non-Christians as invariably possessable, including their spirit, bodies, land, and labor. Conquest was informed by a Christian worldview in which a binary between Christian and non-Christian explained why some people could be free and others enslaved or eliminated.[29]

The hauntings of conquest and the mission continue in the lived experience of California Indians. Conquest produced traumas—what California Indian scholar Deborah A. Miranda, citing Eduardo Duran, calls "soul wounds"—that have been reopened repeatedly, including the 2015 canonization of Junípero Serra.[30] In many ways, this book was birthed through the trauma of Serra's canonization, which celebrated California Indian death. The haunting by the mission and the Franciscans is more than an apparition; it has material significance. Sociologist Avery Gordon writes: "If haunting describes how that which appears to be not there is often a seething presence, acting on and often meddling with taken-for-granted realities, the ghost is just the sign, or the empirical evidence if you like, that tells you a haunting is taking place." For Eve Tuck and Christine Ree, hauntings are by "those who have been made killable, once and future ghosts—those that had been destroyed, but also those that are generated in every generation."[31] The Indian, as an identity, is ascribed a meaning of past presence—a haunting. Much of the trauma California Indians experience remains unseen and absent within the historiography, similar to the Indian themselves—neither living nor dead "but interminably spectral"—and yet the historiography of a benevolent conquest is hypervisible.[32] Obscured are Native refusals and resistance to conquest, both in the past as well as to the ongoing systemic structures that articulate everyday life and thought. The haunting of conquest is perpetual, or as Tuck and Ree state, "Haunting lies precisely in its refusal to stop."[33] Native resistance has become so invisible contemporarily that when it visibly manifests, such as in the toppling of a racist statue or the occupation of land, it is understood as evil and blasphemous—as dispossessed incorporeal apparitions threatening to haunt the future rising from the ashes of history to (re)possess the land.[34]

Despite a conquest conceived through the possession of their souls, California Indians have continuously refused to let go of their spirits and become incorporeal non-beings that exist only in the past. Mohawk scholar Audra Simpson critically theorizes how "refusal" has been beneficial to her people's survivance. She explains that the Haudenosaunee maintained their genealogical and political connectedness through refusal, which resonates with California Indian histories: "As Indigenous peoples they have survived a great, transformative process of settler occupation, and they continue to live under the conditions of this occupation, its disavowal, and its ongoing life, which has required and still requires that they give up their lands and give up themselves." The "self" that Mohawk maintain, traced by Simpson, is in refusal to a force she identifies as "imperial, legislative, ideological, and territorial."[35] Building from Simpson's important work, this book argues that an analysis of colonialism and Indigenous refusal must consider the haunting of spiritual conquest.

Until recently, conquest was rarely articulated secularly. Hubert H. Bancroft, an early historian of California, wrote in 1886 that the "period of Spanish occupation" is a history of "spiritual conquest and mission development."[36] In his 1959 biography of Junípero Serra, Franciscan priest

## 12 INTRODUCTION

Maynard J. Geiger agreed with the spiritual purpose of conquest: "Many documents, such as the instructions issued to Portolá by Gálvez, insist that the principal object was to extend the Catholic faith among the pagans of the territory." Geiger explains that the Spanish colonization of California utilized a method he names "pacific conquest—namely, the Christianization and civilization of the Indians through the Spanish mission system."[37] Within *Native Alienation*, I reinsert the spiritual purposes of conquest into my critical analysis of California Indian refusal, which has always responded to the spiritual theft of their lands. Land dispossession and evangelization were the primary purposes of the California conquest, revealing a logic of spiritual possession. California Indians' creative and diverse responses to conquest were refusals to Native alienation, the attempt to eradicate Indigenous ways of life that connect them through kinship to land and each other.[38]

## The Spanish Imaginary

Vastly mythologized and profoundly understudied, California's missions have played a central role in defining the state's identity. Native labor forced under the direction of Spanish priests and soldiers constructed twenty-one missions from San Diego to Sonoma from 1769 to 1823. Starting in the late nineteenth century, professional and amateur historians constructed mythology about the missions as beneficial to the Indians, a process I have named the "Spanish imaginary." This mythology is pervasive in K–12 education and, with few notable exceptions, in California's historiography. *Native Alienation* engages critical mission studies to offer a more complex understanding of California's history by centering the experience and resistance of Native peoples. This volume historicizes the relationship between enslavement, dispossession, environmental degradation, and the construction of the Spanish imaginary, which infiltrates California's everyday existence and identity.

The resistance of California Indians to the missions, historically and in the current moment, is drastically understudied and undertheorized. *Native Alienation* responds to this significant gap by chronicling the long-standing resistance to the power relations that continue to threaten, destroy, and alienate California Indian relationships to place. Few previous works have theorized resistance to the mission beyond singular historicized events of the past. *Native Alienation* locates California Indian resistance beyond historical events' temporal and spatial boundaries. Instead, it views resistance as targeting the logic of conquest and enslavement that continue despite emancipation and inclusion in the settler state.

*Native Alienation* draws from an extensive array of archival documents. Some primary sources I analyze include handwritten Spanish legal documents, including several from 1778 that feature Native resistance at San Juan Capistrano. Although written by Spanish military officials, they provide insight into Native thought on Spanish colonialism and motives for resisting. These archival documents allow me to make crucial connections between the overlapping dynamics of enslavement, place, environmental degradation, and resistance. The archive enables me to retrofit historical memory and respond to the political urgency of amending the historiography. Maylei Blackwell explains that retrofitted memories are those produced through countermemory using fragments of histories that have been "disjunctured by colonial practices of organizing historical knowledge or by masculinist renderings of history that disappear women's political involvement."[39] Furthermore, Blackwell explains, retrofitted histories create new forms of consciousness and desire for social transformations. Retrofitting history is more than a recuperation; it disrupts dominant narratives. To retrofit archival documents, I give them an Indigenous reading—what Deborah A. Miranda describes as "a reading that enriches Native lives with meaning, survival, and love."[40] The archive ultimately helps us better understand who we are and can be used to genealogically meditate on our histories. *Native Alienation* analyzes history and recovers stories of Native resistance and refusals to the missions and their afterlife. It also assists in transforming the ways we understand California Indian lived histories that have long been trapped in a fantastical, romanticized Spanish past. This book pushes beyond the limited scope of a history text in its use of transdisciplinary theory to critically analyze historical events and the ongoing impact of conquest.

At its core, this book tells stories. As Native novelist Thomas King writes, "The truth about stories is that that's all we are."[41] California Indians are the stories they tell about themselves, which often disrupt the stories told about them within the traditional disciplines of history and anthropology.

*14*   INTRODUCTION

Some of the stories that California Indians tell were collected by historians and anthropologists who had agendas and biases when they collected data from their informants.[42] Learning to read the archive and sifting through the racism to tell the stories that highlight Native lives is a challenge. As L. Frank Manriquez (Tongva and Acjachemem) explains, learning how to reconnect with the ancestors within the collections can be "heart-breaking." While visiting a museum collection in France, Manriquez could hear and feel the "boxes of my people's lives, and they were like muffled crying coming from these shelves and these boxes."[43] The archive, as Black studies scholar Sandra Harvey clarifies, "exists as a historically created set of colonial power relations that forecloses our status as sovereign and complex political subjects even as we often turn to it for proof of our existence."[44] Retrofitting the memories of the ancestors through the colonial archive is a form of trauma that some of us choose to expose ourselves to in a refusal of their existence only as ghosts filed away in non-Indian collections.

Drawing from theoretical and methodological approaches developed in Native and Indigenous studies, Chicana/x studies, Latin American studies, and Black studies, *Native Alienation* approaches critical mission studies from a disciplinary intersection that understands the celebration of conquest as a celebration of California Indian genocide. Furthermore, conquest cannot be separated from enslavement, land dispossession, and white supremacy; I do not compartmentalize conquest as the separate logics of slavery or settler colonialism. The conquest of California depended upon enslavement *and* settler or military occupation. My research emerges from the evidence that colonization works as a process of erasure, that "settler colonizers come to stay: invasion is a structure not an event."[45] Settler colonialism in California, as in much of Latin America, comprised both land dispossession and forced labor during the Spanish and Mexican regimes into the early decades of American colonialism. Native studies scholar Shannon Speed elaborates, "In places like Mexico and Central America, such labor regimes (*encomienda, repartimiento, hacienda*) were often the very mechanisms that dispossessed indigenous peoples of their lands, forcing them to labor in extractive undertakings on the very land that had been taken from them." Furthermore, she states that Indigenous peoples were subject to "both territorial dispossession and bodily exploitation." Robin D. G. Kelley also provides a compelling example of settler colonialism in South Africa where the colonizer "wanted the land *and* the labor, but not the people." Kelley argues that under this system, "the native is simultaneously 'eliminated' and exploited."[46] Both Kelley and Speed's consideration of settler colonialism as more than land dispossession mirrors the way *Native Alienation* applies settler-colonial theory to its analysis of California history, where the settlers eliminated, dispossessed, and exploited the labor of California Indians.

In most of the book, however, I do not use the term *settler colonialism*, as I prefer to use *conquest* to move beyond the discourse of settler colonialism as only land dispossession and erasure, as articulated by Patrick Wolfe and other settler-colonial studies scholars, without bodily exploitation or possession of Native peoples. *Conquest* also enables me to move beyond the binary of settler colonialism (Native/settler) and its debate. I discuss conquest as a structure that consumes land and life, subsuming the corporeal into its project without consent. As Black studies theorist Tiffany King writes, "the relations of conquest have far from abated" and still need inclusion in critical inquiry "among scholars in Black studies, Native studies, ethnic studies, settler colonial studies, and other critical discourses."[47] Conquest is structured through genocide and slavery—often discussed within the context of the United States as Black slavery (racial chattel) and Indigenous genocide. Conquest in California, however, functioned through the simultaneous genocide and enslavement of California Indians whose land and bodies were possessed by a white supremacist regime intent on possessing their souls as well.

The possession and expansion of space in California depended upon the unrestrained use of the Native body and soul. Learning from Black studies scholars such as Hortense Spillers, Saidiya Hartman, and Orlando Patterson, I argue that conquest produced a California Indian fungibility, similar to Black fungibility, that rendered them possessable, exchangeable, and disposable. The Spanish conquest of California intended to establish and maintain empire in the eastern Pacific by possessing the bodies and souls of the Indigenous peoples already living there. This project depended upon the captive Native body from which, as Spillers argues, "we lose any hint or suggestion of a dimension of ethics, of relatedness between human personality and its anatomical features, between one human personality and another,

*16* INTRODUCTION

between human personality and cultural institutions." The Indian within the missions is just an Indian, a mission Indian, a neophyte—they remain merely a captive, demarcated through their captivity. As Spillers argues, conquest disrupted thousands of years of culture, starting in the fifteenth century with the invention of Blackness, transported across the Middle Passage through and devoid of time and space, repeatedly undergoing change alienating the being from their land and heritage.[48] As the cornerstone of the California conquest, the mission possessed and counted the number of souls at the missions, including those who were baptized, married, confirmed, and buried by the church. Junípero Serra, for example, reported that it was his duty to give the governor an itemized report of "the number of souls and the properties belonging to each mission." In his enumeration of 1778, he wrote, "When they are all added up, there would appear to be two thousand, nine hundred and forty-seven Baptisms."[49] The fungible, accumulable, and disposable Indian was counted as a captive corporeal soul possessed and delivered to God through baptism, similar to the slave ship log that counted Black bodies being transported for delivery to slave auctions.

As Saidiya Hartman explains, "The experience of slavery made *us* an *us*, that is, it had created the conditions under which we had fashioned an identity. Dispossession was our history."[50] The mission slave regime reconfigured distinct sovereign peoples and villages into Indians (gentiles and *neofitos*) and later Native Americans. Before the mission, there were no Indians in California. Before the mission, there were no Juaneños, Gabrielinos, Luiseños, or Serranos. These names are the *us* that were created by the mission slave system and later by Mexican and American colonizers without consent. Not only were these tribal identities changed and reorganized, but the people themselves were divested of their peoplehood, including their names for themselves, their sovereignty, their total social organizations, and their languages that provide meaning to their worlds. Once missionized, the only identity and social system that Indians could have was in relation to soldiers, fathers, and the church. And even after the adobe mission walls had crumbled, no longer holding them captive, and church and state had begun legally emancipating them in 1826, the identities formed through missionization would continue to shape their social relations, alienated from their precolonial selves. The opposite of dispossession is not possession, though, as Leanne Simpson and Native feminists have argued.[51] The opposite is returning to a rite relationship with the land as kin—the ultimate form of resistance that many California Indians are struggling for—at the center of decolonization and a futurity based on relationality in which the *us* is formed outside of alienation and enslavement. Indigenous futurity is thus premised on all people living in relationality as stewards of the earth. This is an alternative reality to the historical alienation of land and kin at the heart of slavery and colonization.

To discuss and theorize the spiritual conquest of California through the enslavement of California Indians at the missions, I rely on Black studies and the Black radical tradition. The theories produced about slavery and Blackness far exceed anything produced in Native studies about conquest as both genocide and enslavement. Furthermore, scholars of the California missions have largely disavowed slavery, and few, if any, studies have theorized the logic behind enumeration lists of Indians as possessions.[52] Instead, colonization has been written about as a natural progression; as historian Steven Hackel writes, "Spanish exploration, conquest, and colonization were carried out by soldiers and administrators, who scoured frontiers in search of Indian kingdoms to conquer and plunder, and by Catholic missionaries, who were often among the most zealous and intrepid agents of colonial expansion."[53] For Hackel and many mission studies scholars, conquest was something "carried out," not a long-term genocidal structure that perpetually possessed Indian bodies and their souls, a structure in need of study through critical theory.

*Native Alienation* examines what I call the Spanish imaginary—the historiography and popular culture that romanticizes the missions. Through its romanticization, the history erases the effects of missionization on Native people, and in particular, the experiences of Native women. I borrow from Chicana studies scholar Emma Pérez's use of the "colonial imaginary" and apply it to California's mission project. Via Foucault, Pérez argues that all history consists of discursive formations. The colonial imaginary forms interstitial gaps—the unheard, unthought, and unspoken.[54] This is most evident in how California Indian women are often disregarded within the historiography and their leadership in refusal and resistance. In the praxis of disrupting the colonial imaginary, the stories of California Indian women are

## 18 INTRODUCTION

vital to filling the interstitial gaps, particularly those that have romanticized and sexualized them in the discursive formations of history.

I use primary and secondary sources to construct an Indigenous methodology that does not tell the story of colonialism in strictly chronological order. My research aims to understand how we got here and where we are going, linking the past to the present and, in turn, theorizing a decolonial future. To do this, I situate the experiences and knowledge praxis of California Indians, specifically focusing on my tribal nations, Taraaxam and Acjachemem, and our relatives from Southern California as a genealogical meditation. I begin each chapter with an alternating story of Taraaxam and Acjachemem resistance, retrofitting the archive and improving our understanding of resistance and conquest.

## Disruptions

In 1987 Rupert Costo and his wife, Jeannette Henry Costo, disrupted the Spanish imaginary in their edited volume, *The Missions of California: A Legacy of Genocide*. The Costos wrote their book in response to the campaign for Serra's canonization: "this book was born—out of necessity, the necessity to have the truth known in the context of the project for Serra's canonization." Building from that work, *Native Alienation* responds to a canonization that has already occurred. My book is only possible because of the interventions the Costos, other California Indian scholars, and their accomplices have made. Like *The Missions of California*, this book centers Native love for their lands and their ancestors. This love endures despite centuries of what Rupert Costo called "the rapacity of three invasions—Spanish, Mexican, and American" that facilitated a nonconsensual alienation. These invasions devastated the populations of Native people who have lived in California for thousands of years. Still, they were unsuccessful in completely crushing their spirit to resist, as Rupert Costo demonstrated through his dedication to the California Indian peoples.[55] It is unfortunate that more than thirty years after *The Missions of California* was published, my book is even necessary. It remains necessary to continue telling the truth because the pervasive discursive myth of the missions still has power. We must repeat the truth until we completely change the discourse of conquest. Moreover, outside California

Indian communities, their histories remain relatively unknown, including within the fields of Native studies and ethnic studies. What I have gathered and constructed in the following chapters is only a fragment of the story.

*Native Alienation* is a disruption to California mission historiography and a genealogical meditation on the practices of California Indian knowledges that informs their resistance. It offers disruptions, generally understood as the process of unsettling something—a break, disturbance, or interruption in the normal continuation of an event, activity, or process.[56] Specifically, I disrupt the imaginary of mission studies scholars who, for example, disavow the enslavement of California Indians by the Spanish missions despite primary source literature that describes Natives as enslaved, including by California Indians themselves. This disavowal functions much as in Holocaust deniers who, despite all evidence necessary, will not concede that genocide occurred, or those who say that Israel is a perpetual victim and thus incapable of genocide against Palestinians. Many historians who have studied the missions also conclude that *genocide* is not an appropriate descriptor. Historian James A. Sandos, for example, writes: "Some have even directly and wrongly accused the Franciscans of genocide."[57] Sandos is not alone in his assessment.

Disrupted are the everyday imaginings of architecture permeating a landscape that has been profoundly altered for the settler to inhabit. Cities such as Santa Barbara and San Juan Capistrano were developed using mission motifs, and nearly every suburb in California has mission-style homes with red-tiled roofs and stucco walls. However, the disruptions analyzed also include conquest itself, which wholly disrupted Native ways of life and caused a radical change to their existence. For example, mission studies scholar Lisbeth Hass characterizes conquest as "the process that extends the political, economic, and social domination of one empire, nation, or society over another one." Although Hass, in her significant scholarship, explains that conquest "involves the systematic acquisition of land," she does not consider Native forced labor, on which the Spanish or Mexican colonial project relied, as essential to conquest or Native alienation.[58] Furthermore, she does not define conquest as a spiritual project despite centering the mission in her historical analysis, and, most problematically, she does not write about conquest as genocide.

*Native Alienation* disrupts the historiography of the conquest of Cali-

*20* INTRODUCTION

fornia. It argues that conquest is an ongoing structure of spiritual possession that has retained its "spiritual" aspect long after conquest's secularization—the action or process of converting something from a spiritual to a nonreligious possession.[59] Conquest's logic of spiritual possession functions through heteropatriarchy, exploitation, and consumption—it is a predatorial logic. As a land-centered project that perpetrates genocide on the Native population and relies on the exploitation of labor, conquest is rationalized multifacetedly, including through theology, science, and other racialized discourse. It is also often considered beneficial—bringing civilization and advanced technology to the wilderness.

## Structure of the Book

I begin chapter 1 by contradicting the mythology of a benevolent conquest of California by examining slavery and California Indian resistance. The list of scholars who disavow slavery at the California missions is extensive. The scholarly conclusion that Indians were not enslaved has primarily been rooted in an inadequate definition of slavery based on chattel, coupled with the Spanish imaginary. According to leading scholars in Black studies, property is not constitutive of enslavement.[60] A theoretically rigorous analysis of slavery at the missions could potentially transform the discourse about California's conquest and settle the prolonged debate on how to define California Indians' coerced labor and captivity. To date, few scholars have argued that California's missions comprised a slave regime. This chapter centers on Native women's experience of enslavement and sexual violence within the *monjerío*, the women's dormitory/prison where girls as young as six were separated from their families.

Chapter 2 critically examines the Spanish imaginary and its influence on California's architecture, which was built to resemble Catholic missions. I explore the construction of the Mission Inn (1903) and Sherman Indian School (1902) in Riverside, California. Both buildings were designed by the same architect, using an early form of an architectural style that would later be used throughout California. Mission Revival–style architecture adds to popular understandings of California missions as benevolent. The beauty of the architecture conceals the brutality of the mission system. Furthermore,

I examine tourism as critical to the selection of the Mission Revival style and the location of the Indian boarding school, which had pronounced resemblances beyond architecture to the violent regime of the mission. This chapter explores the Spanish imaginary to disrupt the everyday experiences of Californians. The built environment surrounding us is not benign—it seeps with genocidal aspirations.

In chapter 3, I argue that the colonial violence against land and Indigenous people in California can be best understood as apocalyptic. This chapter explores the use of apocalypse in theological and literary terms, comparing the fictional environmental devastation of Cormac McCarthy's novel *The Road* to the real colonial violence against Southern California's largest riparian ecosystem. The Santa Ana River, during two and a half centuries of colonialism, has been devastated—both destroyed and brought extreme grief. Humans have been separated from this environment by its damming and entombing in concrete.

In chapter 4, I examine resistance to Serra's canonization, focusing on two events held in 2015. The first is Walk for the Ancestors—a walk begun by a California Indian woman and her son from the northernmost mission at Sonoma to San Diego. I was part of a delegation from the Juaneño Band of Mission Indians (Acjachemen Nation) that welcomed them to San Juan Capistrano, where we talked about the mission's history and held prayer for the ancestors. The second event was a guerrilla-theater trial of Serra that found him guilty of genocide and crimes against humanity. I acted as an expert witness at the trial. Furthermore, chapter 4 disrupts the Catholic Church's apologies for its involvement in colonialism.

Then, in chapter 5, I provide answers and complicate the question Duane Champagne and Carole Goldberg pose in their 2002 article, "Ramona Redeemed? The Rise of Tribal Political Power in California."[61] Ramona is the title character of Helen Hunt Jackson's 1884 novel, which aided the creation of the Spanish imaginary and popularized tourism to the state. Jackson's romance novel closes with the end of the Spanish/Mexican *rancho* period and the Native population's dispossession. Finally, in the conclusion, I argue that despite economic gains made by some federally recognized tribes who choose to have gaming, California Indians remain dispossessed, and their histories of genocide and enslavement are celebrated. Nevertheless, they are a community rising, and their nations are actively addressing systemic racism in creative ways.

Through the five chapters of this book, I intervene in the historiography of California to better explain the afterlife of conquest, offering what I have named "Native alienation" to describe human collective disconnection from a nonexploitive relationship to land. California Indians are centered throughout, yet I hope that a diversity of scholars and communities can build upon my broader intervention, rethinking the stakes of conquest and its afterlife, which has demanded an alienation of humans from the earth.

# ONE

## Slavery and Disavowal

### *Native Alienation*

On the night of October 25, 1785, the priests and soldiers at Mission San Gabriel were targeted for execution by Taraaxam leaders of six independent and sovereign villages who had come together to rid their land of colonizers. In his 1787 report about that night, Spanish legal adviser Galindo Navarro wrote that gentile (nonbaptized) Indians "forced their way into Mission San Gabriel" armed and "intent on killing the missionary Fathers and the soldiers." Navarro reports that the soldiers at the mission had received advance notice and "were waiting for the Indians and managed to surprise and apprehend them."[1]

Several scholars and amateur historians have told the story of the Taraaxam uprising of 1785 under the leadership of Toypurina and Nicolás José. Toypurina is perhaps the most famous Taxaat woman, and rightfully so. She resisted colonialism as a woman leader; her story is both inspiring and tragic. The story's details are often misunderstood and taken to dramatic lengths, including Thomas Workman Temple II's influential 1958 article, "Toypurina the Witch and the Indian Uprising at San Gabriel." Historian Steven Hackel critiques the overdramatization and fictionalization in Temple's account and suggests that the other leaders, including Nicolás José, should receive more attention for their role in the uprising.[2]

Navarro wrote that the "principal instigators of that plot" were "neophyte Indian Nicolás José, who was from the mission, and the gentile Indian woman Toypurina, who was from the *ranchería* Jaichivit." In his analysis of the events, Navarro felt that Toypurina was instrumental in planning the attack, describing her as "reputed to be the most clever and shrewd among those of her nation." Navarro, in his reading of the trial transcript, provided Nicolás José's motivation for organizing a defense against Spanish violence and states, "he was angry with the Fathers and with the corporal of the escort because they would not allow him to perform his dances and his gentile

*24*  CHAPTER ONE

indecencies. Nicolás José availed himself of Toypurina so that she would induce the Indians to revolt."

From the Spanish military writings on the uprising, Nicolás José encouraged Toypurina to join his effort because she had the influence to persuade "the six *rancherías* into banding together for the fight." Toypurina provided leadership and militarily planned the attack. According to Navarro, Toypurina "made them believe that when they arrived at the mission they would find the Fathers dead as a result of her crafty powers." Following her strategy, "The only thing the Indians would have to do would be to overpower the corporal and the soldiers, whom they would catch off guard and unprepared." In her coerced confession, Toypurina explained that Nicolás José had influenced her and that "she was angry with the Fathers and the rest of the people from the mission because they had gone to live and settle on their land." Hackel suggests that Toypurina was upset by the priests and soldiers and the neophyte interlopers living at the mission, settling on her people's land. His assertion may be correct; resentment toward Native interlopers (Indians living on land or territory they do not have genealogical responsibility for) by Taraaxam people continues today. However, she targeted only the priests and militarily orchestrated only the soldiers' deaths, not neophytes'—whom she planned to free from their captivity by executing the guards. It is difficult to believe that Toypurina, as a Taxaat from the village of Japchivit in the San Gabriel Mountains, would have had a sovereign view of the land at Mission San Gabriel as hers, casting neophytes from elsewhere as enemies, as Hackel asserts. The only other plausible reading of "the rest of the people from the mission," as stated by Toypurina, that includes neophytes would be her disgust with those who had willingly converted. Finally, Weshoyot Alvitre (Tongva) argues that Toypurina orchestrated the uprising while pregnant, a fact most scholars have not commented on.[3] Toypurina's pregnancy could also have influenced her decision to resist for the benefit of Taraaxam future generations.

This summary of events, written by the Spanish governance, can be retrofitted to better include Taraaxam reasoning, motivation, and methods for resistance at Mission San Gabriel in 1785.[4] The Taraaxam resisted in response to settlers' living on their land without permission and to the priests' and soldiers' prohibiting the neophytes from practicing their precolonial dances, spiritual ceremonies, and religions—part of the Native alienation of the mission that disconnected the Indians from their ancestors' ways of life. Resistance is more than an event. Haunani-Kay Trask states, "resistance takes organization, planning, and a tenacity that develops and sustains individual and group capacities."[5] Toypurina and Nicolás José organized through their culture in their capacity to resist imperialism. The two reasons for Taraaxam defense against colonialism, often termed *rebellion*, can be analyzed through Spanish records as a response to Spain's logic of conquest of California, which required Native slavery and Native alienation: the elimination of the Native to clear the land through multiple dispossessions and the spiritual possession of California Indian minds, bodies, and souls. Andrés Reséndez shows in *The Other Slavery* how the causes of the Pueblo Revolt of 1680 included slavery and the exploitation of Indian labor by the missionaries and military; similarly, this chapter theorizes Indian resistance to the California missions as a response to enslavement.[6] The Kumeyaay in 1775, the Acjachemem and Payómkawichum in 1778, the Taraaxam in 1785, the Chumash in 1824, and the thousands of refusals: the California Indians defended themselves from the gratuitous violence of slavery at the missions, pueblos, presidios, and ranchos.

Taraaxam violence in 1785 temporarily unified six independent villages against Spanish colonialism. Violence was a cleansing force; it could enable the Taraaxam to cure the colonial infection of their land. This infection initiated land dispossession and the transformation of Indigenous relationships to place, characterized by the consumption or possession of another's life.[7] Violence emboldened the Taraaxam to collectively imagine liberation from the brutal force of conquest, which involved genocide, enslavement, and environmental damage. Their agency as demonstrated within the archive allows us to appreciate their complex lived experience beyond being read merely as victims of unspeakable terror or as the beneficiaries of a "superior" culture. The Taraaxam, as Trask writes about Native Hawaiians, are "stewards of the earth, our mother, and we offer an ancient, umbilical wisdom about how to protect and ensure her life."[8] The Taraaxam undertook collective resistance in 1785 through their intelligence as stewards of the earth.

The colonizer saw his actions not as violence but as benevolence; he was there for the good of the Natives. This is clear within the trial transcripts from the 1785 uprising and the second question asked of the accused: "After they had been warned and advised repeatedly to keep the peace and tranquility,

## 26 CHAPTER ONE

why did they come armed to kill the Fathers and the soldiers when they had never been harmed by us at all?"[9] Through their presumed authority and violence, the colonizer attempts to control what is considered harm and crime. The colonizer deems Native worlds and the acts of resistance to conquest that they inspire as evil. "The 'native,'" according to Frantz Fanon, "is declared impervious to ethics, representing not only the absence of values but also the negation of values. He is, dare we say it, the enemy of values. In other words, absolute evil."[10] The Spanish declared Taraaxam resistance in 1785 as violence without precedent, for the Indians had not been harmed by them. Peace was the responsibility solely of the colonized subject, despite that Spanish colonialism in California existed only because of Spanish self-imposed authoritarian violence.

All those who were arrested for their part in the 1785 uprising were physically and spiritually punished for their wickedness, though they had harmed no one. The governor of California, Pedro Fages, oversaw their sentencing and punishment:

> In addition to the time they have spent in prison, each of the five Indians who participated in the matter pertaining to the first question will receive the punishment of twenty to twenty-five lashes as a means of changing their behavior. This punishment will be carried out in the presence of everyone so as to serve as a warning to all. They will receive from me the most serious reprimand regarding their lack of gratitude. I will reproach them for their wickedness. And, I will show them how they were tricked into allowing themselves to be controlled by the woman whose cunning acts have no power against those of us who are Catholics.
>
> With these and other appropriate admonitions, they will be set free with the precautionary warning that the slightest indication that they are reverting to their previous behavior will not be tolerated. We will make them understand that they are being punished with moderation, out of compassion and love we have for them. For in that manner, we can assure ourselves that they are completely reformed.[11]

The uprising leaders, Nicolás José and Toypurina, were banished from San Gabriel and their world and homelands, Tovaangar. The weapons the Taraaxam used to defend their lands and lives were not the arms they carried but their humanity. It was not aggression or anger that motivated the Taraaxam but freedom and their love for Tovaangar. Translated, Tovaangar means "the world," but it is more than the physical earth or Taraaxam traditional territory. Tovaangar represents Taraaxam relationality to all things. Tovaangar is Taraaxam intelligence, responsibility, reciprocity, relationality, way of being, and future. Furthermore, Tovaangar represents Taraaxam spatial history and human geography in relation to the power of a conscious and living land. Removing Nicolás José and Toypurina from San Gabriel and the greater Los Angeles area was a calculated method to remove them from Tovaangar, their land-based intelligence system, spirituality, kinship, heritage, and spatial histories—it was Native alienation.

The Spanish government officials markedly focused on Toypurina's role in the uprising. Her involvement was spectacularly "wicked" within the Spanish gendered system. She was described as "crafty," with "cunning powers," respected and feared by other Indians for her "superstitions," having "spells," and "corrupting the Christians." In their report, the Spanish used all the metaphors one might use to call a woman a witch or *hechizera*. The report stated that Toypurina was the principal instigator who had persuaded and "tricked" other gentiles (nonbaptized pagan Indians) into participating in the uprising, including sending the male chief, Tomasajaquichi, into battle. To reform Toypurina, the Spanish coerced her into being baptized a Christian, transferred to a mission far from her home, and married her to a Spanish soldier (Manuel Montero) whom she had children with. Toypurina's baptism and removal from her homelands by the Spanish severed her from her kin and denied her of her ancestors. In 1786, as a prisoner at Mission San Gabriel, she gave birth to the child she had been pregnant with during the uprising. The baby boy was baptized with the Spanish name, Nereo Joaquin. In 1787, five months before the death of her son, Toypurina was baptized at Mission San Gabriel, and the priests renamed her Regina Josefa. Her baptismal record indicates she was twenty-seven years old and married to an unnamed gentile Indian. After her banishment from Tovaangar, she married Manuel Montero in 1789 at Mission Santa Cruz. Two of Toypurina's children with Manuel Montero were recorded at their baptisms by the Mission San Luis Obispo priest as razón and as half mission, like the contemporary baptismal records of my ancestors.[12]

Only through Christianity and heteropatriarchy, through having her

28 CHAPTER ONE

spirit, sexuality, and gender controlled, would Toypurina be set "free," and the Spanish thus assured she would not revert to her former wicked behavior. Reform from her evil ways meant being possessed and reduced from her precolonial life. Transforming Indigenous conceptions of gender and sexuality was central to the spiritual conquest of California enacted through enslavement. The example of Toypurina demonstrates the foundational method of missionary control over the Native body and sexuality through possession and Christian marriage, alienating Indians from the heritage of their ancestors, lands, and informal kinship relations.

The example of resistance to conquest in 1785 by the Taraaxam/Gabrieleño at Mission San Gabriel demonstrates a rare contemporary California Native perspective on colonialism and the reasons for their insurgency. It also displays Taraaxam reliance on their culture and spirituality as a means for resistance, what we might now consider, in the words of Native feminist scholar Leanne Simpson, radical Indigenous nation-based resurgence. The insurgency was not organized to repossess the land from those who had dispossessed it. The Taraaxam intended to rematriate and return the land to a rite relationship beyond patriarchy's stranglehold. Their purpose was with responsibility and relationality that was political, cultural, social, and spiritual, while being reciprocal, complex, nonlinear, affirmative, and generative.[13] Taraaxam had lived for thousands of years as stewards of Tovaangar, and Toypurina's legacy lives within each new generation that carries their identity, culture, and demand for land back. Their purpose was the same as all enslaved, ex-enslaved, and those avoiding becoming slaves. According to Saidiya Hartman, their desire is for their kin, as slavery severed kinship and denied ancestors.[14] For the Taraaxam and other Native people, the land is their kin. Moreover, freedom for Native peoples has always been collective and not regulated through individual rights granted by state governments. As Black studies scholar Angela Y. Davis writes, freedom is a constant struggle for a collective life free from violence, exploitation, and oppression.[15] Expanding on Davis's meaning of freedom, I argue that freedom should always include the more-than-human. Anticolonial collective organizing must be about more than human freedom; it must center the power of the earth and human beings' responsibilities, which colonialism alienates us from.

This chapter's opening story of resistance at Mission San Gabriel in 1785 allows me to reposition resistance and refusal as confrontations with conquest and its logic of spiritually possessing Native land, bodies, and souls that predate the European invasion of the Americas. Colonialism, as Linda Tuhiwai Smith argues, "brought complete disorder to colonized peoples, disconnecting them from their histories, their landscapes, their languages, their social relations, and their own ways of thinking, feeling, and interacting with the world."[16] In this book, I name the disorder *alienation*.

This chapter critiques the scholarly disavowal of the enslavement of California Indians by the missionaries and provides a more complex discussion of enslavement beyond slaves as property or labor. My critique of mission studies' disavowal of Indian enslavement by the missionaries is informed by Black studies' theorizations of what slavery entails beyond chattel. My critique is not personal or dismissive of any authors' scholarly contributions. It is a critique meant to intervene in the field, which has struggled to define Indian captivity and labor at the missions. Furthermore, in this chapter, I analyze the inextricability of slavery from conquest vis-à-vis the Doctrine of Discovery. I argue that land dispossession and loss of sovereignty are contingent on enslavement, just as slavery enforced through conquest is contingent on land dispossession.

## Enslavement at the Missions

Mission studies scholars have long debated how to define California Indians' coerced labor and captivity at the missions. Scholars have used a number of terms to describe Indian laborers, including *wards*, *vassals*, *peons*, *serfs*, *inmates*, *laborers*, and *children*. The vast majority of scholars who have studied the mission, even those critical of the institution, have disavowed slavery. Critical scholars have used terms such as *slavery-like* to explain how the conditions resembled slavery but were not enslavement.[17] Furthermore, many historians have described the intent and ideology of the colonizer and defended the mission as differentiated from slavery based on the absence of chattel. Scholars' anxiety with using the term *slavery* to describe the mission system appears rooted in their inadequate definition. Slavery is much more complex, as I will demonstrate, than the simplistic definition applied by many mission studies scholars who have relied on one question to make their

*30* CHAPTER ONE

determination: Were Indians bought and sold? This simplistic definition of slavery, dependent on human chattel, misidentifies the complex violence of enslavement central to the conquest of California that violently dominated Indians, dishonored them, and natally alienated them from their ancestors.[18]

The conversion of Indians to Christianity and the "apparent anomaly" of the "Catholic church stoutly declaring slavery a sin, yet condoning the institution to the point where it was itself among the largest slaveholders," as Black Studies theorist Orlando Patterson explains, "has baffled so many Anglo-American historians."[19] By disavowing slavery, scholars have unwittingly and resolutely contributed to romanticized understandings of Spanish colonialism. They have also erased racial and colonial brutalities, legitimating missionary morality and Indian wickedness. Scholarship supported by theory that identifies Indians as slaves could transform the discourse about California's conquest that has too often narrated its benevolence.[20]

Scholars have long compared missionization in California to enslavement, even as they have disavowed the presence of slavery itself due to the absence of chattel. For example, historian Benjamin Madley, in an otherwise excellent article, asserts that the California missions "blurred lines" between slavery and incarceration. He confidently writes that the "Franciscans could not legally buy and sell California Indians. Thus the system cannot be strictly defined as legalized chattel slavery." However, he confirms that Franciscans held Indians as "unfree laborers while seeking to morally transform them."[21] Madley compares the missions to slavery, concluding that their characteristics were closer to imprisonment. Like many fellow scholars, Madley alleges that "unfree" Indians held captive and forced to labor at the missions should not be considered slaves since they were not chattel. Madley's assertion that slavery is limited to chattel aligns with most mission studies' scholarly thinking.

Historian James A. Sandos claims that there are stark contrasts between chattel slavery and the treatment of Indians, principally the purposes of the for-profit plantation and the mission, whose only profit was spiritual conversion. Sandos asserts that critics of the missions, including contemporaries whose firsthand accounts depict enslavement, misunderstand the status of Indians as children who required discipline and guidance. He argues that the priests did not buy and sell Indians, "something that no Franciscan father could do to his son or daughter." According to Sandos, the neophytes owed a debt in return for the spiritual instruction they received, what he names "spiritual debt peonage."[22] The forced labor they provided was in payment for their debt. Sandos's definition of slavery is contingent on Indians as property, and he argues that priests were instead in loco parentis—legally responsible for Indians (children) as parents.

Anthropologist Kent Lightfoot writes about the scholarly debate of whether neophytes were enslaved at the missions. He states: "Mission scholars differ in their opinions as to whether the labor system in the missions constituted communal, slavery, or feudal-like conditions." He remarks that this is not a new debate, as many of the contemporary Europeans who visited the missions also grappled with whether the Indians were slaves or not. In his opinion, the labor system of the missions "combined some aspects of communal principles and some of enslavement, and is probably best described as a form of forced communal labor." In Lightfoot's comparative analysis, he found that the missions resembled plantations: the neophytes could not leave without permission, they were forced to labor, they extracted surplus from the mission estates, and they were loaned out to the presidios and pueblos without compensation for their labor (though compensation went to the mission). However, he concludes that despite the similarities between the plantation and the mission, the Indians were not enslaved "because the padres could not legally sell or own the neophytes."[23] Lightfoot's conclusion is based on slavery as a system dependent upon chattel and the question of whether the missionary fathers could sell Indian bodies.

Chicanx literature scholar Rosaura Sánchez examines the primary source texts of the Californios—their testimonios. She, like many scholars, has difficulty defining Indian forced labor and captivity at the missions and makes a comparison to slavery: "The Indians who were proselytized and brought to the mission were tied to it almost as bonded servants." She further explains: "They were not serfs in the strict sense of the word, but they had no control over their labor power or over the means of production." Despite not having control over their labor, Sánchez concludes that Indians were not slaves of the missions: "For all practical purposes they were enslaved, except that they were not *property* of the mission or of the church. They could not be sold, but their labor could be leased to the *presidios* or townspeople, for example, and

## 32  CHAPTER ONE

their wages went to the mission coffers."[24] The definition Sánchez applies in her analysis of enslavement is contingent upon humans as physical property able to be traded for money.

Scholars Laurence Shoup and Randall Millikin found similarities between the missions and slavery: forced labor, physical abuse, a caste system, denial of property rights, restrictions on technological development, frequent resistance, and an inability to leave. They concluded that missionization was "similar to feudalism" but in praxis "resembled slavery."[25] One of the elements of slavery they found missing from the missions was the sale of people.

Historian Steven Hackel argues that "Indian laborers at the missions were neither enslaved nor indentured"; instead, they "were a semi-captive labor force." Demographer Sherburne F. Cook writes, "The term slavery has been uncritically applied" based on a lack of "personal ownership."[26] Economist Marie Duggan declares an end to the debate of whether Indians were enslaved or not: "Whatever mission Indians were, they were not slaves—if only because Indians were not property and African slaves were."[27] Historian Lisbeth Haas also distinguishes neophytes from African-descended slaves "by their legal status as chattel." Theologian George Tinker calls the missions "virtual slavery," and historian James J. Rawls describes Indians inhabiting a "twilight zone between freedom and slavery."[28] Both professional scholars and amateur historians have disavowed slavery. Others, such as journalist Alison Lake, leave it to the reader "to decide for themselves whether the mission system was an instrument of slavery and indoctrination and to what extent it was a product of its time and its origin in Spanish colonial doctrine."[29]

One of California's first historians, Hubert Howe Bancroft, wrote in 1886 that the Indians were toiling "practically as slaves."[30] Bancroft notes the similarity but ultimately disavows the enslavement of California Indians by the missionaries. Historians Damon B. Akins and William J. Bauer, in their excellent 2021 book *We Are the Land*, indicate that the mission "labor system resembled slavery" and "exposed Indigenous People to violence." They also reference James A. Sandos's "spiritual debt peonage" and contend that once baptized, Indians were required to live the rest of their lives in the missions, unable to leave, in return for being educated about God.[31]

Whether the scholar was studying the missions in 1886 or today, as of this writing, most have compared Indian labor and captivity to slavery, yet they ultimately deny that Indians were enslaved at the California missions. Those who have named the violence as enslavement have not sufficiently argued how their studies disrupt the more prevalent disavowal based on a limited conception of slavery as constituted by property. The academic breadth and number of scholars who disavow slavery at the California missions are extensive. The researchers quoted here, and many others, have long compared the missions with slavery, and most could not dismiss the comparison completely. The scholarly conclusion that Indians were not enslaved has largely been rooted in an inadequate definition of slavery that reduces enslaved people to chattel.

## Slavery and Social Death

According to Orlando Patterson, property is not constitutive of slavery. He defines slavery as "the permanent, violent domination of natally alienated and generally dishonored persons." Although chattel plays an important role in discussions of slavery, it is not one of Patterson's constitutive elements. "To define slavery *only* as the treatment of human beings as property fails as a definition," Patterson argues.[32] His seminal work on slavery, extensively cited in Black and ethnic studies, contrasts with the definition applied by most mission studies scholars (from many fields) who rely on a definition of enslavement contingent on property.

Patterson outlines three constitutive elements of the slave relation. First, slavery is based on violence and coercion, and most distinguishably, the potential for the slave's total powerlessness to the authority of the enslaver.[33] Powerlessness is often enforced through continuous and routine violence as motivation for compliance with coerced labor and captivity. The violence of slavery also exceeded the routine, according to Saidiya Hartman, who stated that violence included "abuses that were beyond description: excremental punishments, sexual violation, and tortures rivaling anything the Marquis de Sade had imagined."[34] Historians have provided extensive documentation of the unimaginable violence used to enforce the Indians' Christian domination at California's missions. Early California historians, such as Bancroft and Theodore Hittell's 1885 *History of California*, catalog violence

34    CHAPTER ONE

at the missions, as do many current scholars. Moreover, primary source documents written by Russian and European explorers and merchants who visited the missions from the late eighteenth to the mid-nineteenth century documented violence as well.

Several travel narratives compared the treatment of the Indians with slavery, including the first non-Spanish foreign travelers to California during the mission period. Jean François Galaup de La Pérouse visited Mission San Carlos Borroméo de Carmelo in the Monterey Bay in 1786 and compared Indians to Black slaves in the Caribbean:

> The colour of these Indians, which is that of negroes; the house of the missionaries; their store-houses, which are built of brick, and plastered; the appearance of the ground on which the grain is trodden out; the cattle; the horses; everything, in short, brought to our recollections a plantation at St. Domingo or any other West-India island. The proselytes are collected by the sound of a bell; a missionary leads them to work, to the church, and to all their exercises. We observed with concern that the resemblance is so perfect that we have seen both men and women in irons, and others in the stocks; and lastly, the noise of the whip might have struck our ears.[35]

Some of the fiercest critiques of the mission and comparison to enslavement come from the Spanish themselves. In 1780 California Governor Felipe de Neve stated, "the Indians fate [was] worse than that of slaves."[36] In 1798 Spanish missionary Padre Antonio de la Concepcion Horra wrote, "The treatment shown to the Indians is the most cruel I have ever read in history. For the slightest things they receive heavy floggings, are shackled, and put in stocks, and treated with so much cruelty that they are kept whole days without a drink of water."[37] The missions' gratuitous terror has been well documented, and mission apologists cannot refute the violence through their justifications—most commonly that the Indians were punished as children. This argument has been circulating in California mission historiography ever since, most notably in the work of James A. Sandos.

The scholar's argument of the Indian's treatment as children derives from the priests. For example, Father Estevan Tapis states in a letter to Father Fermín de Lasuén in 1800:

As regards the Indians, these are the punishments we use with that judgment, appropriate, absolute, and our very own, with which natural fathers punish their legitimate and beloved children. We have conceived these neophytes, seeking them with zealous solicitude and reducing them so that they embrace Christianity. We were the ministers at their baptism in which they received the life of grace. We assist them with the holy sacraments and do what is necessary and useful to instruct them in the maxims of Christian morality. We use that authority, then, which God gives to fathers for the good education of their children, now exhorting, now chiding, now punishing whenever necessity calls for it.[38]

The priests understood their position as innately superior. They believed they were culturally and spiritually capable and responsible for determining punishments for other adults who they viewed as children based on race, origin, and spirituality. The priests' role as arbiters of violence was justified by their position as men of God. In the priests' determination, Indians were dishonored as children, heathens, and animals, possessable by the church, state, and ultimately, God. Through the priests' reasoning, they may have whipped the Indians as any father would his child. Still, the priests additionally viewed the Indian as nonhuman and gente sin razón, increasing the amount of pain a priest was willing to inflict on Indian flesh.

The priests determined what was punishable, what was considered criminal, and what was against the law of God, rendering the Indian powerless in making these determinations. The priests' routine use of cudgels, whips, irons, stocks, shackles, and imprisonment were assaults on the body as much as on the soul as penance for sin. The punishments were spiritual, not mere punishment to the flesh. Just as the penance after confession today may be in repeating Our Fathers and Hail Marys a certain number of times, at the mission, it was routinely a penance of twenty to twenty-five *azotes* (lashes), enduring grotesque humiliations, and being put in stocks on display or wearing shackles and irons that made it possible to continue being productive workers. The most common crimes the neophytes were punished for included having sex outside of marriage, stealing from the mission or military, refusing to perform assigned tasks, and committing fugitivism (abandoning the faith, taking with them valuable possessions, and returning to their

36  CHAPTER ONE

wickedness). Additionally, they were punished for murder, assault, armed robbery, conspiracy to rebel, and destruction of mission or military property.

Above all else, the priests sought to control and punish Indian sexuality that was non-monogamous, premarital, and queer. Controlling Native sexuality through routine violence functioned to indoctrinate them into the faith and often relied on other Indians who had been selected for positions of power. For example, women's punishments were not always public spectacles. Robert Heizer writes, "Women were punished separately and privately, being flogged by other women in the female quarters. Public punishment of women caused much unrest among the men, hence the privacy."[39] The Spanish views of the Indians as nonhuman necessitated routine violence. As mission priest Father Fermín de Lasuén explained, "It is evident that a nation which is barbarous, ferocious and ignorant requires more frequent punishment than a nation which is cultured, educated and of gentle and moderate customs."[40] The mission slave institution relied on routine violence and the threat of violence to control the bodies and souls of the Indian slaves that the priests had determined were not fully human, even after baptism.

The second and perhaps most important constitutive element of slavery, according to Patterson, is natal alienation: the process of severing the slave from their genealogical relationships so that their social standing only has meaning through enslavement. The violence of enslavement extracted labor and held the slaves in captivity; however, it also included processes for creating slaves. These processes repeatedly transformed free humans into slaves, including their children, creating generational temporality. Grace Hong describes natal alienation as a "process of severing someone from forms of meaning articulated through normative kinship, so that person no longer has meaning and value as an uncle, a grandchild, a cousin, a son of the tribal chief, a wife of a tradesman. Instead the slave's only tie to any social group is as the possession of the master."[41] In addition, Patterson emphasizes that enslavement culturally isolated slaves from the social heritage of their ancestors: "That they reached back for the past, as they reached out for the related living, there can be no doubt. Unlike other persons, doing so meant struggling with and penetrating the iron curtain of the master, his community, his laws, his policemen or patrollers, and his heritage."[42] Indian neophytes, such as Nicolás José were prevented from and punished for dancing, singing, and continuing the non-Christian ceremonial ways of their ancestors that taught them the laws and protocols of their culture and governance. Moreover, missionized Indians who fled from the mission to reclaim their ancestral roles in their community were swiftly hunted down by soldiers and severely punished, as were those who provided sanctuary for fugitives.[43] The missionaries criminalized Native life, making it next to impossible for neophytes to integrate their ancestors' worlds into their lived experiences.

The missionaries, with the assistance of the Spanish military, systematically removed Indians from their home communities and villages—a strategy called *reducción* in Spanish. This legal scheme reduced the number of Indian villages and congregated Indians to a village under the control of the mission, termed *congregación*. As Duane Champagne and Carole Goldberg explain about Mission San Fernando:

> The movement of Indians to the mission and away from their villages and settlements was an attempt to discourage kin-based lineage relations, erase lineage land-ownership, and displace lineage leadership. Traditionally non-differentiated lineage territories, kin-based leadership, and kin-organized economy were disrupted and congregated into land-trust relations and a more differentiated economy that was managed and controlled by the missionaries.[44]

The congregación villages were often multicultural, composed of Indians from different villages, clans, tribes, and linguistic groups with the goal of detribalization. The Spanish objective was to break Indigenous reliance on kinship connections, communal ownership, and relationality to lands and economies, thereby making the Indians reliant on the social organization of the mission. Franciscan scholar Francis Guest, an apologist for mission violence, explains the natal alienation of the mission in its intent to separate Indians from their ancestors: "the Spanish mission system, in virtue of its long established policies and methods, separated baptized Indians radically from their habitat in the forest, from the ways of their forefathers, from their native observances and customs, from their entire culture." Hugo Reid, a Scottish immigrant, became a Mexican citizen and married Victoria

Bartolomea, a Taxaat maniisar (daughter of the tomyaar) from the village of Comicranga.[45] In 1852 Reid wrote that the Taraaxam "language has deteriorated so much since the conquest," indicating the extent of the alienation from their heritage that missionized Indians had survived. Reid remarks that before colonization, the Indians of Los Angeles "were the free, natal possessors of the soil, living contented in a state of nature."[46] Although Reid may present a romantic view of precolonial Native life, it is evident that the mission, with its congregación villages, enforced a legally sanctioned cultural genocide that natally alienated neophytes from their land and heritage.

Building on Patterson's description of natal alienation, I argue that slavery for Indigenous peoples is alienation from human–land relationships. Through an Indigenous worldview, land is more than a resource or material object; it shapes Natives' social world, forming identities and relationships. Vine Deloria Jr. explains that "American Indians hold their lands—places— as having the highest possible meaning, and all their statements are made with this reference point in mind."[47] Both pre- and post-mission Southern California Indians, for example, identified with their village of origin and familial ancestral relationships contingent on place rather than on a tribe with centralized governance composed of many villages. The mission enforced a natal alienation that attempted to isolate Indians from their ancestors' villages and worlds—what I term Native alienation. Tovaangar is an example of the relationality of place radically connected to Indigenous intellectual practices and identities. Each village had a unique way of understanding its relationship with Tovaangar. The kinship and responsibility held together by Tovaangar was threatened by conquest's logic of replacing their kinship systems with those based on the mission, which meant to destroy their sense of place. Tovaangar guided Taraaxam resistance to colonialism through direct action and violence or refusals, including maintaining obligations to the land, animals, plants, ocean, and waters. The effects of Native alienation are beyond an acculturation project, as some historians have described the mission.

The Native alienation enforced by the mission slave system was meant to dislocate the Indian, to make them a people of nowhere except with God. Saidiya Hartman argues that slavery can be equated with the loss and denial of kin, identity, and the loss of a mother, including a mother country—a homeland.[48] If the earth is mother and provider of sustenance, then the loss and denial of obligation and relationality to place as central to one's identity, and culture is a loss of knowing oneself and one's past inseparable from land/mother. In the European view, according to Deloria, time is the central narrative of the world. Europeans derive meaning from historical, time-centered development.[49] Spanish conquest was predicated on the Indians losing themselves, forgetting their own names and kin, and replacing worlds based on relationality—Tovaangar for the Taraaxam—with time and the narrative of humans' limited presence on earth and their souls' everlasting existence in heaven or hell. Like the Middle Passage, the mission was a slave ship on land that some neophytes survived. In the words of Saidiya Hartman, there is a routine of violence to slavery—"whippings, humiliation, and separation from kin."[50] The everyday life of the neophyte was conditioned through violence and death, including a social death separating them from their ancestors and relationship/responsibility to place—this is Native alienation.

Separation from a people's responsibility to place, history, culture, language, kinship, and religion doesn't happen overnight. Native alienation is an extractive process limiting access to Native worlds in the making of slaves. It works through generations of people. At the mission, the children of the neophyte slaves were also possessions (this aspect is comparable to chattel slavery) and were even further removed from the world of their ancestors than their parents. As Saidiya Hartman notes, "The mother's mark, not the father's name, determined your fate."[51] Within the mission slave regime, a neophyte mother birthed a neophyte child baptized soon after birth—the possession of the mission. Scholars have debated whether baptisms, conversions, and, therefore, captivity by the missionaries were consensual or forced. Several firsthand contemporary accounts within the travel narratives explain that they were forced.[52] However, it can be deduced that most of the Indians who came to the mission willingly at the beginning of the colonial period did not understand the language of a system that would hold them and their children captive in perpetuity, a system such as that had never existed. Indians who came to the mission willingly later most likely came because of colonialism's effect on their traditional ways of life and environment—their food sources. They came without choice, pushed to the mission rather than pulled by conversion. Whether the Indians came to the mission willingly or

40    CHAPTER ONE

not, the children of neophytes had no choice in determining for themselves if they wanted to be baptized and have that "indelible mark" upon them for the rest of their lives, binding them to the mission till death.[53] The baptisms of second-generation (or later) neophyte children were not consensual. They were born into a system of forced labor and captivity that sought to replace Native worlds, a system they could not freely choose to leave.

Reproduction was tethered to making neophytes possessions in service of Spain's economy, governance, and nationalized religion. The priests encouraged and even demanded marriage and reproduction, punishing Indian women who had difficulties reproducing or had miscarriages. Unmarried women lived in *monjerios* (gendered prisons for unmarried girls), and marriage came with advantages. Through marriage, women would be released from their maximum-security imprisonment within the monjerío, where conditions involved lack of sanitation, institutionalized disease and sexual violence, and an individual sleeping space of only seven feet by two feet, not much more than that of the slave ships of the Middle Passage.[54] Through marriage, couples could have separate housing with more space within the congregación villages, often just outside the mission compound. Like many plantations in the American South, the mission slaves who had married were allowed to grow a garden and have chickens, providing much-needed food as the nutrition provided by the mission was often inadequate. Married couples had more time to themselves that wasn't regulated by the bell for Mass and labor, providing them an opportunity to socialize, have sex, gamble, sing, have secret ceremonials, and even foment rebellion. The small amount of freedom allowed through marriage and the selective incorporation of individuals into authoritative positions were, as in the plantations, techniques to pacify the neophytes and to monitor their actions, preempting rebellion.

Reproduction was central to a conquest based on the possession of souls. The priests required Indians to reproduce and punished women who had miscarriages. Many Indian women refused to have children conceived through rape. They induced miscarriages and aborted their children. The priests, according to Hugo Reid, interpreted every miscarriage and stillbirth as abortive and blamed the woman for the death of her child and the loss of a soul to possess. Reid explained that the priest at Mission San Gabriel, José María Salvedea, punished the women with a cruel and humiliating penance:

when a woman had the misfortune to bring forth a still-born child, she was punished. The penalty inflicted was, shaving the head, flogging for fifteen subsequent days, iron on the feet for three months, and having to appear every Sunday in church, on the steps leading up to the altar, with a hideous painted wooden child in her arms![55]

Men and women were held responsible for reproducing. If a couple was fighting, Redi states, the priest tied them together by the leg until they agreed to get along.[56] These acts of violence against neophytes reinforced the possession of Indian slaves as part of a conquest that benefited the Spanish empire and the Catholic Church. Children of neophytes were born separated from the world of their ancestors. All they would know was life at the mission and its social organization.

Patterson's third constitutive element of slavery is a general, sociopsychological dishonor. Patterson specifies that slaves had no names of their own; they held no honor; all honor went to their masters. Slaves often blamed themselves for their mistreatment, expressing psychological violence. Patterson explains this as "the outward show of self-hatred . . . prompted by the pervasive indignity and underlying physical violence of the relationship." The missions were physically, spiritually, and psychologically damaging.[57] Neophytes were made to believe they were captives of the missions because their race, culture, and lives before Christianity were inherently inferior. California Indian poet Deborah A. Miranda states that the mission created intergenerational trauma that continues today with the accompanying loss of self-respect and self-esteem.[58] Although it is nearly impossible to understand the psychology of individuals enslaved, we can recognize the loss of honor and the loss of authority over their lives. Scholars have rarely attempted to explain the Indians' experience of loss, the psychological effects, or the dishonor they accrued through baptism and the associated loss of freedom to leave the mission. Furthermore, as Dakota scholar Waziyatawin asks, "What kind of mental harm is done to a people dispossessed of their homeland?" Studies of the psychological damage of enslavement and genocide are lacking beyond the body of scholarship by Eduardo Duran.[59] However, the archive adds to a better understanding of Native loss.

Through archival sources, we know that gendered and sexual control over

42  CHAPTER ONE

Indian lives and bodies was dehumanizing, humiliating, and psychologically damaging. Practices of psychological terror upon Indians at the mission were coupled with attempts by the priests to demand reproduction through monogamy. The priests could be brutally cruel toward Indians who had difficulty conceiving or had miscarriages. They were blamed and punished for both. Lorenzo Asisara, a neophyte from Mission Santa Cruz, reported one such incident. A Native woman was asked by Father Ramon Olbés, "Why she did not give birth?" Olbés ordered her husband to appear before him and asked him the same question. "The Indian pointed towards heaven (the Indian did not know Spanish) as if he was indicating that only God knew why." The priest asked through an interpreter "if he slept with his wife, and the Indian answered yes." Unsatisfied with the answers to his questions, the priest put the couple in a room to make them have sex in front of him. "The Indian [male] refused but he was forced to show his member [penis] in order to make certain that it was functioning properly. Then, the priest took the woman and put her in a room; the husband was sent to the guards with a pair of shackles."[60]

The priest continued interrogating the woman about her sexual activity and repeated his irrational question, "Why can't you give birth?" He then punitively demanded that she undress so that he could inspect her vagina. She physically resisted his forceful effort, and the two began to fight. The priest called out for help as if he were the victim, and the interpreter and alcalde rushed into the room. Father Olbés ordered that she be immediately taken outside, whipped fifty times, and locked in the monjerío. After her flogging, Olbés ordered the woman a penance for her resistance and inability to get pregnant. He forced her to dishonor and humiliate herself by taking away her authority over her life and sexuality. Similar to Hugo Reid's description at Mission San Gabriel, she was forced to carry a wooden doll around as if it were a newborn baby for nine days.

Her husband also served a humiliating penance while imprisoned. The priest made him wear shackles and secured cattle horns with a leather band on his head. He was forced to wear this when he attended Mass. The "other Indians would mock him and bullfight him."[61] The demeaning punishments this couple received for not reproducing were more than bodily harm; they were psychologically damaging spiritual penances. This example demonstrates a grotesque event and displays a structure in which neophytes were dishonored through the mission slave institution. The missionaries and governance treated the Indians not as humans or children but as Father Boscana and others had described them—as animal-like. The Spanish saw the Indians' precontact way of life as but an obstacle to their absorption as productive workers for God and country and to the collective possession of their souls.[62]

Reproduction and the baptism of children to claim their souls were so important to the priests that some baptized babies who had yet to be born. In a brilliant dissertation, Anne Marie Reid researched priests conducting postmortem cesarean sections, which she terms "baptismal caesareans." In one of the burial records of an Indian at San Carlos Mission, Reid found that Father José Viñals interred the body of Galicana Choja on October 25, 1801. In his notes, the priest wrote that he had performed a cesarean operation on the Indian woman "immediately upon her death," extracted the fetus from her uterus, and baptized the child before he died. Viñals gave the child eternal life as God's possession. Reid explains that the Catholic Church prohibits posthumous baptisms. Still, they encouraged cesarean sections to baptize fetuses, even when they would not survive. "Negligence would result in the loss of souls," Franciscan priest Joseph Manuel Rodríguez argued in 1772. The cesarean operation was performed primarily for the baptism of the unborn, not for the health of the infant or the mother. If the fetus was on the verge of death, the priest could perform baptism after cutting the woman open and observing the fetus as living without removal. Reid writes, "From 1779 through 1832, a total of 24 baptismal cesareans were performed on 23 different women," including an eight-month fetus in 1803 at Mission San Gabriel.[63] In proportion to the number of deaths of women during childbirth in California, this number is low, but it is high compared to other regions within the Spanish empire. The body and spirit of the Indians were regarded as separate entities by the Spanish, and both could be possessed even if death was certain. Performing cesarean sections on women to baptize their fetuses can be understood as a spiritual eugenics program. The women's health and death were of less concern than their souls being saved for eternal life. The desirable aspect of an Indian to be reproduced through birth and baptism was not their humanity as individuals but only their souls; their bodies were entirely fungible.

44  CHAPTER ONE

While the priests attempted to control Native sexualities and reproduction, many simultaneously raped Indian girls. Sexual abuse and the rape of children by priests and soldiers were symptomatic of colonialism since the beginning of the conquest. Few oral histories of Indians who were born during the mission period exist; only six Indians born during the mid-nineteenth century have published accounts.[64] One of the six, María Solares (Samala Chumash), specified that her grandmother had been an "esclava de le mission." Solares reported that her slave grandmother had run away "many, many times, and had been recaptured and whipped till her buttocks crawled with maggots."[65] Another of the Indians was Lorenzo Asisara (Costanoan), who told us the story about the couple punished because they hadn't reproduced. His account of the mission corresponds with Solares' assessment of the mission as a slave institution. He states that at Mission Santa Cruz, "the Spanish priests were very cruel with the Indians . . . and they made them work like slaves." Asisara also explained the sexual violence by the priests at the missions. He states that Father Luis Gil y Taboada was "easily infatuated" with Indian women. He would kiss them, and "he would have relations [sex] with them until he caught syphilis and lesions erupted on the skin."[66] Many priests had reputations for their relationships with Indian girls, including priests that Asisara identified who later replaced Father Taboada at Mission Santa Cruz. Asisara's experience and memory are limited to one mission. Still, it can be assumed that numerous priests at other missions similarly abused Indian girls, especially when they viewed Indians as human only in body, not in mind. Fernando Librado, a Chumash Indian, provides yet another Indian voice that documented the priests' abuse and how the mission system imposed structural sexual violence against Indian women. Librado explains how the monjerío imprisoned Indian girls and made them easily accessible for the priests to rape:

> The priest had an appointed hour to go there. When he got to the nunnery [monjerío] all were in bed in the big dormitory. The priest would pass by the bed of the superior [maestra] and tap her on the shoulder, and she would commence singing. All of the girls would join in. . . . When the singing was going on, the priest would have time to select the girl he wanted, carry out his desires. . . . In this way the priest had sex with all of them, from the superior all the way down the line. . . . The priest's will was law.[67]

Sexual violence at the missions was a dehumanizing dishonor routinely used against slaves. As Cheryl Harris has written, slaves "were more than a source of labor; they were a source of nonterritorial property."[68] Saidiya Hartman further considers the captive female body under racial slavery as something that could be "traded as a commodity, worked to death, taken, tortured, seeded, and propagated like any other crop, or murdered." Hartman reminds us, "The work of sex and procreation was the chief motor for reproducing the material, social, and symbolic relations of slavery [that] . . . inaugurated a regime of racialized sexuality."[69]

If the mission scholars quoted earlier had analyzed the Indian experience of missionization through Patterson's three constitutive elements, their findings concerning slavery may have been different. The questions they asked would at least be more complicated than the single determining question of whether Indians were bought and sold. Through a more critical and interdisciplinary approach, scholars may established that Indians experienced a social death through missionization in which their enslavement was permanent; they were violently dominated through forced labor and captivity, generally dishonored, and natally alienated from the worlds of their ancestors. The Taraaxam resistance at San Gabriel in 1785 responded to the mission regime's social death that required land, labor, and their complete powerlessness through spiritual possession. Furthermore, the mission demanded Natives' alienation from the heritage of their ancestors and their relationship with place.

## Slavery Is Foundational to Conquest

Slavery has long been foundational to a Western logic of conquest and land dispossession, from West Africa in the mid-fifteenth century to California at the end of the eighteenth. As Black studies theorist Jared Sexton argues, the loss of sovereignty is contingent on slavery.[70] One of Christopher Columbus's first acts of genocidal violence against Indigenous peoples in 1492 was not only murder and land dispossession but enslavement justified through religion. Cedric Robinson traced the origins of racial capitalism to histories of "invasion, settlement, expropriation and racial hierarchy" within Europe before the American conquest.[71] While 1492 is a significant date in the conquest of the Americas, more than a half-century earlier, in 1434, the first

46   CHAPTER ONE

Portuguese ship passed beyond Cape Bojador to the west coast of Africa, which was critical to the development of slavery and enabled the first African captives and gold dust to be transported to Portugal in 1441. Ultimately, this resulted in the conquest of the Americas and the transatlantic slave trade.[72] Three years later, in 1444, the Portuguese held the first slave auctions. Slavery enforced through Portuguese conquest was more than a historical event; it set into motion anti-Blackness and anti-Indigeneity, the two inseparably linked through African indigeneity and European markers on non-Christian bodies and souls as possessive logics that would be brought to the Americas in 1492 and later to California in 1769. In *God Is Red*, Vine Deloria Jr. asks, "Where did Westerners get their ideas of divine right to conquest, of manifest destiny, of themselves as the vanguard of true civilization, if not from Christianity?"[73] Deloria's question can be expanded to ask, where did Europeans get their idea that some humans can be possessed? In the logic of conquest, non-Christians were viewed as violable and their lands and bodies as possessions, sanctified by papal law.

The development of a logic of spiritual conquest that includes enslavement, genocide, and the conversion of the Natives predates the invasion of West Africa or the Americas. In 1341 a Portuguese-sponsored ship brought back four Indigenous captives from the Canary Islands, and in 1344 Pope Clement VI issued the papal bull *Tuae devotionis sinceritas*, which authorized the conquest and conversion of the Natives to Christianity.[74] In 1351 Pope Clement VI sent Franciscan missionaries (the same order sent to California) and twelve previously captured and converted Indigenous Canarians to convert the Native peoples of the Canary Islands. After a century of warfare, enslavement, and conversion, the Portuguese completed the conquest of the Canary Islands, and today, the Indigenous people are possessed and eviscerated: disemboweled body and soul from their homelands.

Prince Henry of Portugal's reasons for rounding the cape to the west coast of Africa in 1434 included finding a passage to India, possessing trade goods, knowing more about his Muslim enemies, and "increas[ing] in the faith of Jesus Christ, and to bring to Him all the souls that should be saved." Gomes Eanes de Azurara, who chronicled the conquest of Guinea, estimated that between 1441 and 1446, the Portuguese had taken and converted or baptized 927 captives. In one act of violence, Azurara states that Prince Henry took a young boy from a fishing village to "train him for a priest, with the purpose of sending him back to his native land, there to preach the faith of Jesus Christ."[75] The boy died before he was trained. Nearly four hundred years later, in 1832, Father Antonio Peyrí abducted Luiseño Indian children Pablo Tac and Agapito Amamix from their kin at Mission San Luis Rey, California, to train them as priests. Before they could be inducted through traditional ceremony into Luiseño manhood, they were kidnapped and spent two years in Mexico City before being taken to Rome. Because of colonialism, Tac and Amamix had experienced what Tac calls being *ahicho* ("poor and also orphaned") in the Luiseño language.[76] Tac and Amamix would both die without their families while learning to become priests, as the boy from Guinea had four hundred years before.

Shortly after the Portuguese entered the slave trade and the conquest of West Africa, beginning with Guinea, the Catholic Church extended papal law that spiritually and politically justified conquest and slavery, including the possession of land and people. Dating back to the twelfth century, theological law governing territorial sovereign claims for Christian monarchies was enhanced by the papal bull of 1452 by Pope Nicholas V. *Dum diversas* authorized Portugal to conquer the Muslims and pagans and possess them in perpetual servitude. In 1455 *Romanus pontifex* added to *Dum diversas*, authorizing the Portuguese to "invade, search out, capture, vanquish and subdue all Saracens [Muslims] and pagans whatsoever, and other enemies of Christ where so ever placed, and the kingdoms, dukedoms, principalities, dominions, possessions and all movable and immovable goods whatsoever held and possessed by them and to reduce their persons to perpetual slavery."[77] Through theological law, the church deprived Africans of their lands and their political and personal freedoms. The pope and Portuguese viewed them as possessions: body and soul. Theological law rationalized the enslavement of West Africans because they were non-Christians.

After Columbus had claimed the "New World" for Spain, Pope Alexander VI issued the bull *Inter caetera* in 1493, giving Spain authority and rights to possess the Americas. As previous bulls had indicated, the people's souls were also to be possessed: "Moreover, we command you [Spain] in virtue of holy obedience that . . . you should appoint to the aforesaid mainlands and islands worthy, God-fearing, learned, skilled and experienced men, in order

48 CHAPTER ONE

to instruct the aforesaid inhabitants and residents in the Catholic faith and train them in good morals."[78] The bulls of Pope Alexander VI, including *Inter caetera*, modified the previous bulls that had given Portugal sovereign control over lands discovered and provided Spain with sovereign rights to new lands discovered in the Caribbean. As applied to the Americas, the papal bulls divided lands between the Portuguese and the Spanish, with the ecclesiastical responsibility of converting the Indians. The bulls justified war against the non-Christians to provide entry for Catholic missionaries. While Alexander VI modified political rights, he neither amended nor nullified the enslavement of Muslims and pagans. Alexander VI included additional language that issued the above command to formally instruct pagans in the Catholic faith.

*Inter caetera* expedited the transatlantic slave trade and the fungibility of Indigenous and Black bodies. According to author Pius Onyemechi Adiele, Pope Leo X, in cooperation with the kings of Portugal and Spain "gave the license for a direct importation of 4,000 Black African captives as slaves into the Spanish New World for the same purpose of using them to replace the dying West Indian population, who were being worked to death at the sugar plantations and on the gold and silver mines by the Spanish Conquistadors."[79] Millions of humans would follow this initial foray into the trade of Black bodies as cargo through the Middle Passage.

Simultaneous with the importation of African slaves to the Americas, the Spanish were performing a script read aloud to claim new lands and justified the kidnapping and enslavement of Indigenous peoples. Juan López de Palacios Rubios wrote the *Requerimiento*, which was first used in 1514. As one author explains, this document was often read "to trees and empty huts."[80] It was read by the Spanish while aboard ships approaching new islands or to Indians already captured. Despite being pure performativity, its content included the threat of violence and the convergence of enslavement and forced conversion that the Spanish relied on to obliterate Native sovereignty:

> If you do not [submit] . . . I certify to you that, with the help of God, we shall
> powerfully enter your country, and shall make war against you in all ways
> and manners that we can, and shall subject you to the yoke of obedience of
> the Church and of their Highnesses; we shall take you and your wives and

your children, and shall make slaves of them, and as such shall sell and dispose of them as their Highnesses may command; and we shall take away your goods, and shall do you all the mischief and damage that we can.[81]

The Spanish threat of enslavement was dependent on Indians' submission to the church. The *Requerimiento* blamed those who did not obey "and refuse to receive their lord, and resist and contradict him" for the "deaths and losses which shall accrue from this."[82] The *Requerimiento* read by the Spanish provided Indians with little choice other than to submit and convert to Christianity or be killed or enslaved.

These papal bulls, collectively known as the Doctrine of Discovery, regulated dispossession (of land and sovereignty), enslavement, and the possession of pagan bodies and souls. The doctrine facilitated the conquest of West Africa and the Americas, the transatlantic slave trade of Africans, and the enslavement and genocide of Indigenous peoples. The papal bulls did not demarcate between Africans and Indians; both were viewed as pagans. Although the Doctrine of Discovery was amended over the centuries, it resolutely developed a logic later deployed by the missionaries and Spanish military that I call a logic of spiritual possession—the enslavement of the Indians of California and theft of their lands for God and country. This logic has been rewritten as a benevolent project that taught the Indians of California new skills and a new religion. The mythology created about the conquest of California erases the gratuitous terror and disavows Indian enslavement. The story of Toypurina is one of resistance to slavery and the isolation of being severed from kin and denied ancestors. In the next chapter, I interrogate the mythology of the California conquest as strengthened by Americans, whose built environment glorifies the mission system. This mythology, which I call the Spanish imaginary, erases the foundational violence of enslavement in the structure of conquest, which was established long before Europeans came to California.

# TWO

# Hallucinations of the Spanish Imaginary

*Mission Revival Architecture*

José Francisco de Ortega, lieutenant and commander of the San Diego Presidio, wrote in his official capacity about a planned rebellion in 1778 organized by the neophytes and gentiles at Mission San Juan Capistrano. Ortega wrote, "The cook, an Indian native to San Juan Capistrano, strongly warned them [the priests and Captain Guillermo Carrillo] that the gentiles from the mission were planning to kill the Reverend Padres and all of the soldiers." Carrillo investigated the accusation brought to him by the cook and "found it to be very true."[1] Ortega explains that the "heathens of the Sierra and from La Laguna, Las Flores, San Mateo, and all the surrounding areas had combined" to attack the missionaries and soldiers. Ortega's report provides limited details, but those he did include allow me to retrofit the Acjachemem reasons for rebellion at San Juan Capistrano and better understand the methods of conquest in California.

Ortega evaluates why the Indians at San Juan Capistrano and the surrounding independent villages organized to "kill the Reverend Padres and all of the soldiers." He states, "The reason that they give for this is that the Indian Capitancillo was insulted by his daughter's marriage to an Indian from Baja California.... In addition to this, they are insulted by the Reverend Padres and soldiers and say that they are devils who have come to ruin their seeds on their lands." The Indians, Ortega reports, held a ceremony led by an old man from the "Sierra"—an area not under Spanish control. Ortega explains, "With the other gentiles present, they rejoiced in their special evil ways, in remembrance and renewing their anger and similar concerns about the Indians who died in the arroyo of San Mateo."[2] Unfortunately, Ortega does not provide more discussion of what had happened at San Mateo, the Acjachemem village of Pánhe, that caused the death of Indians there. The large village of Pánhe was quickly renamed by the Spanish, and the land was used as a cattle ranch. Pánhe was the origin village for the largest number

## 52 CHAPTER TWO

of Indians baptized by the Franciscans at Mission San Juan Capistrano. Pánhe is located in southern Orange County, in a canyon near present-day Marine Corps Base Camp Pendleton, world-famous surf spot Trestles, and California State Parks' San Mateo Campground.

Ortega writes of no accountable party for the deaths at Pánhe, but he implied that Spanish soldiers were responsible. According to Ortega, tensions were still high among the Acjachemem. Past Spanish violence and anxieties of further violence were part of the reason behind the Acjachemem's organizing resistance to colonialism to defend their land and life. Ortega's statement provides the prevailing Spanish view of Indian worldviews, indicating that Indian religion and ways of life were "evil." The goal of conquest was to alienate and eradicate, in all its forms, Indigenous "evil" from the landscape, replacing Native life with white life—European "civilization" and its cultural hegemony—this is Native alienation.

Acjachemem and presumably Payómkawichum (Luiseño, "People of the West") from several traditional villages, including Pánhe, Amaugenga, and 'Uchme (also known as Las Flores, located south of Mission San Juan Capistrano on the coast near Las Pulgas, Las Flores Creek, and Oceanside, California) fomented rebellion against Mission San Juan Capistrano. The village of Amaugenga may refer to a small village in the Santa Margarita Mountains. Independent villages came together to kill the priests and soldiers. By late February 1778, a little less than a year and a half after the founding of the mission, the Indians affected by Spanish conquest had already experienced the severe trauma of colonialism, including effects on their land and environment, multiple forms of violence, forced heteropatriarchy, and captivity.[3] The uprising was in defense of Native humanity, out of responsibility to place, and in resistance to slavery and Native alienation.

According to the documentation of this mostly unknown event, the Indians from a large area had organized to kill those responsible for their families' captivity. The forced separation of families included the chief's daughter from the village of 'Axachme, who had been baptized and married to a Christian Indian named Leonardo from Baja California without the consent of her family and kinship system. In the mission records, I found that the third marriage at Mission San Juan Capistrano on June 12, 1777, was between Leonardo from Mission San Borja and María Margarita, whose Native name was Sucucainem.[4] María Margarita was held at the mission, according to the 1778 report, unable to "leave because she was already a Christian."[5] Having been baptized with an "indelible mark" upon her, she became the priest's captive possession, body and soul.

Similar to the events in 1785 at Mission San Gabriel (chapter 1), the methods of rebellion were not limited to arms but were contingent upon their culture and spirituality. At Mission San Juan Capistrano, the Indians brought arrows to kill the soldiers, but "for the Padres arrows were not necessary; [they] would kill them with herbs." The Indians combated colonialism spiritually by witching the priests to their deaths. Through ceremony and song, they organized their attempt to free their people and rematriate their lands. Slavery is a system that alienates people from the protection of their lineages; freedom is the opposite. Freedom from slavery is the recuperation of lineages, the systems that provide order through kinship, and the worlds of ancestors. To be free, the Natives affected by Mission San Juan Capistrano organized to remove the settlers from their lands, reunite their families, and rematriate the land into their kinship.

Through retrofitting this archival document, it is possible to recognize that the Acjachemem at Mission San Juan Capistrano viewed the soldiers and priests as a scourge causing great harm to the people and their land. Ortega wrote, "It was more noticeable in their songs that they were crying out that the Reverend Padres and soldiers are devils who have come to steal their land. Since they [Spaniards] have lived here, it hasn't rained, and there are no seeds." Although devils are a Western concept, Ortega's use of the term explains the intense hostility felt by the Acjachemem. Moreover, they were determined to act against the Spanish dispossession of their lands and the priests' spiritual authority to possess their souls. The environmental changes signaled things to come and gave the independent villages the purpose of organizing to defend their land and life. For people who lived in relation to the environment as stewards of their land, choosing to rely on the bounty of the local flora and fauna, a lack of rain coinciding with the arrival of the Spanish was an important signal directly from their relatives and ancestors to fight against the colonizers. The lack of rain was a critical indicator for the Acjachemem of colonialism's violence to the land. The same signals are more than apparent in today's drought and the gratuitous violence to Acjachemem homelands.

The uprising at San Juan Capistrano extended to Mission San Diego.

## 54 CHAPTER TWO

According to military letters, on March 16, 1778, an Indian from the village of San Dieguito warned the Padre of San Diego, Fray Fermín Francisco de Lasuén, that the Indians of Pamó, particularly their chief, were preparing arms to kill Christians. Furthermore, he explained to Lasuén that there were other villages in the conspiracy and that they had killed a fugitive neophyte from San Juan Capistrano.[6] San Junípero Serra and the governor of California acknowledged the insurrections at San Juan Capistrano and San Diego as a serious problem, the leaders were arrested, and the violence against the missions was stopped. They did not show concern for why the Indians had organized together or why the gentiles had killed a fugitive neophyte.

On April 6, 1778, Serra sent a letter to Father Fermín Lasuén and indicated that there had been "unrest" among the Indians in the southern missions, including San Juan Capistrano:

> According to what he confided today, Sunday, to Father Dumetz, the Governor does not consider important the unrest in your mission down there and in Mission San Juan Capistrano. He says that if they killed the Indian named Clement—about which I have heard nothing from the Fathers of San Juan Capistrano—it was because he had escaped and had a mind to do them some injury, and if the prisoners at the said mission confess that they intended to kill, etc., that proves nothing. If you were to ask them if they wanted to kill the Pope, they would answer yes. They did not do any real damage to the mission, and so the whole affair amounts to nothing.[7]

Approximately two weeks after this letter, Serra wrote a second to Father Lasuén indicating that the prisoners would be sentenced to death.[8] He told him to "administer solemn Baptism to them in the prison itself" on "the evening before" they were to be executed. For Serra, they would not be "deprived" of baptism, and they could have patience for the "heavy cross" they bear and "anything else that might help them to die well." He finishes his letter about the uprising by reassuring Lasuén that he will insist that the mission be provided with additional soldiers to make sure it is "well defended and in a position to add to the number of our Christians, no matter how much it may displease the Pamo Indians, and the one with the hoofs."[9]

This unpublished episode of Native resistance highlights the generative refusal of the Acjachemem, Payómkawichum, and Kumeyaay to abandon culture and accept Spanish conquest. It also displays the spiritual possession of their lands and their souls' alienation from the heritage of their ancestors. Through their culture and kinship networks, they found the ability to organize independent villages to fight against the logic of conquest, which included slavery and the kidnapping and sexual exploitation of women and those beyond a gender binary. The history of the California missions has largely been written, with few exceptions, to exclude rather than center events such as the one I begin this chapter with. If historians include such events, they write about them as isolated and not through a lens attempting to better understand the effects of colonialism from a Native perspective and Native demands for freedom that continue today.

Historians who exclude resistance to the missions have fashioned a fantasy past for the Americans who followed Spanish and Mexican colonialism. Indians refusing the priests and Christianity, sometimes violently, did not fit into the narrative of benign and beneficial colonialism. Through our built environment, we have collectively been induced into a hallucination of the past—the Spanish imaginary—that conceives of the missions as beautiful despite a history of gratuitous violence.

## Hallucinations of the Spanish Imaginary

The bells of the mission ring jarringly into the dark desert night. Their sonic intonations demand we forget their original purpose: compulsory prayer and forced labor. Simultaneously, the bells' vibrations are a call to remember and a call to forget. They function today as remnants of a genocidal before and a collective hallucination. Today's much-refurbished mission structures, such as Orange County's Mission San Juan Capistrano, serve the local economy as valuable tourist destinations that receive thousands of guests annually.[10] Visitors are eager to experience the mythology of the old missions, with their white adobe walls, red-tiled roofs, arches, corridors, bells, and lush, carefully manicured gardens. Contemporary mission sites heavily influence visitors' perceptions of California's mission system, obscuring for commercial purposes the mission system's profoundly negative impacts on California Indian life (and death).[11] The hallucinatory powers of the mission bells sonically

## CHAPTER TWO

transport tourists to a time that never was: the Spanish imaginary. Instead of entering sites of violence and death, visitors experience beauty and tranquility at the refurbished missions.

The nightmare of the Spanish imaginary has been reproduced in the physical landscape. Few California structures better illustrate the colonial ambitions of Spain (then Mexico, then the United States) than Riverside's Mission Inn.[12] With its historic connection to Indian boarding schools, which, as one writer put it, "were a knife stabbed into families and clans— the heart of Indian Country," perhaps no other hotel's legacy better epitomizes the colonial beast unleashed by self-indulgence, greed, excess, and distorted reality.[13] Opening its doors in 1902, the Mission Inn consciously drew from Spanish colonial architecture's style and functions, incorporating Spanish Christian iconography and symbols of the landowning rancheros (Mexican Californio cattle ranchers) who dominated California until the United States seized it in the late 1840s. This architectural style, known as Mission Revival or Spanish Colonial Revival, lived on after the Franciscans abandoned the missions, well beyond the Mexican colonial era, and—as the Mission Inn reveals—long after the United States officially attempted to "civilize" Native Americans in such institutions as Sherman Indian Boarding School, founded nearby one year after the hotel's founding.[14] The Indian boarding schools' goal was very similar to that of the missions, namely, to alienate Indians from their heritage and kinship with the earth.

The Mission Revival architectural style, now synonymous with Southern California, continues to exert its malign influence upon the land. It is an enduring symbol of the anti-Indian ideology that informed the greed and violence of the Spanish, Mexican, and American colonizers who invaded California, for which those colonizers have no alibis. The Spanish introduced the genocidal architecture that integrated capitalist goals into their collective colonial fantasy of a benign, peaceful era populated by saintly missionaries and happy Indians who did not resist colonialism and conversion. The stories opening this book's chapters tell of resistance that contradicts the Spanish imaginary. The Americans who later seized California from Mexico seized upon that historical imaginary as well. Americans charged with controlling California's Indigenous peoples turned to the Spanish colonial model in their efforts to transform Native peoples. Other newcomers summoned the

Spanish imaginary to boost local economies, crafting structures and whole neighborhoods in the Mission Revival style in hopes of attracting new settlers—and their wealth—to Southern California. Mission Revival architecture survives today as the physical embodiment of the Spanish imaginary. The enduring legacy of Mission Revival architecture is its suppression of genuine histories of California Indians, before and after the missions, which has been misinterpreted, mistaught, misrepresented, repackaged, and sold for non-Indigenous profits.[15] Instead of slavery and violence at the missions, many historians (amateur and professional) have written about the priests as good fathers disciplining their children and teaching them new skills.

Iconic Mission Revival structures such as the original Sherman Indian Boarding School and today's Mission Inn can be analyzed as social constructs with profound implications for those who pass through their doors. Existing scholarship has missed the fundamental reality of Mission Revival architecture: it is the physical embodiment of an anti-Indian ideology, motivated and informed by successive waves of colonizers for capitalist purposes. To be sure, historian Carey McWilliams was ferociously critical of mythic representations of California history, what he called the Spanish "fantasy heritage."[16] McWilliams correctly identified life in the missions as "a nightmare for the Indians," and questioned whether Indians "profited by the experience to the slightest degree." Indeed, writing soon after the end of World War II, McWilliams compared the missions to the Nazi death camps, where prisoners' state of chronic undernourishment meant that they could not run away.[17] Ironically, for American newcomers, the Spanish imaginary was a useful nativist tool: Mission Revival architecture helped boosters market California to tourists, integrated Anglos into the systems of racial dominance that underlie Spanish and Mexican colonialism, and supported American newcomers as they blended California into the ongoing project of US nation-building.[18]

Other scholars have followed McWilliams's lead. Emma Pérez labels the historiography produced by traditional scholars as "colonial imaginary," an approach that silences women, ignores people of color, and denies the existence of nonheteronormative forms of sexuality. Phoebe S. Kropp asks the question guiding this chapter: "Can we read the history of a place in its buildings?" and answers "yes." Kropp notes that Anglo boosters of Los

Angeles invested that city with a romanticized Spanish history and fashioned that fantasy into its built environment. Likewise, William F. Deverell explores the hypocrisy inherent in that city's devotion to an imaginary past: Angelenos annually celebrate La Fiesta de Los Angeles while simultaneously disregarding contemporary Mexican residents.[19]

Building on these works I posit the term "Spanish imaginary" to explicitly engage not only the Spanish fantasy past but, more importantly, the active myth-making that followed the American conquest of California, a process that suppressed Native peoples' histories and experiences and obscured the Native genocide, enslavement, and violence that were hallmarks of Christian Spanish colonial practice.[20] Placing the histories and experiences of California Indians at the center of the Spanish imaginary, I explicitly analyze the operation of US Indian policy in a built environment that mythologized Spanish California as a pleasant, beautiful, and peaceful place. More importantly, I examine how late nineteenth- and early twentieth-century promoters of the Spanish imaginary in Southern California actively enforced the state's anti-Indian policies and practices.

## Mission Revival and the Spanish Imaginary

Architecture tells us useful things about a place and its history. Architectural style is symbolic and representational; it organizes systems of thought and authority. Because buildings provide conduits for human interactions, architecture shapes the organization of societies, imposing builders' social and cultural hierarchies onto the built environment. Architecture is simultaneously a capitalist product, a design solution for extracting value from real estate (e.g., the financial transactions through which title to landownership changes hands), and the manufacture and sale of goods (e.g., aggregating products for sale to consumers in boutiques and other physical settings). From a single building to the more extensive arrangements of entire city blocks into residential, commercial, and industrial spaces, with streets, walkways, and green spaces, architecture is the physical embodiment of how a culture arranges itself. The ways that societies arrange their structural and infrastructural space are intersectional, touching upon notions of race, space, gender, sexuality, and class. In this way, architecture is a social construct that tells stories about a place's history and people. However, architecture is often misunderstood as, in the words of philosopher Henri Lefebvre, "the intangible outcome of history, society and culture."[21]

Before Spanish missionaries, soldiers, and colonists arrived, Indians were California's architects. Natives built their structures of found and tended-to natural materials, creating homes and communal structures that were essentially part of the environment. California Indian buildings were temporary by design, leaving few traces on the landscape. The settlements of California Indians showed them living lightly, responsibly, and sustainably. Native ways of using the environment contrasted profoundly with that of early European settlers, who valued the land primarily for the extractive resources it could provide.[22] The Acjachemem used the same materials as the Taraaxam to make their kiicha (house), including pivéesash (tule) and $ahát (willow). Their homes were round and domed, and they spent most of their daily lives outdoors. The ceremonial dances connecting them to the earth and their ancestors were performed outside on level ground, rendering the spirit world into corporeal existence.[23]

The first non-Indigenous settlers to impose their architectural vision upon the land were Spaniards. Between 1769 and 1784, Franciscan missionary Junípero Serra established California's first nine missions. A far cry from their early twentieth-century restorations, early mission buildings were initially no more than crude camps, marked by stick-and-mud structures with thatched roofs. These early mission structures were followed by the more familiar adobe buildings, assembled with forced Indian labor. Some of the first adobe structures completed in California served to imprison unmarried Native girls as young as six years old.[24] The Spanish pueblos (towns) were organized around rectangular plazas used for religious festivals and markets to exchange crops and other goods. Government buildings and the homes of prominent citizens fronted the plazas, with meandering lanes lined with tiny adobe, tar-and-stick-roofed houses linking residents. Small farms ringed village outskirts and, beyond them, open ranges for Spanish cattle, horses, sheep, and goats. Knitting settlements together were open *zanjas* (ditches) that carried water for drinking, irrigation, and drainage. Poor and disorderly, early Spanish architecture showed the colonizers' attempts to impose European systems of social organization upon the land.[25]

*60* CHAPTER TWO

After Mexican independence in 1821, Mexican Californio rancheros (cattle-raising landholders) built large adobe homes, typically one-story, tile-roofed structures with long covered porches and often an inner courtyard, like the missions. Architectural forerunners of the California ranch-style house, Mexicans typically built their homes on hills surrounded by open space as a precaution against Native attack. Missions dramatically changed in the 1830s when Mexican authorities ousted the Franciscan missionaries, installed local parish priests, and turned mission lands into private properties. Structures at the original twenty-one Spanish missions and their *asistencias* (small sub-missions) quickly fell into disrepair.[26]

Americans were the next group to impose their architectural vision upon California's landscape. The first American structures in what would become Riverside were barns and board-and-batten shacks. Like the first missions, says archaeologist John Goodman, early Riverside was less a town than a camp. Soon after the city's 1875 founding, American home builders introduced architectural styles named for Queen Victoria, forms that had long been popular along the Eastern Seaboard of the United States.[27]

In the 1880s American newcomers rediscovered California's disintegrating Spanish missions. Amateur and professional preservationists, boosters, and entrepreneurs launched campaigns to restore these colonial structures. Adobe by adobe, in a style that came to be known as Mission Revival, Americans redeveloped these former Indian prisons, often for commercial purposes, especially tourism. Mission Revival style spread quickly throughout early twentieth-century California, becoming the region's signature design. City leaders in Santa Barbara and San Juan Capistrano, for example, built their communities' identities through the wholesale adoption of Spanish colonial architecture. Phoebe Kropp observes that "Anglos did not inherit" this version of California's past; rather, "they produced it."[28]

At the same time, American newcomers began producing fanciful histories of Spanish Christian colonization in California. The words *romance* and *romantic* appear often in this literature, usually meaning "idyllic," "peaceful," "happy," and "picturesque." Prominent Southern Californians such as Charles Fletcher Lummis, explains one scholar, "realized the value of the Spanish myth, which was loosely based on the factual colonial period of California," and actively fashioned that myth "into a nostalgia for the seemingly simple times of the days of missions and ranchos."[29] These treatments skimmed over the genocidal Spanish treatment of Native Americans, both physical and cultural. Professional and amateur historians—none of them Indigenous—produced tragic tales about California's lost innocence, in which the inevitable march of American Manifest Destiny ended California's peaceful pastoral era under Spanish and later Mexican control. Infusing their new Mission Revival commercial and residential structures with the Spanish imaginary, American newcomers melded Spain's colonial logic with the United States' long-standing patterns of white supremacy, including Native dispossession, slavery, and genocide.

## "Is There Money in It?"

Two of the best examples of how Americans in California used the Spanish imaginary to support their economic goals are the Sherman Indian Boarding School and the Mission Inn. Central to the history of both institutions is Wisconsin-born Frank Augustus Miller (1858–1935), the influential Riverside businessman who helped Southern California realize the commercial potential of the old Spanish missions. Miller came to California with his family as a teenager; their first home was built in 1875 by an Indian named Miguel on unceded Cahuilla and Taraaxam land. The following year, the Millers expanded the original adobe structure. As the Glenwood Cottage, it offered room and board for twelve guests. In 1880 Frank purchased the inn from his father for five thousand dollars and took over management of what had become the Glenwood Inn.[30]

Miller's vision for his business expanded in 1895 when he and a group of Southern California businessmen including architect Arthur Burnett Benton and reformer-businessman Charles Fletcher Lummis founded the Landmarks Club of Southern California to preserve the missions and other sites of historical interest.[31] As an article in the *Sacramento Daily Union* explained, founders planned "to undertake the immediate and permanent preservation from decay and vandalism of the venerable missions of Southern California." They would finance repairs "and take such measures as may be necessary to protect the buildings from further ravages of the weather." The club committed itself to "conservation of any other historic monuments, relics, or landmarks which may properly be deemed part of our public inheritance of history or romance."[32]

## 62 CHAPTER TWO

In his 1886 annual report, club secretary Arthur Benton asked and answered the key question about mission restoration: "Is there money in it?" He assured Californians that they would be rewarded for their investment in historic preservation, especially of the crumbling missions. "There is money in it," wrote Benton, "for these same missions serve now and will continue in a[n] ever increasing ratio in the future to attract the best class of tourists." And it was to those tourists, Benton assured his readers, that "California must look for no small part of her material advancement."[33]

Miller was familiar with the Mission Revival architectural style when he joined the Landmarks Club, having seen examples at the 1893 World's Columbian Exposition. He also worked closely with club secretary, architect Arthur Benton, who oversaw the group's restoration work, including its first project at Mission San Juan Capistrano.[34] Miller learned more about that mission at an 1896 Landmarks Club symposium. As the *Los Angeles Herald* reported, speakers gave "very entertaining descriptions" of the old mission, including highlights regarding "the village life of the Indians that clustered about its sides," and its "many guest chambers" offered to "all travelers and wayfarers, friends and foes," who had once stopped there to rest.[35]

Not surprisingly, in their mission restorations, the Landmarks Club glossed over many unsavory aspects of mission life and Indian resistance to their spiritual conquest. For example, one of its first projects was recreating Mission San Juan Capistrano. Although the monjerío was among the first buildings constructed at Mission San Juan Capistrano, the Spanish imaginary dictated that restorers misidentify the monjerío as "guest rooms" and the *jayuntes* (male dormitories) as "soldier's barracks." No mention is made of the sexual violence of Spaniards against Native women and children at the restored mission. In 1777 Junípero Serra himself admitted that "the soldiers, without any restraint or shame, have behaved like brutes towards the Indian women."[36] Careful scrutiny of original records in rebuilding the mission would have revealed that syphilis and other sexually transmitted infections were rampant at San Juan Capistrano. Mislabeling the monjerío as "guest rooms" was purposeful.[37] Acknowledging sexual violence or the racialized gender dynamics at play in the monjerío would have defeated the Landmarks Club's objective of luring tourists to Southern California.

In addition to mission restorations, Miller and other boosters found other ways to promote the Spanish imaginary. Examples include John Steven

A view of Mission San Juan Capistrano from the southeast, showing the church and the belfry, ca. 1886. University of Southern California Libraries, California Historical Society Collection, 1860–1960.

A more recent view of Mission San Juan Capistrano with its lush manicured garden, palm trees, and statue of Junípero Serra with an Indian boy, 2019. Wikimedia Commons; California Digital Newspaper Collection, Center for Bibliographic Studies and Research, University of California, Riverside.

*64* CHAPTER TWO

McGroarty's *The Mission Play: A Pageant Play in Three Acts*, a stage performance that presented the end of the Spanish colonial era as a tragedy. McGroarty wrote much of the play at the Mission Inn and completed it in 1911.[38] Garnet Holme first staged his *Ramona Pageant*, a live performance based on that famous novel, in 1923; the outdoor production repeated annually until 2019 and returned to the Ramona Bowl stage in Hemet, California, in 2022.[39]

Another example of local promoters' commitment to the Spanish imaginary is Riverside's pervasive city symbol. According to a local newspaper, Frank Miller patented the trapezoid with a double-cross and a mission bell design in 1908. Mission Inn literature later explained that the cross represented the "rain cross" used for centuries by Indians praying for rain, a symbol Miller reportedly learned from Navajo inmates of Sherman Indian High School.[40] City leaders and entrepreneurs have since ensured that the symbol would become synonymous with Riverside.

Given his commitment to the Spanish imaginary, it is unsurprising that Miller chose his Landmarks Club colleague Arthur Benton to redesign the Glenwood Inn as a Mission Revival showpiece. Benton's design blended elements from Mission Carmel, where Junípero Serra is buried, and Mission San Gabriel, which provided the model for the hotel's *campanario* (bell tower).[41] Several sources tell us what Miller was thinking when he designed the hotel. Benton explained that Miller wanted to "perpetuate the spirit" of the Spanish missions' "old architecture," and to incorporate the details "and ornamentation as found in the missions," which Miller admired "for their own beauty and historic interest" above their "specific fitness for modern uses."[42] Miller biographer Maurice Hodgen agrees, writing that Miller aimed for "an environment of beauty and quiet" that reached backward "to create the imagined spirit of California's Franciscan missions." Miller and Benton's collaboration resulted in the reimagined Mission Inn, which reopened in 1902.[43] The hotel earned high praise from the *Los Angeles Herald*, which called it "indeed a new departure in hotel building." The new hostelry included "a long, low, cloistered building of the Mission type," which enclosed "a spacious court . . . surrounded by magnificent old trees and palms. In the court the old adobe or casino adjoins the stately campinile with its sweet chime of old Mission bells."[44]

In addition to the Mission Inn, Miller and Benton also worked on a new Indian boarding school Miller hoped to build in Riverside. It would not be

Postcard of the Glenwood Mission Inn, Riverside, ca. 1913. The exterior image displays Mission Revival–style architecture. "Glenwood Mission Inn, Riverside, Calif." Miriam and Ira D. Wallach Division of Art, Prints and Photographs: Photography Collection, New York Public Library Digital Collections, accessed February 23, 2024.

the first local off-reservation boarding school; the first had been founded in 1892 in the nearby community of Perris. Miller led efforts to relocate the school to Riverside, citing the inadequacy of the school's water supply. As it happens, Miller owned an interest in the water company that served Perris Indian School. He also held an interest in the Riverside water company that would supply the new school, rights to the land upon which the Perris School stood, and rights to the land of the school's proposed new site in Riverside.[45]

Mission Revival was an even more appropriate architectural style for an Indian boarding school than it had been for Miller's hotel. After all, the institutions served identical functions for their sponsors. Like the Spanish missions, Indian boarding schools existed to control Native bodies. Through them, administrators intended to eliminate Native cultural and spiritual practices and alienate Indigenous peoples culturally into replicas of their colonial masters. The choice of Spanish colonial architecture makes further sense in that both missions and Indian boarding schools utilized Native bodies for their labor, and both based their operational logic on Native

*66* CHAPTER TWO

peoples' difference, or Indians' availability as a threatening Other who required physical as well as cultural control.

Miller's efforts to relocate the Perris Indian School coincided with his discovery of the Spanish imaginary. In an 1899 letter, Miller explained that he was "especially anxious" to relocate the school "as it will mean a great deal to tourist business." He noted the popularity of Helen Hunt Jackson's 1884 novel *Ramona*, a romantic story about California Indians flourishing under the compassionate care of Spanish missionaries and Mexican rancheros.[46] More importantly, wrote Miller, "every other tourist" to California had read Jackson's novel, and each represented tourist revenues lost to Riverside, since "a great many people drive over to the Perris School, a distance of about thirty-two miles, round trip."[47] For Miller, harnessing the Spanish imaginary was the key to capturing those dollars.

Miller was not alone in grasping the commercial potential of Jackson's novel. Southern California boosters rushed to capitalize on *Ramona*, generating advertisements and brochures about the missions to lure tourists to "Ramona Country," where the traveler might experience mission history and behold what remained of California Indians before they disappeared completely.[48]

Miller succeeded when the Indian boarding school reopened in 1903 on Magnolia Avenue in Riverside. The school was renamed to honor Congressman James S. Sherman, who chaired the Indian Affairs committee responsible for funding the school.[49] As anticipated, visitors flocked to the relocated school. As historian Kevin Whalen writes, with its white stucco walls and arches, red-tiled roofs, and bell *campanarios*, complete with Indian children inside, Sherman became a Bureau of Indian Affairs showcase, "a grand homage to the Spanish fantasy."[50]

Miller's contemporaries understood his role in relocating the school. When Riverside celebrated the laying of its new cornerstone in 1901, US President William McKinley sent Miller a letter of congratulations. The cornerstone ceremony included sixteen Perris Indian School inmates, who performed "Oh, Columbia, We Hail Thee," a song celebrating the freedoms that, in theory, alienated Native children would enjoy upon their graduation from Sherman. The singers followed up with renditions of "America," "The Star-Spangled Banner," and the ironically named "My Native Land."[51]

Like all Indian boarding schools run by the federal government's Bureau of Indian Affairs (BIA), education at Sherman was designed, in the words of Carlisle Indian School's Richard Henry Pratt, to "kill the Indian and save the man."[52] Success to the BIA meant stripping Native children of their names, languages, religions, and cultures, and indoctrination in white, middle-class ways. The end goal was to transform Native Americans into punctual, responsible, low-waged American laborers and farmers. The schools were also directly connected to the General Allotment Act, also known as the Dawes Act of 1887. This policy focused on detribalizing Native nations by breaking up reservation lands held in trust and granting land allotments to the individual heads of households. Instead of removal, treaties, and war, this new liberal policy era focused on encouraging Native peoples to be agriculturalists. The boarding schools functioned to teach Native children how to farm their allotments, and the school's curriculum centered on the skills to be self-sufficient farmers within a capitalist system. For example, the school's math curriculum asked students to use simple arithmetic to solve problems concerning land allotments. The Dawes Act proved to be one of the most disastrous policies for Native nations, resulting in a loss of approximately ninety million acres of reservation land.

In California as elsewhere, the BIA's Indian boarding school system of alienation meant removing Indian children from their families and communities. In 1891 Congress authorized the BIA to "make and enforce . . . such rules and regulations as will ensure the attendance of Indian children of suitable age and health at schools established and maintained for their benefit."[53] Indian boarding schools were built off-reservation, often hundreds of miles away from students' families and communities. Students received year-round schooling, with many living at the school for a decade or more, usually with little to no contact with parents or kin. The schools placed Native children under the complete control of BIA teachers and staff so that they would forget their former ways of life and learn to act, talk, and think in ways that white, middle-class, Christian educators deemed appropriate. Many scholars have characterized federally mandated boarding schools as a US policy of assimilation. As Dakota scholar Waziyatawin argues, "that presentation is much too benign." It would be much more accurate to describe the schools as genocide, as outlined in the United Nations Convention for the Prevention and Punishment of Genocide.[54]

The BIA made schooling compulsory for Native children. To punish

## 68   CHAPTER TWO

parents who refused to send their children to boarding schools, in 1893 Congress ordered the BIA to "withhold rations, clothing, and other annuities" to reservation parents and guardians "who refuse or neglect to send and keep their children of proper school age" in BIA boarding schools.[55] And yet, despite BIA efforts, Native students resisted alienation. Just as Acjachemem builders embedded sacred stones and shells into the walls of the great stone church at Mission San Juan Capistrano, and as the Taraaxam subverted colonialism in artwork at Mission San Gabriel, so too did Native students at Indian boarding schools like Sherman draw on their Indigenous cultures to withstand the challenges and violence of their daily experiences.[56]

BIA boarding schools shared essentially the same goals as California's early Spanish missions: administrators were determined to Christianize, reeducate, and detribalize California Indians. Like the Spanish and Mexican missionaries who kidnapped and enslaved California's Native peoples before them, early twentieth-century settlers forced Native families to relinquish their children to state-run Indian boarding schools. A 1902 *Los Angeles Herald* article lamented Indian parents' reluctance to enroll their youth in the Sherman Indian Boarding School. Where African American Southerners were "eagerly seeking education" at Booker T. Washington's Tuskegee Institute, the *Herald* mused, no such clamor for education greeted administrators at Sherman. Instead, "education was compelled to seek the Indian." Looking "at these beautiful buildings, complete and awaiting their inmates," the *Herald* wondered why force was needed to fill Sherman's dormitories and classrooms.[57]

Like the Spanish missions after which it was modeled, Sherman separated students by gender. Sherman was by no means identical to the Spanish missions; however, school administrators followed the logic of Spanish Christian colonial formulas, from enforcing white, middle-class notions of appropriate men's and women's work to ensuring that students replaced the beliefs and practices of their families with the forms and observances of Christianity.[58] The boarding school operated through a reformed version of Spanish conquest reliant on Indian bodies as spiritual possessions, violable to colonial violence. Spaniards constructed monjeríos and *jayuntes* at the missions. Missionaries locked Native girls as young as six overnight in the monjerío, intending to enforce Native sexual chastity before marriage, making the monjerío the first prison in California. Next, missionaries educated neophytes in gendered tasks to support the Spanish global-imperial project. Males learned such skills as agriculture, blacksmithing, and cattle raising; females learned Spanish methods of cooking, cleaning, and textile production and care. Mission success relied on the forced labor of Indians regardless of gender, from forming adobe bricks to erecting mission structures and producing mission goods for consumption and sale.[59]

The Sherman Indian Boarding School's gendered structure was a continuation of the mission's heteropatriarchal logic, including a gendered division of labor. Gradebooks show that Sherman boys took courses in agriculture, blacksmithing, carpentry, engineering, masonry, painting, and shoe and harness repair. Girls, on the other hand, learned American methods of cooking, sewing, laundering, nursing, and poultry raising. Sherman intended to train Native children for what administrators saw as work appropriate to their sex and race. As was true of the missions, the economical and efficient operation of the school relied on the forced labor of both sexes. Boys engaged in construction work at the school, such as building the hospital, workshops, farm buildings, and an auditorium, while girls cooked, cleaned, and laundered for school inmates, administrators, and employees.[60] During a time of rapid economic change in the United States, as the dominance of industrial manufacture gave way to a service-based economy, Sherman students learned trades that would place them at the low-waged end of the labor pool.

A gendered division also marked Sherman's "outing system," by which administrators placed Native child laborers in private white-owned households and businesses. According to Kevin Whalen, Sherman functioned as "an employment agency," offering Native children "as cheap workers" to Riverside employers. Sherman sent Native girls as young as ten years old to serve white households as babysitters and cleaners. Their youth and powerlessness combined to make them susceptible to sexual violence. They were also profoundly underpaid, their meager wages offset by deductions for their room and board. Whether the workers were seasonal or year-round, employers deducted the cost of their meals from their wages. Sherman administrators did little to protect their students from these and other forms of exploitation. Boys working on private farms and ranches were often required to bring bedding so that they could sleep outdoors.[61] The school's educational program fit neatly with the economic goals of local business leaders.

From the beginning, Miller integrated the Sherman School into his hotel

A group of Sherman students ironing in a laundry, ca. 1910. Sherman Indian Museum Collection, https://calisphere.org/item/ark:/86086/n2gq6z9f.

A group of Sherman students working as blacksmiths in a shop, 1900–1930. One is replacing a horseshoe while another repairs a wagon. Sherman Indian Museum Collection, https://calisphere.org/item/ark:/86086/n26d5tg2.

and other commercial enterprises. Guests at the Mission Inn could ride the Pacific Electric Railway, in which Miller was an investor, back and forth between the hotel and school. A 1919 advertisement for the Pacific Electric Railway noted that, for a $3.50 ticket, tourists might travel from Los Angeles to Riverside to experience the magic of the Spanish fantasy past: "At Riverside the car passes down famous Mount Rubidoux crowned by the Junipero Serra cross, to Sherman Indian School." After touring the school, visitors could return to the Mission Inn, "where ample time is given for a tour" of that building and its grounds.[62]

Tourists often wandered Sherman's halls. As the *Los Angeles Herald* reported, the school's "grounds and buildings were visited by hundreds of visitors" each year. Great crowds flocked to the school for tours, entering "the classrooms and buildings to see how the Indian youth are cared for and educated." Just as Miller had envisioned, the school functioned as an educational institution and a human zoo for white tourists. Tourists came to witness, as one historian argues, Native American children in "the march from savagery to civilization."[63]

Frank Miller collaborated with Sherman officials to secure Native students to entertain hotel guests and exploit their labor. In 1903, for example, President Theodore Roosevelt came to Riverside and stayed at the Mission Inn. Miller requested that Sherman superintendent Harwood Hall loan the hotel Native workers for the duration of Roosevelt's stay. "I want half a dozen of your most intellegent boys," wrote Miller. He asked specifically for "George and John," whom he wished "to wait on the President as bell boys." This, he assured Hall, would be an excellent opportunity for the boys, "and I think that the President will enjoy seeing them." More importantly, Miller expected George and John to "impress" Roosevelt with "what an education does for the Indian boy." Miller also requested that Hall send Sherman girls to the hotel to "serenade" the president.[64] In these and other exchanges, Miller discussed Indian children as though they were simply props, human cogs in the Spanish imaginary—as fungible bodies to profit from.

The rebranded Mission Inn invited guests to a celebration on February 24, 1903. The *San Bernardino Sun* noted that it allowed the public to "inspect it inside and out." "Thousands visited the hotel" to view "its elegant accommodations for the incoming guests." The opening included a "grand opening ball" for those in the "fashionable society." Opening day festivities

A postcard depicting students drilling in gendered formations on the Sherman Institute campus with spectators present, ca. 1910. Sherman Indian Museum collection, https://calisphere.org/item/ark:/86086/n2b56m0h.

concluded, noted the *Los Angeles Herald*, with a ceremonial raising of the US flag. With Stars and Stripes "floating over the new hotel," guests heard "patriotic songs" performed by "the Sherman Institute Band."[65] The flag-raising ceremony, with its performance by Native child prisoners from the Sherman School, demonstrated the success of Manifest Destiny and the racial ascendence of Anglo-Americans in California.

Miller's contemporaries lauded him for his foresight. Writing in 1905, eugenicist and Stanford University president David Starr Jordan rhapsodized over the Mission Inn. "It has been left to you," he wrote, "Frank Miller, a genuine Californian, to dream of the hotel that ought to be, to turn your ideal into plaster and stone." Miller's gift to "mountain-belted Riverside" was "the one hotel which a Californian can recognize as his own." "No one," Jordan vowed, could leave the hospitable Mission Inn "without a resolve to come back again." The hotel was more than a hotel: it symbolized "the region where such things are possible—to the region where in time all noble things shall be possible."[66]

## Mission Revival's Long Shadow

The Sherman Indian Boarding School and the Mission Inn illustrate how Mission Revival architecture and the Spanish imaginary support the goals of American capitalism. As non-Indigenous settlers, Miller and others appropriated more than colonial Spanish architecture: they also benefited from their conquest, enslavement, and dispossession of the state's Indigenous peoples. Untold numbers of Mission Inn guests have taken at face value its benign rendering of the mission era, incorrectly concluding that the missions were pleasant, peaceful, and beautiful places.

The Spanish imaginary continues to distort popular conceptions of the state's history. Beginning in the 1920s, for example, California's public school teachers presented fourth-grade students with fanciful lessons about the mission era. Underscoring this chapter's central argument, these lessons typically asked students to build models of the missions, often out of sugar cubes, as though the architecture was the key to understanding colonial Spanish California. Students learn through such curriculum of a benign colonialism that Indians had no reason to resist. For many students (and teachers), fourth grade was the first and last time they learned anything about California Indians. As a result, say the authors of a recent study, students gained "a limited and distorted perspective of the history of the state." Moreover, this instruction prioritized the Spanish over the Indigenous peoples who were here before them. Only recently have fourth-grade public school teachers begun to rethink lessons about this era.[67] The long shadow of the Spanish imaginary has disavowed California Indian voices and scholarship, including their persistent argument that the missions enslaved them and their ancestors.

Symbols of the Spanish imaginary survive throughout California, from Riverside's tolling bells to the hundreds of bells that line El Camino Real ("the highway of the king") that once, as the mythology states, connected California's Spanish missions. Los Angeles's Olvera Street offers tourists a trip into the past at a supposedly authentic Mexican marketplace developed by the city of Los Angeles within its El Pueblo de Los Angeles Historic Monument. Statues of Franciscan missionary Junípero Serra are another powerful symbol. For generations, educators from kindergarten through university have taught that California's history began with Serra.[68] A 1904

74   CHAPTER TWO

newspaper article, for example, proclaimed Serra's importance as a "physical influence upon the history of the West—the first white leader to come into the wilderness, where he labored lovingly." Eight decades later, a 1984 newspaper poll found that two-thirds of Californians still considered Serra the most important person in the state's history. Non-Indigenous scholars continue to emphasize Serra's significance and that of other missionaries, both in state and national history. Native scholars, on the other hand, emphasize the complicity of Serra and other missionaries in Spanish violence against Native Californians. For Native scholars, missions were instruments of genocidal Spanish policies and practices.[69]

Regarding timing, it is worth noting that the placing of bells along El Camino Real and statues honoring Serra coincided with California's embrace of Mission Revival architecture. They coincide as well with the push around the United States—not only in the South—to erect monuments honoring symbols of the Confederacy. In the decades following the American Civil War, opponents of racial equality erected monuments to Confederate heroes. Proponents of memorials to various Confederate leaders presented the men as cultural heroes who dared to resist Reconstruction and the reordering of racial hierarchies it represented. The erection of Confederate monuments intensified in the 1920s as white Americans moved to codify Jim Crow and the social and political disenfranchisement of African Americans. Statues honoring Robert E. Lee, like those valorizing San Junípero Serra, romanticize a fantasy past that is intrinsically linked to the preservation of white supremacy, typically by violence against people of color.[70]

The power of the Spanish imaginary explains why, in the 1930s, Californians chose Junípero Serra to represent them in Washington, DC's National Statuary Hall. Serra fulfilled a similar symbolic function for white Californians as statues of Robert E. Lee did for white Southerners: dispossession of California Indians and the seizure of California from Mexico. As historian Laura E. Gomez explains, Californians' selection of Serra as a state hero helped to resolve thorny questions about inclusion and exclusion in the American polity.[71] Monuments to Serra, like Mission Revival architecture, helped Americans in California to build a polity based on conquering, then excluding, people of color.

Southern California communities continue to raise the Spanish imaginary flag. Published in 2003, Riverside's architectural heritage guidebook offers a benign explanation of the purposes of Mission Revival architecture. "Instead of reacting to Eastern styles, which focused on the Colonial Revival style architecture," they championed Mission Revival as "an assertion of the state's individuality."[72] In asserting American settlers' pride in the region's "rich Hispanic heritage," Riverside glosses over the violence with which Spain, Mexico, and then the United States wrested control over the land and its people.

Riverside's city symbol, a trapezoid with a double-cross and mission bell, continues to promote Frank Miller's vision of the Spanish imaginary. Local leaders placed the icon on bridges and streetlamps and attached the Raincross moniker to a downtown plaza and a public high school. Entrepreneurs and artists followed suit: visitors today can buy Raincross jewelry and tattoos, stay at the Raincross Hotel, rent an apartment at the Raincross Promenade, visit their elders at the Raincross Senior Village, or get medical care from the Raincross Medical Group.[73]

The city retains its commitment to the Spanish imaginary through its web page. At this writing, Riverside's web page confirms that its "unique City Raincross Symbol" is based on "a replica of the mass bell used by Father Junipero Serra, missionary priest and founder of the California Missions," commissioned by Frank Miller for the Mission Inn and later given to the city for its use. Even though no mission was ever located there, Riverside admits that it uses its symbol for commercial purposes. "Playing on the nostalgia for the state's Spanish heritage and the romanticized images of the missions and the Indians," the website explains, American settlers "worked together to market Riverside as a Spanish Mediterranean Mecca."[74] For many California Indians, Riverside's decision to use this symbol is analogous to a German city adopting the image of a concentration camp as a marketing tool. The Spanish imaginary, with its various symbols, including architecture, statues, and mission bells, memorializes a romanticized history that erases Native experiences, including resistance, and functions as state- and corporate-sponsored white supremacist propaganda.

———

Despite its willful misrepresentation of California history, the Spanish imaginary will undoubtedly continue to shape how residents and visitors understand the region's past. If asked, few residents of Riverside (or California, or the United States, Canada, Mexico, etc.) would likely be able to identify which tribe's traditional and unceded territory they reside on. They also would have few stories to tell of Native resistance, obscured as it has been through the Spanish imaginary. Yet Riverside residents would be able to identify the Mission Inn and perhaps recognize the name of Frank A. Miller, whose legacy of shaping the Spanish imaginary and integrating it into Riverside's built environment was honored by the city in its naming of a middle school and a regional memorial park after him.

Analysis of the founding of the region's first missions from a Native perspective reveals that there is a need to reassert Native peoples into the history of California, those who attempted to escape the gratuitous terror of the mission, and the many generations of California Indians who lived before colonization. By identifying the Spanish imaginary where we find it, by understanding the commitment to white supremacy embodied in this long-standing collective hallucination, this chapter asks that precolonial spirit to return and the beauty of Native generative refusals to continue and offer us guidance into a future of environmental changes wrought by colonialism.

The environmental devastation coupled with the violence of conquest is apocalyptic—ending Native worlds. With a focus on land and water, specifically the Santa Ana River, chapter 3 connects the violence of conquest, which demands dispossession and the social death of the enslaved, with environmental devastation and the legacy of romanticizing Indian death and the disavowal of slavery at the missions.

# THREE

## Apocalyptic Colonialism

### *Environmental Devastation of Wanáw Waníicha / Kahoo' Paxaayt / Santa Ana River*

On September 6, 2015, the Juaneño Band of Mission Indians, Acjachemen Nation (Belardes) passed a historic resolution opposing the canonization of Junípero Serra and called on Pope Francis to rescind the Doctrine of Discovery and support the United Nations Declaration on the Rights of Indigenous Peoples. The Acjachemen Nation, as a sovereign political body, sent the pope and Vatican its formal opposition to the canonization of Junípero Serra, continuing the legacy of the Acjachemem ancestors who had repeatedly resisted the spiritual conquest of their lands and souls at Mission San Juan Capistrano.[1] The tribe's opposition to the canonization targeted Serra's uplifting of "Church and State doctrinal policies aimed at the eradication of Indigenous cultural, linguistic, and spiritual beliefs and practices." Furthermore, the tribe stated that the spiritual conquest has had "far reaching and long lasting negative impacts on the Indigenous Peoples of the hemisphere and around the world as a result of such policies and practices."[2] The Acjachemen resolution against the canonization of Serra concretely connects the spiritual project of conquest on their traditional territory with the global colonial project of white supremacy and land devastation.

According to Tribal Chairman Matias Belardes, "The process of sainthood and canonization is symbolic—and Father Junipero Serra was a symbol of colonization. It is the uplifting of this symbol . . . to which we object." Belardes explains that Serra "was a man of his time, and that time was a period during which the very humanity of our Ancestors was called into question by the legal and religious doctrines espoused by the Church and State."[3] Belardes and the Acjachemen Nation argue that Serra and similar men of their time chose not to see the humanity of Indigenous peoples and do not deserve to be celebrated. "The context of the 'time' that Serra was 'a

78 CHAPTER THREE

man of," according to Shawnee-Lenape scholar Steven Newcomb, "was a context expressed in numerous papal edicts of the fifteenth century issued by popes who were men of their time." Among the directives of conquest that Serra and other colonizers carried out were to "invade, capture, vanquish, and subdue, all Saracens, pagans, and other enemies of Christ," to "reduce their persons to perpetual slavery," and to "take away all their possessions and property."[4]

To judge Serra as a man of his time, the Acjachemen argue, is to understand his time as one replete with white supremacist ideologies intent on subduing and enslaving non-Christians, including Indigenous peoples of the Americas and Africa. Serra was a man of his time who uplifted and fulfilled these racist edicts, not a man who challenged them. Celebrating Serra is a celebration of Indian death. In fact, in his writings, there are many instances where he celebrated Indian death:

> In the midst of all our little troubles, the spiritual side of the missions is developing most happily. In [Mission] San Antonio there are simultaneously two harvests, at one time, one for wheat, and [one] of a plague among the children who are dying.
>
> Conquest would thus be hastened to a most notable degree, assuming a harvest of many souls for heaven.[5]

The death experienced in California was not limited to humans, as colonialism invariably harmed nonhuman life and the environment. The Acjachemen Nation's resolution states that their territory and environment have been "heavily and forever altered as a result . . . of the Doctrine of Discovery and the subsequent imposition of the Spanish Mission System on our Ancestors and the Ancestors of surrounding Indigenous Nations."[6] The Acjachemen Nation linked the devastating environmental impact on their lands to the Doctrine of Discovery, which implemented land dispossession and the possession of Native souls through baptism and alienation, beginning in California with the mission system. Their 2015 resolution closely resembles the statements their ancestors had made more than two hundred years before, in 1778 (chapter 2), immediately linking colonialism to environmental devastation and the long-term impact it would have on their people. By 1778, only two years after the founding of Mission San Juan Capistrano, the Acjachemem had already observed that their "seeds," which made up their principal food source, had been reduced, that it had not rained, and that their rivers, streams, and springs had been harmed by the violence of colonialism. Scholars who have studied the environment and rainfall through tree ring data during the mission era confirm Acjachemem experiences of multiple drought periods beginning shortly after the arrival of the Spanish.[7]

The resolution passed by the Acjachemen Nation was a refusal of the canonization of Serra and the ongoing celebration of California Indian death. It was also a refusal of the simultaneous celebration of the devastation to the environment. When studied together, the violence of colonization in California against land and people can best be understood as apocalyptic, ending their ancestors' worlds and socially alienating them from their relationships and obligations to place. The largest riparian ecosystem in Southern California—the Wanáw Waníicha in the Acjachemem language of Chamteela, Kahoo' Paxaayt in the language of the Taraaxam, and the Santa Ana River in a hybrid of Spanish and English languages—brings into focus the environmental devastation to Acjachemem and Taraaxam homelands.

## Apocalypse

In *Bad Indians: A Tribal Memoir*, Ohlone-Costanoan Esselen and Chumash scholar Deborah A. Miranda explains that California Indians had their worlds come to an end. They are the survivors of "a great holocaust: out of an estimated one million Indigenous inhabitants, only twenty thousand survived the missionization era." The first chapter in her significant and critical tribal memoir is titled "The End of the World: Missionization, 1770–1836." During this era, an estimated 80 percent of the precolonial California Indian population perished. Miranda provides a "genealogy of violence" from which the primary methods of conquest in California can be analyzed: sexual violence, murder, capital punishment, invasion, paternalism, missionization, land theft, and slavery. Building on Eduardo Duran, Miranda explains that California Indians, through the processes of colonialism centered on

*80* CHAPTER THREE

Native dispossession and the dominance of foreign authority, inherit a soul wound: "a wound which we negotiate everyday of our lives." The mission, as Miranda clarifies, "was meant to suck in Indigenous peoples . . . strip them of religion, language, and culture, and melt them down into generic workers instilled with Catholicism, Spanish values, and freshly overhauled, tuned-up souls." The devastation of colonialism, as Frantz Fanon explains it, included having Native "customs and the agencies to which they refer . . . abolished because they were in contradiction with a new civilization that imposed its own." Historian Jack D. Forbes explains it this way: "From the native viewpoint, the missions were a catastrophe of indescribable proportions."[8] The spiritual conquest of California was devastating to people and land. It was the end of the world, an apocalypse.

The biopolitical control exerted by the Spanish and Franciscan priests was apocalyptic, aimed at alienating individual and collective ontology, memory, ancestral heritage, and relationships to land. The logic of spiritual possession names the corporeal, cultural, social, psychological, spiritual, and racial colonial terror enacted with the intentionality of ending Native worlds through the coming of Christ in sheep's clothing. The missionaries cannibalized the bodies and souls of Native peoples and their lands to extend and maintain empire through their evangelical slave regime.[9] The consecutive colonial eras of Spain, Mexico, and the United States distinctively regimented racial colonial violence, which continues today. California Indians are the survivors of an apocalypse that began with the missionary and Spanish military's invasion, continues through the mass settlement of California Indian lands, and has completely altered many of their landscapes, sacred places, and environments. Much of the landscape within the traditional territories of the Taraaxam and Acjachemem (Los Angeles and Orange Counties)—lands they continue to call home—are radically disfigured and desecrated. The Santa Ana River in Orange County provides a site that almost completely captures an apocalyptic scene from a movie. In many locations, it has little life—only concrete—barren of plants, water, and animals. Comparing the early writings of the Spanish, who described the river as full of water and life with its current state, devoid of being, is best described as apocalyptic. The devastation to the environment is colonialism.

Lawrence Gross explains, "To put it in a word, American Indians have seen the end of their respective worlds. Using vocabulary from the study of religion, this should be correctly termed an apocalypse." The word *apocalypse* is Old English, via Old French and ecclesiastical Latin from Greek *apokalupsis*, from *apokaluptein* "uncover, reveal," from *apo-*, "un," and *-kaluptein*, "to cover."[10] Apocalypse, translated literally from the original Greek, means "a disclosure of knowledge, a revelation." In this translation, Christianity appropriated apocalypse to refer to the revelation given to John and the end of the present age where good will triumph over evil. In a Christian understanding, the apocalypse is an event yet to come. Within Christian theology, a branch of study known as eschatology originates from the Greek *eschatos*, "last," and *-logy*, "the study of." *Eschatology* is a theological science concerned with death, judgment, heaven, and hell. Apocalypse is referenced in theological study and the Nicene Creed as both an earthly and spiritual end time with the second coming of Christ, His judgment of the living and the dead, and the resurrection of the dead into His kingdom with no end.[11] However, the word *apocalypse* has commonly (secularly) become known as representing "the end of the world"—the end of the human race.

The apocalypse is viewed as something yet to come in the form of spiritual revelation, nuclear holocaust, astronomical catastrophe, alien invasion, ecological and geophysical disasters, biological pandemics, zombie infections, warfare, or another science-related cataclysm. In general, fiction and films have told the story of the apocalypse and the post-apocalypse in two ways: utopian idealism or a dystopian wasteland. In utopian idealism, the story revolves around the rebirth and resurrection of humanity into a society without social injustices. The dystopian wasteland, however, often focuses on the resolve of a lone American white male Christian survivor who had previously been middle class—the targeted audience and the population who, from an American exceptionalism point of view, has the most to lose.[12] The story is told from the point of view of the heroic survivor and simultaneously displays other surviving humans as cannibalistic, scraping out an existence in an anarchic state of corruption. English scholar Hannah Stark argues that dystopian literature is a "repository of our already existing fears, projected into a future world." Furthermore, she explains climate fiction is "exemplary in this case because it shows us the terrible future of the planet that we already suspect may come to pass."[13]

*82* CHAPTER THREE

An example of a fictionalized apocalyptic dystopian future is the novel and subsequent film *The Road*, written by Cormac McCarthy. The plot of *The Road* centers on a man and his son's struggle to survive an earth ravaged by environmental destruction. Within the dangerous postapocalyptic world that McCarthy creates, the man and boy travel through the aftermath of an undisclosed extinction event scavenging for food and avoiding thieves, rapists, and gangs of cannibals. The environment they traverse is devoid of vegetation, and the sky is perpetually gray. *The Road* warns about future environmental catastrophes and relies on Christian biblical narratives of Revelation. As Stark notes, "The representation of this world is heavily reliant on the eschatological imagery of the book of Revelation. The intertextual references to this great apocalyptic text include the increasing darkness, the blackening sun, the charred earth, lightning, earthquakes, a dead ocean, and poisoned bodies of water."[14] The representation of the post-apocalypse in the novel contrasts with the time before, of unspoiled nature. The environmental change in the novel is significant to the plot and divides time between before and after the unnamed event that caused the bleak circumstances the protagonists negotiate. McCarthy describes the land after as "barren, silent, godless," where there is "nothing living anywhere." The trees have "raw dead limbs," in a "waste of weeds" with "dry seedpods" and "dead seaoats." The before exists only in the protagonist's dreams of blue skies and a fertile green landscape. McCarthy writes that the streams in the mountains of the before were full of brook trout, and within the deep glens lived plants and animals that "were older than man and hummed with mystery." The protagonist is a man old enough to be born before: "a being from a planet that no longer existed." Stark elaborates, "the man questions whether his own ancestors watch him, and dreams of them casting 'fey sideways looks upon him.'"[15] The apocalypse dispossessed the world he knew before, the world created and ended by his ancestors—a world his son will never know.

The fictional apocalypse in *The Road* brought devastation to land and humans, alienating the survivors from the experience of their ancestors, who lived in a place that no longer exists. The survivors merely endure, in contrast to the full lives and the world they thrived in before. They were alienated from their environment, which was fertile and provided sustenance. In many ways, the postapocalyptic setting of fictional stories such as *The Road* can be compared to the history of California Indians after the mission system, when land and people were devastated (destroyed and brought to overwhelming grief) by conquest. The Indians used multiple strategies to survive, including by becoming thieves themselves, blending into the dominant society as wage laborers, and doing all they could to avoid the settlers, particularly in Northern California, where the American colonizers were determined to enslave or kill as many Indians as possible and passed laws to make it legal. In downtown Los Angeles during the 1850s, there was a slave market where American citizens purchased Indians to exploit their labor after they had been imprisoned for vagrancy and consuming alcohol. In comparison to *The Road*, the cannibals of the apocalypse in Indians' reality were the Americans who devoured people and place.[16]

The apocalypse, as written about by French philosopher Jacques Derrida, exists only in the realm of discourse. He argues, specifically about a nuclear apocalypse, that it "is a speculation, an invention in the sense of a fable." Concerned with temporality, he writes, "nuclear war has no precedent. It has never occurred, itself; it is a non-event."[17] In philosophical discussions, the apocalypse is seen solely as a work of fiction, as a fear of a future without a historical basis. However, for California Indians, the apocalypse has already happened. It is in the past, or as Heidegger might prefer, the "no longer," the "before." Deborah A. Miranda explains that the end of the world "is not science fiction to California Indians."[18] As she clarifies, the cause of the apocalypse (mass death and environmental devastation) was the spiritually transformative set of events to human and more-than-human life in California that began with Junípero Serra and his spiritual mission of evangelical slavery.

The post-apocalypse continues today through mass settlement and rapacious capitalist development, dispossessing California Indians from the worlds of their ancestors. Those who exist in the after can only ever know the after. Survivors of an apocalypse can only imagine and dream of the before, the world of their ancestors—a world gone forever. This is Native alienation. To borrow from Pablo Tac's writings, we can apply the Payómkawichum/Acjachemem word *ahíichu* to provide a Native perspective on the apocalypse. Villiana Hyde (Luiseño) uses *ahíichu* in song lyrics in the book *Yumáyk Yumáyk*: "My mouth became stiff. And my mouth lost its feeling

## CHAPTER THREE

in death and nothingness. My mouth is lonely (I have no one to talk to)." In the final line of the song, *ahtichu* translates as "lonely." In the Rincón Luiseño language dictionary, *ahtichu* means "orphan, abandoned child, lonely person."[19] The word *ahtichu* and the song lyrics assist us in understanding what it means to live in the post-apocalypse. *Ahtichu*, in this context, refers to the time and space of abandonment from your history, ancestors, and a worldview reliant on language vitally connected to spirituality and environmental knowledge of place. In the apocalypse, we are lost in the feeling of death and nothingness, lonely as orphaned children whose past worlds are gone forever.

> Nótma pí' puráarya pí.'
> Takwáyya pí' nótma pí' pí'mukvonga yáawaxnga.
> Nótma pí' 'ahííchumay tamáawumal.

## Wanáw Waníicha/Kahoo' Paxaayt/Santa Ana River

The missionized Indians and their descendants can only imagine and dream of their prior worlds and how living in them felt. The "mission Indian" has been alienated from those worlds. However, the ancestors and spirits are still within the land, allowing glimpses of the prior world to be felt, heard, and envisioned. The ancestors continue to exist in the spirit world, untouchable by mortal violence. The Spanish-church dyad could not envision that the Native spirit world could outlast Christian scripture. The spirit world can never be entirely eradicated from the land, no matter the violence inflicted upon the corporeal, psychological, philosophical, and spiritual being of the Native. The land has its own power and its own memory. Native peoples continue to work hard to relearn from their ancestors and the power of the earth despite experiencing *ahtichu*. The Native alienation of conquest could never completely alienate the Native from their ancestors, even when the places held sacred are no longer there or have become unrecognizable. For instance, Southern California's watersheds and riparian ecosystems have been devastated and desecrated, including its largest riparian ecosystem, named Wanáw Waníicha in the Acjachemem language of Chamteela, Kahoo' Paxaayt in the language of the Taraaxam, and the Santa Ana River in a hybrid of Spanish and English languages. The tribes whose traditional territories lay along its banks refuse to allow the river to be completely alienated from their social worlds, from the Yuhaaviatam, whose traditional territory includes the river's headwaters, to the shared coastal territory of the Acjachemem and Taraaxam.

Sustained colonialism in this region of California began on Friday, July 28, 1769, when the Gaspar de Portolá expedition reached the Wanáw Waníicha/Kahoo' Paxaayt (yet to be named Santa Ana) near the present-day colonial city of Anaheim (Orange County, California). Miguel Costansó, a Catalonian engineer, cartographer, and cosmographer kept a journal of their trip north from San Diego on Portolá's failed mission to locate Monterey.[20] In his journal entries, Costansó described the land, the waters, and the Indigenous peoples they met along the way. Catalonian soldiers, leather-jacketed soldiers, Christian Indians from Baja California, and priests accompanied Portolá. Upon reaching the Santa Ana River, Costansó wrote, "It is a beautiful river, and carries great floods in the rainy season, as is apparent from its bed and the sand along its banks. This place has many groves of willows and very good soil, all of which can be irrigated for a great distance." Costansó describes a living riparian ecosystem. It is easy to imagine from his depiction a beautiful river full of water surrounded by the lush greenery of trees swaying in the wind with abundant populations of animals, birds, insects, fish, and humans all able to live because of the life provided by the clean water of the river. His writing displays the river as one that seasonally floods and as a living being, changing the landscape as it naturally fluctuates in size and alternates its course. Costansó's journal also exhibits Spanish conceptions of the environment—as something to be transformed, domesticated, and possessed. Costansó stated, "We pitched our camp on the left bank of the river. To the right there is a populous Indian village; the inhabitants received us with great kindness."[21]

Mission priest Father Juan Crespí also kept a diary as he traveled north with the Portolá expedition. His description of Kahoo' Paxaayt ("the long river") on that same summer day is almost identical to that of Costansó. "About seven in the morning we set out," Crespí explained, continuing their way toward the northwest along the edge of the mountains. Soon, they "came to the banks of a river which has a bed of running water about ten

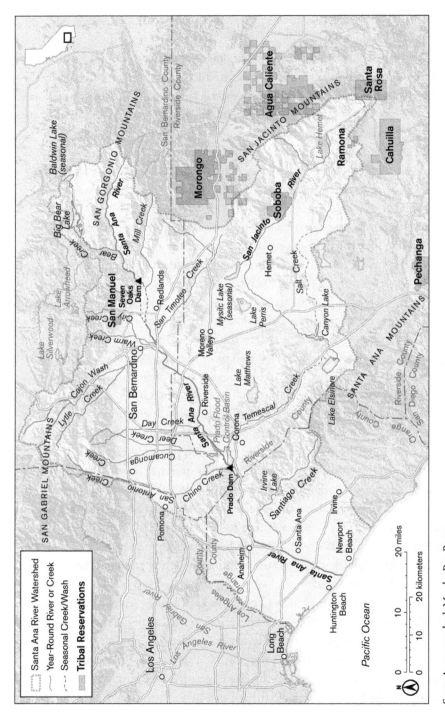

Santa Ana watershed. Map by Ben Pease.

varas wide and half a vara deep"—approximately 27.5 feet wide and 1.5 feet deep. He explains, "It is not at all boxed in by banks. Its course is from northeast to southwest.... It apparently has its source in the range that we have in sight on the right, about three leagues from the road that we are following." Crespí correctly traces the origins of Wanáw Waníicha to the mountains above what is now called San Bernardino, flowing toward the southwest for approximately 96 miles until it empties into the Pacific Ocean. The river's watershed spans 2,840 square miles and has more than 50 tributaries.[22] Crespí's description also states that they followed a "road"—a well-worn trail used since time immemorial by the Indians for trade and travel. In his description, Crespí states, "The bed of the river is well grown with sycamores, alders, willows, and other trees which we have not recognized. It is evident from the sand on its banks that in the rainy season it must have great floods which would prevent crossing it." Crespí also views the river and the land as domesticable, "It has a great deal of good land which can easily be irrigated. We pitched camp on the left bank of this river. On its right bank there is a populous village of Indians, who received us with great friendliness."[23] This was most likely the village of Hotuukgna.

Costansó and Crespí's descriptions of the Santa Ana River on a late July summer day starkly contrast the river's current state of possession. Much of the lower Santa Ana River, below the Prado Dam, is ecologically dead, having its ecological life and power as a living being suspended through domestication. What had been a perennial (continuous) and powerful river has been reduced to a domesticated and ephemeral river—only flowing as a reaction to rainfall or runoff. Kahoo' Paxaayt, in the same area where Costansó and Crespí describe it as a "beautiful river," is now channelized and entombed in concrete. It has very little, if any, vegetation. Many fish, animals, and plants the river supported no longer exist and are extinct, including the California grizzly bear, the Southern California kit fox, the gray wolf, and the river's steelhead trout.

The last California grizzly bear was reported killed in 1908 in the Santa Ana Mountains, above the river. Locals had named the grizzly Moccasin John, and they attempted to kill it many times over several years. The hunters set out a light trap they would normally use to catch mountain lions. The trap snapped onto the bear's leg, and it hobbled away. They followed the metal

Santa Ana River in Anaheim, with Angel Stadium "A" in the background. Photo by Downtowngal, Wikimedia Commons, https://commons.wikimedia.org/wiki/File:Santa_Ana_River_Anaheim.jpg.

marks left by the bear's escape path for more than five miles. With a pack of dogs, the hunters cornered the bear. The dogs attacked and subdued it long enough for Ed Adkinson to shoot the bear with a .30-30 rifle. As sensationalized in a newspaper article: "The bullet struck her in the left shoulder, and Moccasin John went down. Another shot followed the first. The four men came up, and Moccasin John was still snapping at the dogs. Another bullet was fired and she was dead." The newspaper details the skinning and investigation of the bear to prove it was a grizzly. "With her death goes the last of her kind in the Santa Ana Mountains," the article declares as a victory for humans over the wild.[24]

In addition to the extinct fish, mammals, and plants are several more threatened and endangered species. The important ecological relationships between water, plants, fish, insects, animals, birds, and humans have been alienated. The river is a social-ecological dead zone—where humans no longer have a relationship with the environment. Humans treat the lower Santa Ana River as dead and nonexistent. It is not treated as a living being that, if taken care of, would be fully alive and provide sustenance. Instead, Wanáw Waníicha is an afterthought, if it is thought of at all. It is viewed as something humans should be excluded from. The social-ecological death of a place or a river is not necessarily a biological death but an extreme form of the power relations of the domination and domestication of an environment, both physically and in the psychology of people alienated from their environment by spaces deemed uninhabitable.

The social-ecological death of the Santa Ana River is human-made, including its channelization and entombing in concrete, restricting its flow by constructing dams, and its use as a dumping ground for pollution: septic waste, urban runoff, wastewater, chemical and metallic contaminants, and animal manure. As Red River Métis scholar Max Liboiron argues, "pollution is best understood as the violence of colonial land relations rather than environmental damage."[25] The devastation to the environment of the Santa Ana River is directly caused by colonial power relations that view Indigenous land as possessable and domesticable—in a similar manner as they viewed Native peoples and the grizzly bear. In my paper "Our Sacred Waters," I argue that the mission slave regime's attempt to domesticate California Indian women can be compared to the violence enacted against the river.[26] Both the river and Indian women (along with two-spirit and queer folks) were intensely focused on by the colonizers to assist in the development and maintenance of empire in California. Through their captivity within the monjerío, the Franciscans could enforce heterosexuality and gendered labor on California Indian women.

With the first prisons in California, the Spanish colonial violence domesticated Indian women for their perceived purpose as racialized female flesh within the Spanish Christian patriarchal system; the monjerío was colonial violence and Native alienation. The domestication project of the monjerío assisted in alienating the Indian slave from the worlds of their ancestors, including their human–land relationships. The river, too, needed to be domesticated by imprisoning it behind concrete to allow Orange County, much of which lay in a flood zone, to be developed for agriculture, housing, and businesses. The social-ecological death of the Santa Ana River, coupled with the human devastation experienced by Acjachemem and Taraaxam, can best be understood as apocalyptic colonial violence. The geographic space of Kahoo' Paxaayt that remains is viewed as uninhabitable—a space of otherness, homelessness, and danger. Although domesticated and socially-ecologically

*90*  CHAPTER THREE

and geographically alienated and exiled from the lived experience of most residents of Southern California, the Wanáw Waníicha refuses to stop being a river and a problem for the power relations of colonialism.

## The Damming of the Lower Santa Ana River

The Prado Dam is in Riverside County, approximately two miles west of the city of Corona and thirty miles upstream from the Pacific Ocean. It was constructed by the Army Corps of Engineers and completed in April of 1941, authorized by the Flood Control Act of June 22, 1936. It was built at a natural constriction of the lower Santa Ana Canyon, where several creeks join the Santa Ana River. The reservoir created by the damming of the river is in Riverside and San Bernardino Counties. The dam provides flood control and water storage for the growing communities in the counties of Orange, Riverside, and San Bernardino. However, Orange County receives the primary benefits from the dam by controlling floods and any potential damage through flooding. The population within the Santa Ana watershed is one of the fastest-growing in California, home to more than six million people.[27]

In 2019 the Army Corps of Engineers raised concerns about the potential failure of the Prado Dam spillway. This assessment of the dam changed the risk level and increased the urgency of improving it. "Risk factors identified indicate the potential for poor spillway performance, which could have adverse impacts to the downstream population, if a significant flood event occurs," the corps cautioned in a press release. It also noted that downstream from the dam in the Santa Ana River flood zone are twenty-nine cities with more than $61 billion worth of property.[28] The increased risk assessment was produced while work had been under way since 2002 to increase the amount of floodwaters and sediment the reservoir can store. Recent modifications to the dam, spillway, and river channel, including raising the dam embankment and constructing a new outlet that can control the release of water at a higher capacity. It also includes strengthening the river channel to protect infrastructure and development, such as the 91 freeway and railroad crossings. These improvements, according to the US Army Corps of Engineers, "will greatly increase the level of flood protection to the communities of Orange County that are located within the Santa Ana River flood plain."[29]

The purpose of constructing the dam in 1941 and the recent strengthening of the dam, spillway, and river channel originated with discourse about the river as a danger to human/white life reminiscent of language used to describe Indians as dangerous to civilized/white society. The archival record demonstrates the regular flooding of the Santa Ana River, beginning with the first written records the Spanish wrote about it, stating that in the rainy season, it carries great floods. In June 1884 the *Los Angeles Herald* reported, "The Santa Ana River is so high from melting snow in the mountains that it is not fordable." In December 1889 the *Herald* stated, "The Santa Ana river ... [is] out of [its] banks ... flooding the Newport district, west and south of the city, and causing great loss of crops and other property." Again, in March 1895, it reported, "The Santa Ana River is on a *bender* and has broken over the levee. It is flooding the lowlands near Newport. ... There has been no damage yet, but some is certain to occur to the crops growing nicely." In the same article, the *Herald* stated, "A number of new houses are going up in Santa Ana, and many more are in contemplation."[30] Despite the regular flooding of the Santa Ana River, the lower floodplain became an important location for American development and agriculture.

Underscoring the persistent flooding patterns, in November 1900 the *San Francisco Call* reported, "The Santa Ana River is out of its banks tonight and flooding valuable farming lands in a new course to the sea. Low-lying celery lands south of here are partially submerged, and much of the crop will be ruined." In 1906 headlines narrated, "Santa Ana River Goes on A Rampage."[31] And in 1910 the *Los Angeles Herald* reported, "The flood waters which covered thousands of acres in Orange county yesterday morning are subsiding" after the river had destroyed the celery crop "to an extent of $50,000 or $76,000." The flood plain of Orange County at the time was "where the greatest body of celery in the world is annually grown, were covered with water, flooding the celery which was being harvested and shipped."[32] The flooding also temporarily blocked the Pacific Electric railroad between Los Angeles, Santa Ana, and Huntington Beach. Moreover, the *Herald* reported, "Two bridges were washed out. ... The steel bridge of the Santa Fe at Yorba is badly damaged, swaying in the middle. Much trackage is washed out on the Santa Fe between Yorba and Olive." In 1916 bridges were again obstructed by floodwaters, trains were stopped, and property was damaged. "Hundreds of people," it was reported, "were told to flee for their lives."[33]

*92* CHAPTER THREE

The authors who reported the flooding river often provided it with personification, as exemplified in a *Los Angeles Herald* article from 1916: "The Santa Ana River, storm swelled to a width of a mile and a half, is on a *rampage*." Again, in 1921, the "Santa Ana River [was] on a *rampage*." And in 1938 "the Santa Ana River [was again] on the *rampage*, smashing through man-made walls, and carrying dead cows, horses and chickens; parts of houses, thousands of oranges and all kinds of debris."[34] The 1938 flood killed 19 people, left 2,000 temporarily homeless, and covered 68,400 acres with water. That flood was the impetus to construct a dam. To control and domesticate the river from its "rampages" and "benders," it was further channelized, dammed, diverted, and held in reservoirs. And although the river could be dangerous, in fact deadly, the larger reason for controlling the Santa Ana River was not to protect individual life but to protect property and white life—to expand and nourish empire—devouring all that gets in its way. The domestication and domination of the river simultaneously enabled its use as a resource for irrigation, consumption, property, and electrical power. Its ecosystem was drastically changed to support the further development of empire throughout the flood basin in Orange County. Wanáw Waníicha/Kahoo' Paxaayt was turned into a possession through colonialism and viewed by the colonizers as important to the establishment, maintenance, and extension of empire through domination and domestication, alienating it from the human–land relationships developed over millennia by the original peoples of the land.

Orange County was growing; there was money to be made in development and real estate. Santa Ana had to be domesticated into submission so that white men could make their fortunes on the marketing of Indigenous homelands. The Santa Ana River Vision Plan stated, "The magnitude of the event [flooding] served as the impetus for construction of the Prado Dam, thus paving the way for the post–World War II building boom which began the conversion from large agricultural operations to housing and commercial development projects." Another significant flood occurred along the Santa Ana in 1969, two hundred years after the beginning of colonization. This flood, according to the River Vision Plan, prompted the US Army Corps of Engineers to declare "the Santa Ana River to be the greatest flood threat west of the Mississippi River, thus spurring the creation of the Santa Ana River Mainstem Project, which installed concrete lining in the river channel."[35]

Like that of 1938, this crisis was followed by a development boom. The concrete lining imprisoned the river; it forced it into submission, domesticating the river from its continuous "rampages" and "benders." Following the river's domestication, the subsequent decades saw increased property values in Orange County "spurring heavy residential, commercial and industrial development along the Santa Ana River, with little thought given to the river itself other than as a flood control channel."[36] The communities along its banks were disconnected from the earth and the lands they lived on. They took advantage of the capitalist markets during a brief period to destroy that which had manifested spirit for Indigenous peoples for thousands of years, ending the worlds lived before by the ancestors of the Taraaxam and Acjachemem—this is Native alienation and the postapocalyptic world.

The devastation to the environment of highly populated places such as Orange County largely goes unnoticed—it becomes normalized. Similarly, constructing a built environment that celebrates genocide (chapter 2) is often misrecognized. Amid the misrecognition of genocide and its celebration through the canonization of Serra in 2015, Native resistance to conquest has continued in their refusal to acknowledge Serra as a saint, insisting that the mission system was world-ending enslavement. This history should not be celebrated. Those involved in the movement opposing canonization argue that the human and ecological suffering inflicted through conquest and its logic of spiritual possession must be recognized beyond any discursive impulse of benevolence.

# FOUR

## Canonization Fodder

*Resisting the Canonization of Junípero Serra*

"It began with a prayer and ended with a loud *clunk*," reported the *Los Angeles Times*. On June 19, 2020, approximately five dozen Indigenous activists gathered at Father Serra Park in downtown Los Angeles near La Plaza Olvera. Alan Salazar, a Tataviam and Chumash elder, offered prayer and smoke. More than two hundred years before, in 1799, his own family had been taken to Mission San Fernando. He explains that at the mission, they "lost their culture, their language and their lives—and were worked like slaves. . . . I'm talking about my great-great-great-great-grandparents." For Salazar, the cause of the gathering was both a personal and generational obligation. "This is a symbol of oppression, a symbol of slavery, a symbol of our stolen land. . . . It's important that we remove this statue but that's just the first step." With ropes, a group of young activists pulled mightily, and the statue of Serra toppled off its pedestal with a loud clunk to the chants of "Take it down! Take it down!"[1]

The Los Angeles statue of Serra held a cross in its right hand and a model of a Spanish mission in its left. The Knights of Columbus erected the statue in 1932 to teach the benevolence of conquest. For eighty-eight years, the statue celebrated California Indian death, just as the 2015 canonization of Serra by Pope Francis did. The contingent of Indigenous activists that pulled down the statue had exclaimed, "Enough!" in unison. As the *Los Angeles Times* reported, Jessa Calderon, a Gabrielino-Tongva and Ventereño Chumash organizer, leader, and artist, attended the gathering. She described feeling numb watching the statue wrenched from its perch. "I began to cry hysterically," she recounted. "It was like a sense of relief." Calderon's relief did not end her obligations to her people. "Now that this moment is happening, we have a story to tell."[2] According to Calderon, the removal of the statue didn't feel like a celebration but instead "the beginning of healing that

96   CHAPTER FOUR

needs to occur amongst our people." She reiterated the devastation caused
by Serra and the mission system: "This is a man who has created genetic
trauma for myself [and] our ancestry. These ancestors of ours, they struggled
loving themselves because somebody like [Serra] told them that they were
disgusting, told them that they were useless other than for sex and for slavery.
And because of somebody like that, we struggle today as a community."[3]
The toppling of the Serra statue in Los Angeles was not the first and likely
will not be the last statue that activists take down. Whether you agree with
these tactics or not, California Indians have had enough of celebrating their
ancestors' death, romanticizing the conquest, and having the theft of their
lands justified. The Native alienation of conquest has taken a huge toll, and
as both Calderon and Salazar indicated, much more work is yet to be done.

The canonization of Serra into sainthood in 2015 incited California Indians to respond in many ways: protests, gatherings at missions for ceremony
and prayer to honor their ancestors, graffiti and red paint on mission walls
and Serra statues, the beheading of a statue of Serra, moderated debates and
symposia, online petitions, a mock trial, press conferences, art installations,
a 780-mile walk visiting all of the missions, a tribal government issuing a
resolution and sending it to the pope, and the handing of a copy of *News
from Native California* critical of the canonization to Pope Francis. Now,
approaching a decade after the canonization, the persistent uplifting of San
Junípero Serra continues to inspire California Indian refusals. This chapter
highlights some of the actions in 2015 that demanded Pope Francis stop the
planned canonization. It also refutes that Serra had written a bill of rights
for the Indians, which the Vatican used as evidence of Serra's benevolence.
For Deborah A. Miranda, in the days before the canonization, it felt like
"we, the very people upon whom Serra's heroic record of evangelization was
built, are no more alive to Francis than adobe bricks." To Miranda, it felt like
the lives and deaths of California Indians that make "Serra the priest into
Serra, the saint, are inconsequential footnotes in our own history. It is as if
we California Indians and our Ancestors are merely canonization fodder."[4]

## No Sainthood for Serra Tribunal

Under the hot sun, Father Junípero Serra stood sweating with anticipation
next to the judge's table pending the jury's decision. The jury needed only

a few seconds to deliberate whether Serra was guilty of crimes against humanity and genocide. With a resounding "guilty" and calls to "hang him!" the trial was concluded. The prosecutor and her expert witnesses provided the arguments and evidence to convince the jury convening at the Junípero Serra Branch of the Los Angeles Public Library (in South Central Los Angeles) to find him guilty as charged. Nanette Deetz reported from the trial for *Indian Country Today*:

> In the case of Indigenous Nations v. Junipero Serra . . . [he] was brought to court by the American Indian Movement Southern California Chapter on Tongva territory in Los Angeles for the crimes of torture, slavery, rape, theft of California indigenous lands and promoting the intentional death of thousands of California's indigenous people.[5]

The street theater and mock trial of Junípero Serra was a great success as Deetz reported: "The 'No Sainthood for Serra Tribunal' was presented as satire on September 12 [2015] in the form of Guerilla theater, and was serious yet funny, allowing for laughter amidst the pain of the Canonization proposed by Pope Francis." Corine Fairbanks, director of AIM Southern California, stated, "We wanted people to have a voice, and we wanted this protest to be creative and interactive in a positive way." Fairbanks also explained, "There is so much anger surrounding the proposed sainthood among California's Native tribes, that we wanted to be creative and have fun too."[6]

The actors who participated had fun with it, some in costume, despite the seriousness of the gathering. Women played roles representing the Native women at the missions that had been susceptible to sexual violence. The monjerío and violence against women were central aspects of the Indigenous Nation's argument in the trial against Serra. The prosecuting attorney, played by Angela Mooney D'Arcy (Acjachemem), cross-examined the priest with a barrage of tough questions. She forced him to admit that the goal of the mission system was to eradicate Native culture at whatever expense necessary, a fact he and the defense were proud of. This fact, which was also the actual historical goal of the mission system, is one of the elements of genocide outlined by the United Nations Genocide Convention.

Deetz explained the structure of the trial: "At the tribunal, Serra was assigned a public defender, portrayed by Fairbanks, and a defense attorney portrayed by Dennis Sandoval Landau." According to Deetz, "The role of

Junípero Serra was performed by Kevin Head, a professional actor who also organizes community gardens. 'It's tough to play the role of someone so hated. Now I understand why so many California tribal people are angry. The decision to grant sainthood to Serra is wrong,' Head said."[7] The laughter and humor of the theatrical production subsided when the prosecution's expert witnesses presented their testimony. I acted in this role, and made clear connections between the mission system, the Doctrine of Discovery, the spread of venereal disease, slavery, death, sexual violence, institutional racism, and genocide. All of these are celebrated through the canonization of Junípero Serra.

## An Empty Apology

"I wish to be quite clear," said Pope Francis. "I humbly ask forgiveness, not only for the offenses of the church herself, but also for crimes committed against the native peoples during the so-called conquest of America." Additionally, he stated, "Some may rightly say, 'When the pope speaks of colonialism, he overlooks certain actions of the church.'" Francis continued, "I say this to you with regret: Many grave sins were committed against the native people of America in the name of God."[8] These are quotes from Pope Francis's speech and apology during his trip to Bolivia in early July 2015, before the Serra canonization Mass.

Pope Francis attempted to distance the church from the colonial economic structure in his apology speech. He leveled a heavy charge against capitalist economies as he criticized "certain free-trade treaties" and "austerity, which always tightens the belt of workers and the poor." He added, "Human beings and nature must not be at the service of money," and "Let us say no to an economy of exclusion and inequality, where money rules, rather than service. That economy kills. That economy excludes. That economy destroys Mother Earth."[9] The mission system in California was not only rooted in colonialism and Catholicism, but the two were bound to an economy of global trade. Church, military, and trade were inseparable as they functioned symbiotically in an interdependent relationship.

While there were disagreements between the church and the Spanish military, those arguments did not disconnect one from the other. Colonialism functioned through all three. Even today, the Vatican functions through an economic system that requires resources, land, and converts to continue its dominance. Catholicism, simply stated, is more than a belief. The effort to make Junípero Serra a saint continues the tradition of evangelism. To remain a powerful entity, the Catholic Church needs to retain and convert people to the church. Catholicism functions now, as it has in the past, in a much more powerful way than merely a spiritual faith in Christianity. I am using the term evangelism to describe the incorporation of people into the Catholic Church. Through this process, the church gains membership and power through populations that support the church economically and politically. Evangelism was a tool of colonialism utilized by the Spanish to incorporate Native populations into its imperial project while the church collected souls and political power. Today, the logic of evangelism functions similarly where the church extends its reach into the political discourse of nations through its members.

Despite the pope's calculated criticism of capitalism and his gesture toward forgiveness of the church for its "sins" against the Indigenous peoples of the Americas, he offered no solution or suggestions on how tribal nations would heal after more than five hundred years of European and Christian colonialism. "Don't expect a recipe from this pope," he declared. "Neither the pope nor the church have a monopoly on the interpretation of social reality or the proposal of solution to contemporary issues. I dare say no recipe exists." The pope's speech was a deliberate move toward innocence for the church and made without intention to help Indigenous peoples, whose religious conversions continued through coercion. According to the *New York Times*, the apology in Latin America on Brazilian soil was different from Pope John Paul's generalized apology to Jews and other ethnic and minoritized communities at the Vatican in 2000. Francis's apology was specific to the Indigenous peoples of Latin America. "Yet Francis's agenda for the trip," the *Times* reported, "includes bolstering the church" and the idea that Catholicism is integral to the identity of Latin Americans—an identity, Francis concluded, "some powers are committed to erasing, at times because our faith is revolutionary, because our faith challenges the tyranny of Mammon," wealth personified as the devil and worshipped above God.[10]

This is good rhetoric, but why does the Vatican have so much gold if it does not also value wealth? Mirroring my critique of the pope and, by extension, the Vatican's story about wealth, Deborah A. Miranda wrote, "Solid gold candlesticks, expensive vestments, elaborate monuments and cathedrals—none of these are necessary to truly worship the Creator, whether that Creator is Indian or Spanish or something else altogether."[11] Estimations of the wealth of the Catholic Church are unreliable due to much of their holdings being unreported, as well as assets held in property and art. Yet, it is known that the Vatican has a bank, officially called the Institute for the Works of Religion. According to a 2014 article in the *International Business Times*, the Vatican bank holds $7.3 billion in "assets on behalf of its 17,400 customers." The same article reported, "it keeps gold reserves worth over $20m with the US Federal Reserve."[12]

From a 1965 article in *Time Magazine*, "Bankers' best guesses about the Vatican's wealth put it at $10 billion to $15 billion"; "of this wealth, Italian stockholdings alone run to $1.6 billion, 15% of the value of listed shares on the Italian market. The Vatican has big investments in banking, insurance, chemicals, steel, construction, real estate."[13] One can only guess what the Catholic Church is worth today. Miranda wrote, "Someone decided that even if priests couldn't possess gold, God would like gold communion cups, marble in His church, the finest cloth money could buy on His altar."[14] Why, I ask, is the Vatican not melting down all of its extremely expensive golden altars all over the world, flooding the market with gold, affecting the price and the stock market, and investing in the poor who need not churches filled with gold but homes, land, food, clean water, and air? In the Bible, the apostles are not preaching from golden pulpits. Why does the current church (and not only the Catholic Church) continue to need economic investments if it functions outside of, as Francis noted, an "economy of exclusion and inequality, where money rules, rather than service"?[15] The Vatican can be revolutionary, as the pope insisted, but instead, it focuses on empty apologies and continued evangelism.

## The First Hispanic Saint

According to various sources, evangelism is at the heart of Serra's canonization. He is viewed as the first Hispanic saint, as reported by Catholic Online:

"Pope Francis and the Vatican have announced plans to canonize the Blessed Junípero Serra during the Pope's visit to the United States on September 23 [2015]. Serra will become the United States' first Hispanic saint." This article also related the positive impacts on Catholic Hispanics through canonizing Junípero Serra: "Often times, the Spaniards' and the Catholic contribution to the United States' growth and formation is overlooked and belittled," and "Serra's canonization will help Americans realize Hispanics did contribute to the settling of the country." As quoted in the article, Guzman Carriquiry, a Vatican official from Uruguay, said, "A more accurate vision also will help break down walls of separation between what is Anglo and what is Hispanic, between the Protestant and Catholic traditions, between the United States and Latin America." The article added, "Carriquiry believes the canonization of Blessed Serra will allow the United States' Hispanics to free themselves of the harmful mentality that no one likes them." Carriquiry argued that the canonization would enable a better understanding of Hispanics and Catholics as having inhabited large areas of the United States during its birth as a nation.[16]

Steven Hackel, historian and author of a biography of Serra, agrees, "The Vatican sees Serra almost as a patron saint of immigration." He also noted a relationship between immigration and Catholicism: "there's a history behind immigration policy that is rooted in a Spanish Catholic past and not just a Protestant, 18th Century political rebellion."[17] Hackel views the canonization as an opportunity on the part of the church to remind America of its Hispanic past and as a historical context for immigration policies. However, the canonization erases Native peoples and instead focuses on "Hispanic" people (singular) as being the inhabitants of "large areas of the United States," without mentioning Indians as the original peoples of the Americas and as continued living populations.[18] In this discourse, Hispanics replace Indians as the occupants and founders—this is Native alienation.

The erasure of Indians is evident in a statement by Mechelle Lawrence Adams, executive director of Mission San Juan Capistrano: "Blessed Serra is the original founder of California, like an urban planner. As California Catholics, he is a source of inspiration for us."[19] This logic acknowledges no role for the California Indians in California history or the building of the missions. Despite Adams's intimate connection to the local Acjachemem through Mission San Juan Capistrano, her statement about the canonization does not represent Indians as integral to California history. California Indians are erased in this normative version of California history, in which California, not just the missions, was founded by Junípero Serra.

The canonization is meant to retain people of Latin American origins as Catholics and provide them, as Hispanic people, with a patron saint. It is also an attempt to continue the legacy of alienating Native peoples and subsuming them into a "Hispanic" identity. Michael Omi and Howard Winant explain that racial formation in the Americas is tied to processes of colonialism. "When European explorers in the New World 'discovered' people," Omi and Winant write, "who looked different than themselves, these 'natives' challenged then existing conceptions of the origins of the human species, and raised disturbing questions as to whether *all* could be considered in the same 'family of man.'" They conclude, "Race is indeed a preeminently *socio-historical* concept," adding that "racial categories and the meaning of race are given concrete expression by the specific social relations and historical context in which they are embedded," and these "racial meanings have varied tremendously over time and between different societies."[20] In "The Hispanic Spin: Party Politics and Governmental Manipulation of Ethnic Identity," Jack D. Forbes explored the political construct of Hispanic as a racial category tied to the Americas. He asked, "How is it that Original American peoples, including indigenous and mestizo Mexicans and Central Americans can be assigned a 'Spanish culture or origin'?" Forbes answered his own question, stating that the "politics of this move relates to the long struggle of some persons of Mexican extraction to escape from the prejudice directed at persons of Indian appearance by having themselves classified as Spanish-Americans or Latin Americans."[21]

The designation of Hispanic is a continued attempt to erase Native identity and create for Native people a new nationalistic identity that both indigenizes non-Natives and subsumes Indigenous peoples into a politic of white supremacy. Forbes explains that Hispanic, which means Spanish or Spanish-derived, is an "absurd" identity when "applied to Maya, Mixtec, Zapotec, or other American peoples who often do not even speak Spanish (except perhaps as a second, foreign language), whose surnames are often not of Spanish origin, and whose racial and cultural backgrounds are First

American or African or mixed."[22] Forbes argues that the Hispanicization of Indigenous and African-derived peoples is at their expense, enforcing white supremacy. Dylan Rodríguez theorized *multicultural white supremacy*, a term that denotes the practices of inclusion whereby "people of color' are increasingly, selectively, and hierarchically incorporated/empowered by the structures of institutional dominance—government, police, universities, corporations, etc."[23] Pope Francis applies the term Hispanic as an intentional tool of a white supremacist logic to subsume African and Native origins into an identity that does not expunge race but masks it into a multicultural identity with assimilative commonalities such as language and religion, alienating Indigenous and African peoples from the heritage of their ancestors.

The Spanish incorporated Native and African peoples into the colonial project to expand the Spanish empire. The example of my ancestors, the Rosas family (preface), highlights how people of color were incorporated into the colonial project as soldiers and settlers. Furthermore, conquest relied on Indians by including them as alcaldes, a position that functioned as warden, police officer, and municipal officer with administrative and judicial power over other gentile and neophyte Indians. I argue that the gratuitous violence of conquest, while not expressing a need to exterminate Indians, was genocidal.[24] Steven Newcomb explained that the "Spanish Catholic missions of domination shattered the traditional economies and ways of life of the original nations," and this system "was devastating on all levels for original nations that had experienced thousands of years of free and independent life-ways before the colonizers invaded."[25] Native alienation through multicultural incorporation was a cornerstone of the conquest of California and continues to assert its malign influence through the Hispanicization of Indigenous peoples, as the canonization of Serra shows.

The effort to canonize Junípero Serra as the "first Hispanic Saint from the United States" was an attempt to continue the long history of dominance over Indigenous peoples by further incorporating the Catholic Church and Spanish colonialism into the fabric of the United States. As reported by Catholic Online, it is an effort to "promote greater acceptance of Hispanic Americans, recognition of the Catholic contribution to US history, and a more accurate understanding of how the United States became a country."[26] While the effort to accept Hispanics and Catholics is honorable, it promotes

## CHAPTER FOUR

multiculturalism without challenging the long-standing hegemony of white supremacy in which Black and Indigenous peoples of color, including those identified as Hispanic, are susceptible to racist state violence.

## Postcanonization

On September 23, 2015, Pope Francis canonized Junípero Serra in Washington, DC. In the Mass, Francis provided a historically inaccurate narrative of Serra as the protector of California's Native people. He stated:

> Today we remember one of those witnesses who testified to the joy of the Gospel in these lands, Father Junípero Serra. He was the embodiment of "a Church which goes forth," a Church which sets out to bring everywhere the reconciling tenderness of God. Junípero Serra left his native land and its way of life. He was excited about blazing trails, going forth to meet many people, learning and valuing their particular customs and ways of life. He learned how to bring to birth and nurture God's life in the faces of everyone he met; he made them his brothers and sisters. Junípero sought to defend the dignity of the native community, to protect it from those who had mistreated and abused it. Mistreatment and wrongs which today still trouble us, especially because of the hurt which they cause in the lives of many people.[27]

Rather than protecting California Indian people, the Spanish missionaries, with San Serra as their leader, were directly responsible for initiating genocide and enslavement. Many historians, as well as the church, argue that Serra was in opposition to the violence levied by the Spanish military and that he was a man of his time and, therefore, not responsible for the violent punishment he exacted on the Native peoples.

It has often been argued that Serra was not intent on eradicating Native peoples. For example, Steven Hackel, as quoted by *Al Jazeera America*, stated that Serra's "policies and his plans led to tremendous pain and suffering, most of it unintended on his part." This argument transfers responsibility and guilt to the military. In Pope Francis's remarks, he references "those who had mistreated and abused" the Indians in California during the Spanish occupation while Serra was still alive.[28] This argument is remarkably similar to those who currently blame police violence directed at peoples of color on individual bad police officers rather than on a system that has facilitated a historical structure of racial and anti-Black violence. In his statement, Pope Francis also stated that Serra valued Indian customs and ways of life. However, there is a lack of historical evidence demonstrating Serra was a defender of Native peoples or was tolerant of Native ways of life. As I have shown throughout this book, spiritual conquest possessed Native bodies and souls to alienate them from their ancestral heritage.

Gerónimo Boscana, one of Serra's Catholic priests, was stationed at several missions, including San Gabriel and San Juan Capistrano. In his writings, Boscana expresses the hegemonic view of Indians during the time of Serra. It is clear in his writings how he viewed California Indians. He wrote, "The Indians of California may be compared to a species of monkey; for in naught do they express interest, except in imitating the actions of others, and, particularly in copying the ways of the '*razon*,' or white men." Boscana left us with ethnographic writings about the Acjachemem and Taraaxam, which Alfred Robinson later published in 1846 and J. P. Harrington published again with extensive annotations in 1933. Boscana believed that the Indians, "Although ripe in years, they had no more experience than when in childhood—no reasoning powers, and therefore followed blindly in the footsteps of their predecessors."[29] With Serra as president, the mission system did not value the continuation of Indian ways of life undifferentiated from their sacred histories, ceremonies, relationship with place, and languages. The Spanish missions sought to alienate Indian spiritual connections to their ancestors and lands through conversion to Catholicism and Hispanicization.

## The Military or the Church?

Pope Francis shifts the blame for violence against Indians from the priests to the military. From 1779 to 1783, while Junípero Serra was the president of the missions, the Spanish had four presidios, or military bases or forts, at San Diego, Santa Barbara, Monterey, and San Francisco. According to the authors of a report detailing the military in California during that period, the presidios were responsible for "fighting Indians, training, building, guarding, escort duty, dispatch duty, hunting, etc."[30] The pueblos at Los

## CHAPTER FOUR

Angeles and San Jose were supported by soldiers responsible for defense and policing. Soldiers were also attached to the nine missions: San Diego, San Juan Capistrano, San Gabriel, Ventura, San Luis Obispo, San Antonio de Padua, Carmel, Santa Clara, and San Francisco. At the missions, soldiers served as guards, police, and instructors. Spanish soldiers in California were light cavalry, among the best in the world. They were enlisted for ten-year periods with reenlistment opportunities. The core of soldiers that came to California were from the First Free Company of Catalonia, the Catalan Bluecoats. These soldiers had been recruited from Catalonia in 1767.

The remaining soldiers from Mexico were known as "Leather Jackets" (Soldados de Cuera), named for the five layers of leather and deerskin they used for protection against arrows. These were professional soldiers, unlike their portrayal in various media, such as in *Zorro* and the bumbling Sergeant Garcia. They were armed with lance and shield, good for crowd control, a sword, and a trabuco, or cavalry musket. They rode horseback, a major military advantage over Indians on foot, and kept dogs to use against Indians. Presidios were also armed with cannons to defend against attacks by other nations from the sea.

In 1784 priests Junípero Serra and Francisco Palóu prepared a description of all the installations in Alta and Baja California. They recorded fifty-four soldiers assigned to the San Diego Presidio. Six soldiers were assigned to each mission within the jurisdiction of San Diego. These included missions San Diego, San Juan Capistrano, and San Gabriel. Four soldiers were assigned to Los Angeles, and the remaining thirty-two were within the presidio itself, moving among the various properties, including the herds of horses and cattle.

In the Reglamento of 1779, Neve requested a fourth presidio and three new missions in the Chumash region of Santa Barbara and the Channel Islands. He also authorized the establishment of El Pueblo de Nuestra Señora la Reina de los Ángeles near the Río de Porciúncula, later named the Los Angeles River. In early 1780 Captain Fernando Xavier de Rivera y Moncada, governor of Baja California, began to recruit soldiers for the establishment of El Pueblo de Los Angeles. In 1781 Alta California Governor Felipe de Neve offered, as Mary Wittenburg writes, "a generous subsidy to any man willing to enlist in the Spanish army for services on the northwestern frontier."[31] Although Serra opposed the establishment of pueblos, his desire for

Christian women in California aligned to bring settlers to California. The pueblo would be located at a site Father Juan Crespí had previously desired for another mission near the Taraaxam village of Yaanga.[32] That the military governor wrote policy establishing more missions clearly shows the interrelatedness of church and state. Increasing both missions and presidios would also mean a larger military force in California and more priests, exposing a larger number of Indians to the structural violence of Spanish colonialism as it functioned in early nineteenth-century California. Furthermore, establishing pueblos would require families and the beginning of settler colonialism in California.

The canonization of Junípero Serra celebrates him as an individual and praises the colonial structure that allowed him to preach and convert the Native population. He required military escort and military technologies to subdue the Indigenous inhabitants. He was not solely a man of the cloth who brought the word of God and the "joy of the Gospel" to the gentiles, as Pope Francis termed Serra's colonial exploits. Instead, Serra brought a militarized colonial force to reduce Native villages, alienate them into white life, and eradicate their pagan ways of life—their worldviews, language, culture, ceremonies, structures of governance, and kinship.

One of the recruits for the military escort of families from the towns of Los Alamos, Fuerte, Sinaloa, Culiacán, and Rosario to establish the Pueblo de Los Ángeles was Francisco Xavier Sepúlveda (my ancestor). In the Reglamento of 1779, Neve ordered that the recruits be "healthy, robust, and without vice or defect."[33] Soldiers were also to be married to set a good example for the converted Indians and thus extend the Catholic religion and heteropatriarchy. In 1781 Sepúlveda and his wife, María Candelaria de Redondo, and their five sons and one daughter joined the Zúñiga Expedition to travel north from the inland town of Real de los Alamos, Sonora.[34] With the Sepúlvedas on the difficult five-month trip were the Rosas family, including José Carlos, who later married María Dolores from Yaanga. Antonia I. Castañeda wrote, "To quell the sexual violence, strengthen the population base, and provide models of Christian family life, colonial authorities recruited married soldiers and settlers with families. They also provided incentives of land, animals, and supplies to soldiers who married Christianized Indian women, 'daughters of the country,' and remained in California permanently."[35] Central to the politics of conquest for the

## 108 CHAPTER FOUR

Spanish in California as elsewhere was gender, sexuality, and the reproduction of family norms.

In a letter to Antonio María de Bucareli y Ursúa, the viceroy of New Spain, Junípero Serra provided thirty-two suggestions for improvement to the government of the missions in Alta California. These suggestions include the placement of heteropatriarchal norms onto the Native population through the migration of families, such as the Sepúlveda and Rosas families. In a letter dated March 13, 1773, Serra stated that Spain was "desirous of introducing, and spreading, in these extensive territories our Holy Catholic Faith." He stated, "I, with all submission due to Your Excellency, wish to present the following suggestions." Serra numbered each suggestion and provided an explanation and a proposal of how it could be accomplished. Under number 5, he wrote that a trail from Santa Fe to Monterey or San Diego should be explored to facilitate the conquest, which "would thus be hastened to a most notable degree, assuming a harvest of many souls for heaven."[36]

In his thirteenth suggestion, Junípero Serra noted the lack of Christian women and families at the missions: "It is no less important that, when the livestock arrives . . . some Indian families from the said [Baja] California should come, of their own free will, with the expedition." He wanted them to "be distributed, at least two or three being placed in each mission." He specified that bringing families would accomplish two purposes. "The first will be that there will be an additional two or three Indians for work," wrote Serra, indicating a need for more labor in the missions. In 1773 the conversion of the local Native populations wasn't as successful as Serra had desired. His letters indicate his frustration with the slow development of the missions, lack of converts, lack of supplies, starvation, and soldiers who were deserting. In his writings, he expressed that he could not fully understand why the missions in Baja California, from his own experiences there, had been successful from his perspective. At the same time, the Indians in Alta California had proven difficult to lure into his mission project. "The second" purpose, Serra wrote, "and the one I have most in mind, is that the Indians may realize that . . . there are marriages, also, among Christians." He was concerned that the Indians had "been much mistaken when they saw all men, and no women, among us."[37]

In Serra's request for families, moreover, he provided an example where one of the "San Diego Fathers" went to Baja for provisions, "which had run short in that mission," and "he brought back . . . two of the said families." Serra wrote that the Indians at San Diego, both neophytes and gentiles, "did not know what to make of these families, so great was their delight." He believed that bringing women and families was "a lesson . . . useful to" the Indians at the missions. "So if families other than Indians come from there, it will serve the same purpose very well," he wrote. The purpose was to impose a doctrine of patriarchy onto the Natives through the Christian institution of marriage and use the married couples as examples of the proper relationship between men and women, instituting male dominance. These married couples, such as my Sepúlveda and Rosas ancestors, were simultaneously seen as tools of evangelism and conversion.

The colonial processes in California enforced gendered and sexualized power relations. Writing about the colonization of California, Antonia I. Castañeda stated, "Spanish law defined women as sexual beings and delineated their sexual lives through the institution of indissoluble, monogamous marriage." She further stated that "sexual intercourse, in theory, was confined to marriage, a sacrament intended for the procreation of children, for companionship, and for the containment of lust." These were the structures Junípero Serra intended to impose on California Indian people, converting them through the sacrament of marriage and simultaneously imposing on them Spanish and Catholic law. The priests and soldiers, who were male and without families, did not supply the Spanish with the necessary tools to enforce these laws or the ability to provide examples of the normative nuclear family structure; this, according to Serra, was one of the primary purposes in bringing Christian families as settlers to California. "The family, the sociopolitical organization . . . reproduced the hierarchical, male-dominated social order," wrote Castañeda. Systems of gender and sexuality among California Indians precontact conflicted with Spanish norms; "indigenous peoples, in contrast, generally conceptualized females and males as complimentary, not opposed, principals." Edward D. Castillo wrote that women in Taraaxam precontact society "enjoyed a large measure of freedom, respect, and independence," which the colonizer needed to eliminate.[38]

Junípero Serra's sixth suggestion is one that many have pointed to in declaring the priest critical of the military regime in California. Specifically,

CHAPTER FOUR

they argue that Serra traveled to Mexico City to protect the Indians from the soldiers and created a bill of rights for the Indians. Pope John Paul II, who venerated Serra, said that it "deserves special mention" that Serra had frequent clashes with the civil authorities over the treatment of Indians and in 1773 presented a "Bill of Rights" to the viceroy in Mexico City.[39] Monsignor Francis J. Weber, a Catholic scholar and honorary chaplain to Pope Francis, wrote that Serra "showed himself to be a defender of the Indians' human rights in 1773" and "journeyed from California to Mexico City to personally present to the viceroy a *Representación*." This manuscript was the letter to Viceroy Antonio María de Bucareli y Ursúa, which contained Serra's thirty-two suggestions. "This document, which is sometimes termed a 'Bill of Rights' for Indians, was accepted and implemented," wrote Weber.[40] Those who attempt to shift responsibility for the "sins," as Pope Francis termed the gratuitous violence against the Native population of California, blame the military and rely on this bill of rights to declare Serra as the defender of Indians. Another Serra apologist, Ruben G. Mendoza, professor of archaeology at Cal State Monterey Bay, has argued, "A lot of allegations of abuse with regard to Serra have been misinterpreted." Mendoza states, "Serra was not just a man of his time, but a man who was ahead of his time when it came to advocating for the rights of Native American people." Mendoza has claimed that "there is a record of Serra traveling to Mexico City to meet with the then-viceroy and speak on behalf of two Native American women who were raped by a Spanish soldier."[41]

Of "special importance," wrote Junípero Serra in his report, "is the removal, or recall, of the Officer Don Pedro Fages from the command of the Presidio at Monterey." In this request, instead of discussing the mistreatment of Indians by the Spanish soldiers under the command of Pedro Fages, as Weber, Mendoza, and others argue, he presented evidence of Fages's mistreatment of *soldiers*. In his suggestion to remove Fages from his command, Serra presented the protests of the soldiers: "Their grievance is not only because of long hours of work and a lack of food—as I have on numerous occasions heard them declare," but, he says, "because of the harsh treatment, and unbearable manners, of the said officer." Further discussing the soldiers' grievance against Fages, Serra stated that the "men ask their respective Officers to free them in any manner they can from such harsh treatment and oppression." To further push for Fages's removal, he wrote, "there is no other complaint except that they have over them Don Pedro Fages."[42] Serra is clear in his writing that he sought the protection of soldiers from Captain Fages and sought his removal of command in California.

Countering Weber's observance of a bill of rights, reporting for *Indian Country Today*, Christine Grabowski stated, "He neither suggested nor was granted 'rights' *for* Indians." She decisively argues that there is no evidence that Serra wrote on behalf of rights for California Indians: "Indeed, what Serra requested—and what he was granted—was exclusive control over the baptized Indians except with respect to capital offenses." She argues that Serra did not "grant Indians any rights or privileges." Providing evidence of a lack of human rights for Indians under Serra, Grabowski writes, "The abuses of Indian men and women by the soldiers did not stop after he obtained exclusive authority over the baptized Indians. Nor did the Indians themselves think their lives had improved as evidenced by ongoing native resistance such as running away from the missions despite harsh punishments for doing so and launching attacks on the missions at San Diego in 1775 and San Luis Obispo in 1776."[43]

In his thirty-two suggestions, Serra asked for complete control over the Indian population. This was the significant disagreement between church and state, Serra and Fages. Serra asked the viceroy to "notify the said Officer and the soldiers" that the priests would have authority over "the training, governance, punishment and education of baptized Indians" and those "being prepared for baptism." He argued that Indians incorporated into the mission "belong exclusively to the Missionary Fathers." This meant that the free will of Indians, once they were baptized, was suspended, and their bodies and souls became possessions of the church.

Serra asked that the viceroy give the church full control over Indian punishment. The "only exception" Serra noted was "for capital offenses." He advised the viceroy to ensure that "no chastisement or ill-treatment should be inflicted on any of them whether by the Officer or by any soldier without the Missionary Father's passing upon it." Serra desired exclusive control over his missionized Indians in what he argued was a "time-honored practice of this kingdom ever since the conquest." As evidenced in his writing, Serra viewed Indians as possessions of the missions, which he wrote conforms to

*112*   CHAPTER FOUR

"the law of nature concerning the education of the children, and as an essential condition for the rightful training of the poor neophytes." Exclusive control over the Native body and soul and simultaneous implementation of patriarchal norms were the primary arguments in Serra's writings to the viceroy of New Spain, not a bill of rights for the Indians.

The untrue assertion of a bill of rights can be understood as either a clear misunderstanding on the part of Francis J. Weber and others or as a direct political attempt to clear the record of Serra from his "sins" and responsibility of mistreatment of California's Indian peoples. Their colonial imaginary that has created a bill of rights is a denial of genocide that protects the church from responsibility. Grabowski asked in her article, "Why do Catholic websites, publications and spokespersons fail to identify the 'Representación' accurately and explain its provisions in detail?" Attempting to answer her own question, she wrote, "Perhaps it is so their audience will not notice that the 32 points are not 'rights' *for* Indians." She further stated, "Serra did not travel to Mexico City to defend Indian rights or submit a document that anyone identified as an 'Indian Bill of Rights' or a document that could legitimately be 'termed' one. Catholic sources have shamelessly created a fabrication in an effort to make it seem as if Serra deserves canonization."[44] There is little evidence that Serra took any measures to protect the Native population as a whole. If he had written a bill of rights, perhaps the violence against and punishment of California Indians would not have been so great. But Serra was clear on his position of violence against Indians: "That spiritual fathers should punish their sons, the Indians, with blows appears to be as old as the conquest of the Americas; so general in fact that the saints do not seem to be any exception to the rule."[45] Serra viewed using soldiers at the missions as necessary for the spiritual conquest of California.

Although he believed it was the priest's responsibility to punish the Indians, Serra did protect some individual Indians from execution, including Indians who used violence to assert their sovereignty against Mission San Diego in 1775. Steven Hackel states, "One can point to certain moments in the historical record when Serra does protect Indians, but the larger story I think is one in which his policies and his plans led to tremendous pain and suffering."[46] To be clear, the historical record does not support the fabricated story of a bill of rights for Indians.

Edward D. Castillo argues, "Despite the missionaries' awareness that massive Indian death inevitably accompanied Spanish colonization, the Franciscans were determined to save Indian souls and create their particular vision of God's kingdom on earth through the hard labor and abundant natural resources of the California Indians." And Serra himself understood colonialism as a "spiritual conquest" wherein Indians "would thus be hastened to a most notable degree, assuming a harvest of many souls for heaven."[47] With conquest and evangelism, the church, in combination with Spanish imperialism and capitalism, would broaden its world dominance and further enforce heteropatriarchy, white supremacy, and enslavement.

## The Origins of a Prayer

Caroline Ward Holland's grandmother told her not to bring flowers to her grave when she came to visit. Holland explained her Nana's guidance: "Don't bring me flowers when I'm dead. Buy yourself a pair of shoes, you're gonna need them." Holland, a tribal member of the Fernandeño Tataviam Band of Mission Indians, said, "I took that with me my whole life, I'm fifty years old, and that's what I think she meant." Her grandmother meant it in a literal sense: "Buy yourself a pair of shoes, you're gonna need them, because I know you're gonna do this. Today, I don't have to think about that ever again. I know this is exactly what she meant," Holland said.[48] Caroline would use her shoes to walk nearly eight hundred miles for the ancestors in memory of their lives (and deaths) at the California missions.

Holland and her son Kagen followed in the footsteps of their California Indian ancestors. "Wherever their villages were, that's what they were forced to do: walk to the missions," she explained. Holland continued, "We want our ancestors to know that we understand their suffering. And we're going to voice it, so people will know that it wasn't a posh life with the Catholics feeding you, and protecting you. No, it was a horrible existence for them. It's really heart-wrenching, it's sickening, you know."[49]

The mother and son began a 780-mile pilgrimage to all of the twenty-one missions in Alta California. Walking each mile to honor and pray for the ancestors as a direct action in opposition to the canonization of Junípero Serra in 2015. Holland explained the purpose of her and her son's walk: The ancestors "were people just like we are. We want to feel what they went through, and try to let everyone else know what really happened. It's almost like, bringing them to life through what we're doing."[50] To begin such a long walk was courageous. However, it was more than a walk; it was a prayer, a journey for the ancestors. It was an assertion of California Indian resistance and refusal—a rejection of sainthood for Junípero Serra, his legacy and the Spanish imaginary produced from his corpse entombed at Mission San Carlos Borroméo del Río Carmelo. Caroline and Kagen's walk continued a Native protocol of asking for permission as they entered each tribal people's territory, recognizing the people of the land.

It was a Sunday, a day of prayer for the Christian community. San Juan Capistrano has held more than its share of Catholic Masses since 1776, when the mission was founded for the second time. The land has also been part of Acjachemem ceremonies since time immemorial. Yet there have been fewer Acjachemem ceremonies since the coming of the colonizer. November 1, 2015, marked the 240th anniversary since the mission's first founding, which had been put on hold in 1775 when the Kumeyaay fought back, burned down Mission San Diego, and ceremonially killed Father Luís Jayme. On the anniversary of the uprising at San Diego, it was appropriate that Caroline Ward Holland and her son Kagen would walk into San Juan Capistrano to honor the enslaved ancestors.

"Before we can do any kind of reconciliation," Caroline said, "we need to have someone admit to an injury. It was an ugly time for our people." Kagen added, "They go to extraordinary lengths to sanitize the history." Caroline explained, "We have had so much support from all the tribes. They have joined us at each mission and led the blessing."[51] At Mission San Juan Capistrano, the Hollands were met by members of the Acjachemem community, including Adelia Sandoval and Jacque Nuñez, who led the day's prayer and discussed the mission and Serra within the ruins of the great stone church. On the walk in, the Hollands passed by a huge banner of Junípero Serra that honored him as saint. About fifty people came out to honor and support Caroline and Kagen on their journey. Standing within the walls of the old church, the gatherers joined in a circle. Adelia Sandoval stated:

> Our ancestors put these rocks together with their own hands. The reason why I like standing right here, is because this wall has our Acjachemen

medicine in it. As our ancestors were building the wall, they placed in it these shells, and crystals, and obsidian—their own medicine. Today, we can touch these walls, we can feel these shells, and know that our ancestors touched them too. It is a precious gift that they gave us.[52]

Before they moved on, each was asked to touch the walls to remember the ancestors and take notice of the shells placed there in a generative refusal of colonialism.

Mission San Juan Capistrano and its grounds provide a distorted version of history for tourist consumption with "a dizzying array of mission-themed tourist shops. 'First there was Mission San Juan Capistrano,' an Acjachemen friend wryly remarked to us," wrote Caroline and Kagen on their blog. "Then there was Disneyland." They wrote that the gathering was not happy, but "by the time we left the mission, we felt truly uplifted and inspired." Sandoval welcomed people in the Acjachemem language and thanked everyone for their presence:

Today is a very spiritual time, because we're here with our sister from the north of us: Caroline and her son Kagen, who had a moment of inspiration from the divine, from the great spirit, to do something that meant something very powerful. And as California Mission Indians, sometimes we feel very powerless. We feel like we don't have any voice, or we don't have any strength. But Caroline felt something come from within her, and said, I'm going to do something. I'm going to take action.

As the discussion continued, Caroline reflected on the deeply disturbing stories shared by other California Indian people at the previous missions they had stopped at: "There's no excuses for what happened to our people at these missions. Excuses are worse than lies. It's very disheartening to think that they still won't even acknowledge what happened—especially with the missions being tourist attractions today. They're not that, for us." The missions are sacred places for the tribes—where the ancestors were enslaved and where their graves are located. Caroline said, "We are human beings! We bleed, we have jobs, and brothers and sisters and daughters. Their Doctrine of Discovery still says that we are not, that they were the first human beings here in this area." Furthermore, Caroline stated, "Now, our villages are

Walk for the Ancestors at Mission San Juan Capistrano. https://walkfortheancestors.org/wp-content/uploads/2015/11/DSC05485-sm.jpg.

Refusals in the walls of Mission San Juan Capistrano. https://walkfortheancestors.org/2015/11/san-juan-capistrano.

CANONIZATION FODDER   117

their prime real estate. And we have nothing." Jacque Nuñez thoughtfully addressed the canonization of Serra:

> Was I for canonization? No. Did I want to say horrible things? No, that's not my nature. But I knew this: I wanted the Diocese to come to each one of us and say: What your people experienced wasn't OK. And it wasn't right. And we ask, by God, looking at all of us, we're sorry that that happened. And we will promise it will never happen again. I wanted to hear those words. But no one came. We just want our story to be told. We want you to acknowledge our story full of pain. And, know that there should be something done. We are California Indians that have nothing, unless we're a casino tribe, and we're not. So, all we have is the beauty of what God gave us. [In facing these things,] I ask that all of us lead our lives in a way that when we take a step, it is a step of healing, and not hurting.

In their blog, Caroline and Kagen wrote, "Adelia Sandoval stepped forward to introduce a traditional Acjachemen song." Sandoval shared, "It's a time of the harvest, so we're going to sing our harvest song for you, as a gift." Furthermore, she said, "also, it's medicine. In the spring time we plant seeds of prayers, and now, in this time we harvest what we planted."[53] After the prayer songs, the group walked to the cemetery near Serra Chapel—the last remaining original church where Serra performed Mass. Caroline and Kagen led the group in a Tataviam tobacco blessing and asked others to share.

I was there and shared a brief history of the significance of the day we gathered. I told how Mission San Juan Capistrano was first founded in 1775: "But they had a little problem. Mission San Diego was sacked a couple days after the founding. [Kumeyaay people] burned down the mission, and killed the priest, Father Jayme. It was a ceremonial killing." Fearing their tenuous grip on California could be lost, the missionaries buried the San Juan Capistrano Mission bells in the ground and fled with an escort of soldiers back to the San Diego Presidio to reassert control. One year later, on November 1 (the same calendar day as our gathering), Junípero Serra returned with a contingent of soldiers to unbury the bells and refound the San Juan Capistrano Mission. "I've been reading Junípero Serra's writings from that time," I told those who had assembled. I explained:

*118*  CHAPTER FOUR

> He [Serra] was saddened by the fact that they had to leave San Juan Capistrano. Then two years later in 1778, he writes about the Acjachemen rising up, and conspiring to burn down the mission. So, we've had a long tradition of resisting the mission. Resisting the canonization of Serra is just another part of that. We haven't stopped resisting. Even if we've become Catholic, even if we go to church, we're still resisting the effects that it had on our ancestors. What we're doing here is also part of that resistance—we're spreading these knowledges, these truths, and talking about how we can heal from this, how we can move forward. How can we prevent what has happened to us in the past from happening again to our future generations?

I shared these words to help us honor the ancestors and for us to think about our future generations. Corine Fairbanks, of the Southern California chapter of the American Indian Movement, similarly stated, "Remember that some day we're all going to be ancestors, too. And our ancestors prayed for us to be here. And so, you're walking prayers. We're walking prayers." Fairbanks continued: "And you know what, I hope my children will be walking prayers for what's going to come next. And I thank all of you for taking the time to be here, where you could have been doing something else."[54]

At the end of the gathering at San Juan Capistrano, Jacque Nuñez asked everyone to "get close and gather around Caroline and her sons." Nuñez explained that an Acjachemen elder "used to lead many ceremonies like this one. He said that our people need to come together, and we need to touch one another." She instructed everyone to gather close and place their hands on one another's shoulders as a traditional healing song was sung, and the group began singing in unison. "We are not done here, in a lot of ways," Adelia Sandoval said in closing. She elaborated:

> And perhaps, for some of us, this is a beginning. A beginning of really looking inside, and seeing what's really going on. And what is it that we can do next? Because there is always something that we can do next. We can be inspired, and we can continue on. But don't let it fall to the ground and do nothing with this day. Do something with this day. Especially, teach your children. Because that is the most important thing, for they are our future. Let us all go out and speak words of strength and healing. Let's all go forth

with loving action. And whatever comes from this time together that we have had, may it be multiplied a thousand-fold.[55]

The gathering at Mission San Juan Capistrano with Caroline and Kagen Holland was a regenerative refusal. For a few hours, it felt like we were honoring the ancestors and the autonomy of individual conscience through noncoercion and a deep connection between human beings and the elements of creation. The reciprocal relationships between humans and the more-than-human are essential to Indigenous futurity. These relationships are not dependent on state recognition or participation in an environmentally unsustainable economy. Indigenous futurity relies on refusing the violence of incorporation into colonial societies offering recognition as an answer to demands for justice, land, sovereignty, and kinship.

# FIVE

# Ramona Redeemed?

## *The Politics of Recognition and Rematriation*

One of the last coastal open spaces in Orange County is an endangered sacred place and the ancestral village site of the Acjachemem and Taraaxam nations, known as Genga and, more recently, Banning Ranch, then the Frank and Joan Randall Preserve. It is land that the tribes desire to be rematriated—not for economic purposes (despite the poverty, houselessness, and poor health care of some tribal members) but for cultural and sovereign continuity as caretakers of the land whose obligations to place exist beyond the boundaries and violence of the settler state. The 401-acre property is more than an open space; it is one of the few remaining places where the Acjachemem and Taraaxam could have the sovereign capacity to maintain traditional cultural practices through land stewardship. The land has well-documented archaeological sites and is listed on the California Native American Heritage Commission's Sacred Lands Inventory.

The ancestors documented in mission records as originating from Genga were mostly removed to Mission San Juan Capistrano, including Qchàinoque, whose name was changed through baptism on May 24, 1778, when he was 15, to Alexandro. A month after he was baptized, he married Coronni, a 14-year-old Acjachemem whose name was changed through baptism to Agueda. She was from the village of 'Uhunga and baptized *esta mismo dia*—on the same day as her marriage. Qchàinoque and Coronni had two children, a boy and a girl. Qchàinoque died seven years after his removal (*reducción*) from Genga at 22 and was buried in Mission San Juan Capistrano's cemetery on May 20, 1785, 10 days after the baptism of his 2-year-old daughter. The records do not tell us what he died from or the grief experienced by his family and community. However, we know that the deaths of Qchàinoque and the thousands of others who died at the missions devastated the Indigenous populations and their descendants. In 1789 Coronni remarried Cuenànauvit (Spanish name Teofilo), an Acjachemem who had been baptized a month

## 122   CHAPTER FIVE

before their marriage. Coronni died in 1800 at the age of 36. Very little is known about the lives of most Indians who were removed from villages such as Genga, except for the limited records of baptism, marriage, and death written by the priests. The stories of California Indian devastation, like their lands and names for themselves, were not lost or forgotten; they were stolen. Genga is unceded land that Acjachemem and Taraaxam refuse to forget or let go of. They demand that the land be conserved and rematriated to a rite relationship. If the land was stolen, it can be returned. And Genga, the tribes argue, should be returned. The Acjachemem and Taraaxam continue to resist the long history of colonial violence that has attempted to alienate them from their human–land relationships and kin. One way they resist is by demanding and organizing in their capacity for land back.

The California State Coastal Conservancy has determined that the Trust for Public Land will purchase Banning Ranch, and the Mountains Recreation and Conservation Authority will protect the land. The settler capitalist state determined that the living Acjachemem and Taraaxam, whose ancestors were from Genga, could not manage their traditional territory—a place they had lived and successfully stewarded for thousands of years before colonialism. Genga is located west of Newport Beach and south of Costa Mesa, at the confluence of the Wanáw Waníicha/Kahoo' Paxaayt/Santa Ana River and the Pacific Ocean. Land transfer to the Trust for Public Land and the Mountains Recreation and Conservation Authority would also signal the creation of public open space, parks, wildlife habitats, environmental restoration and conservation, and potentially lower-cost coastal accommodations.

Sacred Places Institute for Indigenous Peoples (SPI), whose board and staff includes Acjachemem and Taraaxam (many of whom identify as Tongva), has recommended in letters written in 2022 to the California State Coastal Conservancy that the language used in the land transfer needs to better include the tribes' need to "access and use . . . their ancestral homelands," and that there needs to be a commitment that any use of the land does "not conflict or impair tribal access and use" and that tribal nations and tribal community members must "have equal representation on all decision making bodies for the land." SPI also refuses the generalization of Acjachemem and Taraaxam people as "indigenous tribes" (lowercase). "These are sovereign Tribal Nations," SPI argues, "with whom state agencies have a duty to consult, not a monolithic 'indigenous community.' The staff report should be amended so as to reflect the proper deference that should be accorded to sovereign nations." SPI is working to ensure that if the political and philanthropic forces in the state of California do not find it necessary to return the land to its rightful genealogical caretakers, Acjachemem and Taraaxam at least have access to their unceded ancestral village, ensure protection of their cultural resources, and have decision-making power over the future of the land. SPI also insists that the land be referred to by its precolonial name. "Tribal community members have repeatedly expressed a desire for the site to be identified by its Indigenous place name in addition to the name designated to the site via its purchase by white landholders in 1874." The institute argues that "acknowledging and uplifting Indigenous names for places is a critical step in the work of decolonization and ending structural and institutional racism." Furthermore, SPI writes, "Tribal leaders and community members have consistently expressed a desire for the land to be rematriated" and that tribes are not stakeholders "but rather sovereign nations."[1] The demand for rematriation and government-to-government consultation as sovereign nations is resistance to the continued logic of conquest that has possessed Indigenous lands and bodies to nullify their sovereign capacity and alienate them from their kinship with place.

The Juaneño Band of Mission Indians, Acjachemen Nation (Belardes), and the Gabrieleño-Tongva Band of Mission Indians came together in 2016 under the leadership of Chairman Matias Belardes and Chief Anthony Morales to stop the development of Genga. In total, nine hundred homes, retail spaces, a hostel, and a hotel resort were proposed to be built on the ancestral village. The tribes argued that the developers did not comply with state and federal law and did not consult their tribes about the potential impact on the culturally sensitive land and known archaeological sites. Furthermore, they argued that the permit to develop the site should be denied due to the potential impact on cultural resources and the lack of tribal consultation. "Developers always ignore ancestral lands, the sites of villages, ceremonies, and Native life," Anthony Morales explains.[2] In a 2016 letter from the Juaneño Band of Mission Indians, Acjachemen Nation, to the California Coastal Commission, Chairman Matias Belardes and Tribal Manager Joyce Stanfield Perry addressed the need to "protect and preserve

## 124 CHAPTER FIVE

our ancestral sites." The tribe asked for additional research on Genga, including an "ethnographic study [to] be conducted to document historical and oral traditions of the region we call Genga." The Acjachemen, in the same letter, also argued for the need to establish a "tribal co-management land trust" that would steward "a portion of our traditional cultural landscape."[3] As an outcome of a California Coastal Commission meeting in 2016, at which several Acjachemem and Taraaxam tribal members and leaders provided public comments opposing the development of their lands, the commission denied the development permit in a win for the tribes over the capitalist developers.

Acjachemem and Taraaxam tribal members came together again in 2019 to begin discussions of forming a tribal land trust that they would name the Acjachemen Tongva Land Conservancy. The conservancy was formed to rematriate, protect, and preserve their shared ancestral homelands.

> We seek to reestablish Native people's stewardship of lands integral to our identity and culture. This land conservancy uses traditional cultural knowledge to guard our life ways and conserve the natural environment. We aspire to create awareness of our relationship with nature and to restore balance between ourselves and our environment. We strive to create spaces that can act as vehicles of healing and learning. We perpetuate our mission through community education and outreach, together with cultural and environmental preservation programs.[4]

The Acjachemen Tongva Land Conservancy was established to benefit the Acjachemem and Taraaxam communities outside the politics of recognition. Their vision centers on restoring their relationships to place, not the need or demand to have non-Natives recognize their identities, cultures, or nations. The rematriation of lands in the vision of the conservancy is radical in its absence of seeking reconciliation or redemption with the colonial nation state.

In 2019 California Governor Gavin Newsom apologized to the Indians of California for the state's complicity in genocide. His executive order states:

> WHEREAS, in the early decades of California's statehood, the relationship between the State of California and California Native Americans was

fraught with violence, exploitation, dispossession and the attempted destruction of tribal communities, as summed up by California's first Governor, Peter Burnett, in his 1851 address to the Legislature: "[t]hat a war of extermination will continue to be waged between the two races until the Indian race becomes extinct must be expected."[5]

Newsom's executive order shows the positive change that the State of California has undergone from declaring a war of extermination to apologizing "on behalf of the citizens of the State of California to all California Native Americans for the many instances of violence, maltreatment and neglect California inflicted on tribes." The executive order also created an ongoing process of "Truth and Healing." In 2020 Newsom signed an executive order to join international efforts to protect 30 percent of the earth's biodiversity by 2030. In 2022 the state allocated $750 million in new funding for this effort and created a fund of $100 million to buy ancestral lands to be returned to tribal nations. Still, as of this writing, money has not been distributed for tribal use, and it remains unclear if the state will provide funds to unrecognized tribal nations to protect their land. Acjachemem and Taraaxam, as unrecognized tribes, could benefit from these moneys to purchase their traditional territory as a step in returning the land to a rite relationship.

The state, federal government, and private donors (entities that include the US Fish and Wildlife Service and California State's Coastal Conservancy, Natural Resources Agency, Wildlife Conservation Board, and the Department of Fish and Wildlife, as well as the Randall Family) are giving $97 million to the Trust for Public Land (a non-Native organization) to purchase Genga, ignoring that the land is stolen and the tribes' demand for land back. The Acjachemem and Taraaxam are left to fight to be included and recognized as tribal nations. Their unrecognized status leaves them few opportunities to rematriate their lands to a rite relationship. A critique of the politics of recognition does not answer the consequence of nonrecognition within a system based on exclusion. Yet, without recognition, two land conservancies, the Tongva Taraxat Paxaavxa Land Conservancy and the Acjachemen Tongva Land Conservancy, have both received the first land back in Los Angeles and Orange Counties. The two land conservancies are working to right the wrongs of colonial degradation to the lands that they

*126* CHAPTER FIVE

steward. The first step is land back, and the much more difficult process of rematriation follows.

Even as Genga was being sold to a non-Native land conservancy, Governor Newsom stated, "We know that California Native peoples have always had an independent relations with land, waters, everything that makes up the state of California. Unfortunately we also know that the state has had a role in violently disrupting those relations."[6] The history of conquest and converting land into possession and property under Spain and its missionaries continues in Genga, where a tribal land conservancy could have been funded by the State of California, which admits to its responsibility in the violence of colonialism that alienates Indigenous human–land relationships. The Acjachemem and Taraaxam nations and tribal members want the land to be rematriated, not for economic purposes or simple conservation, but for cultural continuity and the persistence of their relationships and obligation to their land, water, kinship, life, and intelligence systems.

## Redemption Song

Among the definitions of *redeem* is "to atone or make amends for an error or evil previously committed." It can also mean "to save someone from sin, error, or evil," for example, in the sentence "he was a sinner, redeemed by the grace of God." In the Catholic faith, the ultimate redemption was the price paid by Jesus Christ, who suffered and died as an atonement for humans' sins. They also believe that through Jesus's redemption, divine honor has been repaired, and divine wrath has been appeased. Furthermore, redemption from a Christian theological perspective indicates liberation from a life of slavery and sin to the freedom of a new life with God. The secular meaning of *redemption* is often compensation, including regaining the loss of a possession through repayment.

The evil committed against California Indians was simultaneous genocide, enslavement, and land dispossession. The project of conquest natally alienated them from their heritage and human–land relationships. How can California Indian peoples be redeemed for what was taken from them? How can they be redeemed after the evil of an apocalypse and the devastation to land and people? How can they be liberated from enslavement and land dispossession into a restored relationship with their homeland and creator? What is the price to be paid for the sins of colonization? Are Christians willing to redeem themselves from the evil of their ancestors to help liberate California Indians from conquest's continued logic of spiritual possession? Furthermore, what are Christians and non-Christians who live on stolen land willing to do to redeem themselves from the theft they benefit from? Perhaps more precisely: What is justice on stolen land?

In their article "Ramona Redeemed?" Native sociologist Duane Champagne and legal scholar Carole Goldberg conclude that California voters' recognition of tribal sovereignty may finally have redeemed California Indians from the effects of American conquest. Their study explains that the California Indian population decline continued during the American occupation, cutting the population in half between the beginning of the American conquest and the twentieth century. Champagne and Goldberg use Helen Hunt Jackson's 1884 novel *Ramona* and the annual California play by the same name as a metaphor for the impact of colonialism on Southern California Indians.[7] In the story, the title character, Ramona, is an orphaned mixed-race Scottish and Native American whose parents were married at Mission San Gabriel. Ramona's parents are partly based on Hugo Reid (chapter 1) and his Taxaat wife, Victoria Bartolomea. Jackson ensured that Ramona was part Native to prevent readers from being offended by the inclusion of miscegenation in her novel. Ramona was raised in a Californio home by Señora Gonzaga Moreno, who despised the American occupation of California and whose racial politics did not allow her to love her adopted daughter because of her Native ancestry. Señora Moreno is outraged when Ramona and Alessandro Assís (Luiseño from the village of Temecula) fall in love because he is Indian. The señora will not allow Ramona to marry him, so the couple elope. Together, they have two daughters, and the rest of the novel details the lovers' miseries that follow.

The novel describes the Americans' using force to remove Alessandro's tribe from their village at Temecula, and the couple cannot find a permanent community not threatened by the colonial violence of American possession. Eventually, Ramona and Alessandro move to the mountains. Alessandro slowly loses his mind due to the constant humiliation and regret for taking Ramona away from her home with the Morenos. Soon, another tragedy befalls the couple when their daughter, Eyes of the Sky, dies because a white doctor would not treat her. Their love story ends in tragedy. Alessandro, suffering from mental unbalance, accidentally rides away on the horse of an American named Jim Farrar, who follows him and fatally shoots Alessandro. The novel concludes with Ramona in grief, returning to the Moreno household and marrying Felipe, the son of the late señora. Felipe and Ramona must abandon their home because of the Americans' racial politics and the uncertainty of retaining their ranchlands. The novel ends with them moving to Mexico: as Champagne and Goldberg write, "leaving the country to the newly arrived U.S. settlers who make California their home."[8]

Jackson's novel fictionalizes several historical events and places to bring the tragedy of federal inaction and the destitute position of California Indians to the national consciousness. Jackson intended to influence policy that could assist California Indians. She thought her compelling story could help Americans recognize the effects on California Indians by US expansion. She believed her novel could influence the government to pass liberal legislation to ease their suffering. She stated her intention of writing *Ramona* in 1883, "I am going to write a novel, which will be set forth some Indian experiences in a way to move people's hearts. People will read a novel when they will not read serious books."[9] In another quote, Jackson summarizes her view of California Indians at the time, "a more pitiable sight has not been seen on earth than the spectacle of this great body of helpless, dependent creatures, suddenly deprived of their teachers and protectors," that is, priests at the missions, after the missions closed and the Mexican-American War. Jackson compared her novel to *Uncle Tom's Cabin*, stating that she would be thankful "if I can do one hundredth part for the Indians that Mrs. Stowe did for the Negro."[10] Jackson had limited success in her white savior mission to stimulate action for the Indians. But her novel did inspire and influence the development of the Spanish imaginary (chapter 2), which longed for the time of the Spanish missions and their romance—a hallucination that continues to affect the historiography of California.

"The Ramona story," Champagne and Goldberg explain, "symbolizes the marginalization and mistreatment of California Indians during the second half of the nineteenth century." During the 1850s, California tribal nations negotiated eighteen treaties that remained unratified by Congress, leaving many "landless until the rancheria and reservation acts of the 1890s provided tiny, economically undesirable land bases." Federal policies in California did little to assist tribal nations and continued a "disregard for tribal sovereignty and well-being."[11] Unable to continue traditional land-centered ways of life, California Indians depended on wage labor and handouts from the government. Instead of working with tribal governments to support their needs, the policy suggested the "extinguishment of tribal existence." This included the 1920s land claims settlements, which targeted individual tribal members rather than tribal nations. This poorly implemented settlement provided insufficient money for individual tribal members. Moreover, it approved non-California Indians to enroll in tribes and obtain a Certificate of Degree of Indian Blood. The enrollment of non-California Indians continues to affect tribal nations today, including in-fighting over who is a legitimate California Indian. During the 1950s and 1960s, the US government terminated approximately forty reservations and rancherias.

In 1953 Public Law 280 created concurrent state jurisdiction for criminal matters on the reservations, leading to state interference in tribal sovereignty and the federal government to limit services and support for California Indian nations. The lack of support includes a scarcity of money or training for tribal law enforcement, few tribal courts, limited health services, and few tribal schools. According to Champagne and Goldberg, the policies and their implementation throughout the twentieth century "have been administratively, culturally, economically, and politically disadvantaged, even compared with tribes elsewhere in the United States." The lack of resources resulted in "high rates of crime, school dropouts, and substandard housing."[12]

Champagne and Goldberg state that the redemption of Ramona and all California Indians relies on the settler government recognizing their sovereignty. They argue that redemption is the restoration of tribes into the civil systems of the state—mind you, the tribes had never been included in the first place. On the contrary, the State of California excluded California Indians, and during a long period during the nineteenth century, Indians were targeted for extermination.[13] Champagne and Goldberg end their article with a positive outlook for the future of California Indian nations, based on the successful California political campaigns (1998 and 2000) that legalized gaming on reservations through the negotiation of compacts and tribal nations' obedience to federal and state law. Champagne and Goldberg write, "More than one hundred years after *Ramona* was published, the inheritors of the American settlers have helped restore California Indians to a place within the state's political and social landscape, at least for the near term." Gaming, the authors argue, "brought many non-Indian Californians onto reservations for the first time" and raised their recognition of "tribe's continuing existence." They also argue that gaming provided entertainment that most non-Indians wanted access to. Furthermore, the authors insist that the campaigns that ultimately allowed tribes to operate casinos expanded non-Indian recognition, and "tribes benefitted from this new consciousness through political support and significant patronage."[14]

Champagne and Goldberg suggest that Ramona, and therefore California Indians, were redeemed but leave it as a question. I strongly argue that California Indians have yet to sing their redemption songs. Furthermore, I contend that the authors ask the wrong question, using inappropriate terminology. It is not California Indians who need redemption but those responsible for evil. The meaning of *redeem* is inextricable from its fifteenth-century theological definition of "deliverance from sin and spiritual death" and its application through baptism and the spiritual conquest of California. Junípero Serra wrote in 1777 that his purpose was to deliver to God the Indians, who were "redeemed" through the suffering and death of Jesus. Serra wrote that he put his "trust in the Lord, who created them [Indians], and redeemed them with the most precious blood of His Son: He will bring them to the fold in the manner at the time that He will be pleased to do so."[15] Champagne and Goldberg use "redeemed" in its secular meaning of "being paid back," but a more appropriate question, given the content of their article, could have focused on the achievement and limitations of sovereignty and the recognition of Native nations within the setter state. They should have left redemption to theological study.

## The Politics of Recognition

Champagne and Goldberg suggest that through casinos, as an economic opportunity allowed by the settler state, tribes are paid back for centuries of dishonor. However, only recognition by the settler state provides economic advancement opportunities, and more than seventy California tribes remain unrecognized, including the Taraaxam and Acjachemem tribal nations. Moreover, both recognized and unrecognized California tribes are substate groups that have suffered under the hegemonic political power of the United States (and Mexico and Spain before). As Glen Coulthard argues in *Red Skin, White Masks*, building from the writings of Frantz Fanon and Charles Taylor, misrecognition or nonrecognition cannot be contested or made right through "a more accommodating, liberal regime of mutual recognition," and recognition cannot address "the power relations typical of those between Indigenous peoples and settler states." For Fanon, according to Coulthard's reading, the "longevity of a colonial social formation depends" on the state's ability to "transform the colonized population into *subjects* of imperial rule."[16] In other words, tribes are alienated from their heritage through multicultural incorporation.

The tribes who began Las Vegas–style gaming beginning with bingo halls and card parlors in the early 1980s did so to address the endemic poverty of their communities.[17] As Lakota sociologist James Fenelon explains, "The key issues on which all Native American Indian gaming is predicated are Indian sovereignty, economic development, employment, and distribution of proceeds as a means for redress of the many historical and contemporary injustices and inequalities."[18] Proceeds from tribal gaming are distributed, as Jessica Cattelino clarifies, through monetized dividends "converted through a government budgetary process into individualized checks paid directly to tribal citizens."[19] Tribes that ventured into gaming also did so in refusal of state law under threat of colonial violence, and several tribes were raided by police and had their casinos temporarily shut down. State and local governments viewed Indian sovereignty and the operation of casinos as criminal activity. Through the case *California v. Cabazon Band of Mission Indians* in 1987, the Supreme Court ruled that tribes had the right to high-stakes bingo and card games if the state did not have a prohibition against gaming. The opinion of the court argued, as Champagne and Goldberg note, "that states could acquire jurisdiction to regulate tribal gaming if Congress enacted a law clearly manifesting that intent."[20] In response to the 1987 ruling, Congress passed the Indian Gaming Regulatory Act in 1988. The act limited tribal sovereignty to gaming, ensuring that all games other than bingo and traditional

132 CHAPTER FIVE

Indian games would be regulated by state law, and required that the state and tribe negotiate a compact approved by the secretary of the interior. The act established a new federal agency, the National Indian Gaming Commission, which regulates tribal games and management contracts. Indian gaming brought more state and federal oversight over tribal sovereignty, further enveloping tribes into colonial rule.

Tribes that did not back down to state pressures and operated their casinos under the constant threat of state violence saw dramatic improvements in employment, housing, education, tribal members returning to their reservations, and the establishment of cultural revitalization projects.[21] They reinvested in their communities, building infrastructure that was impossible with federal funding or other economic ventures. Champagne distinguishes "tribal capitalism" from capitalism through a tribe's reinvestment in its reservation communities and the tribal rather than individual control of the economy.[22] Tribes also established services that assist the reservation and surrounding communities, including employment, fire, and public safety services. Gaming tribes donate to local charities, organizations, schools, and universities. Champagne and Goldberg note that tribal philanthropy made possible through gaming is in "the native traditions of sharing wealth" and that they "redistributed their good fortune to local community groups, many of which were very grateful for the recognition and support."[23] However, again, these good fortunes through gaming are limited to tribes with federal recognition in states whose laws allow gaming, and the tribal capitalist economies made possible through recognition of limited tribal sovereignty further transform tribes into subjects of imperial rule.

Despite the material benefits of recognition for Native communities, which include better health care and housing, the critique of Coulthard and Fanon should be taken seriously. The politics of recognition and its structure have exploited, dispossessed, and killed California Indians. Mohawk political scientist Taiaiake Alfred maintains that "capitalist economies and liberal delusions of progress" have historically been used as the "engines of colonial aggression and injustice."[24] Working within the system will never radically change the structures of colonialism. However, tribes must make the difficult decisions to, for example, increase the life expectancy of their tribal members by engaging in the capitalist economy. The lived reality for tribal nations is complex and messy, without easy answers on how to be free. Many federally recognized tribes have decided to game, and unrecognized tribes have applied for recognition, not because these decisions move tribes toward decolonization but because they help sustain their tribal nations within a structure of white supremacy constantly working to possess their lands and life.

Although reformist state acts such as the Native American Graves Protection and Repatriation Act, American Indian Religious Freedom Act, the *California v. Cabazon* case, and the Indian Gaming Regulatory Act grant concessions for tribal sovereignty, cultural difference, and economic tribal self-determination and alter the intensity and effects of the domination of conquest, they do not change the power structures. The concessions that uplift tribal sovereignty (nation within a nation), as Coulthard argues, do not address the "capitalist economy constituted by racial and gender hierarchies and the colonial state." Tribes remain subordinated to the state even when their economies place their members into exclusive categories of wealth achievement. The very means to pull tribes out of poverty has further integrated tribes into the capitalist system. Unrecognized tribes often want to be included in the system so that they, too, can take advantage of state concessions, including but not limited to gaming. Tribes whose ancestors fought to defend their lands from the devastation of colonialism have succumbed to fighting to be better included in the structures of the state. Alfred contrasts the fight for inclusion with the goal of traditionally rooted self-determination struggles, which seek to protect the "heart and soul of [I]ndigenous nations: a set of values that challenge the homogenizing force of Western liberalism and free market capitalism; that honor the autonomy of individual conscience, non-coercive authority, and the deep interconnection between human beings and other elements of creation."[25] Recognition and its benefits do not radically challenge the state or provide freedom, which has always meant kinship and the enduring relationships between humans and the earth.

Recognition through the state or from the state's citizens may bring material benefit to tribes and their members, at times more than any individual needs. Still, recognition is not the same as tribal struggles against the longevity of conquest. Recognition struggles are not anticolonial. Coulthard

134  CHAPTER FIVE

explains, "Indigenous struggles against capitalist imperialism are best understood as struggles oriented around the question of *land*." Struggles that Coulthard insists are "not only *for* land, but also deeply informed" by place-based practices, associated knowledge, and "land as mode of reciprocal relationship." Tribal relationships to place guide their resistance against that which threatens to destroy their sense of place. For Alfred, the politics of recognition serve the priorities of capitalist accumulation. According to Coulthard, recognition serves colonial capitalist efforts by "*appearing* to address its colonial history through symbolic acts of redress" that actually "entrench its bases of control through law and policy."[26] If Champagne and Goldberg believe that California Indians may be "redeemed" through recognition and gaming, then the state and its citizens surely must view the historical "wrongs" to have been "righted," negating the need for further transformation.

For Alfred, there is a need to challenge the idea that an equitable relationship between non-Indigenous peoples and a sustainable relationship with the land can be achieved through further participation in an environmentally unsustainable capitalist economy—an economic system that, as Coulthard reminds us, is "at its core" founded on "racial, gender, and class exploitation and inequalities." The same, he says, can be said about "our attempts to negotiate a relation of nondomination with a structure of domination like the colonial nation-state," which, of course, was founded on heteropatriarchy, genocide, and slavery.[27] Tribal attempts to gain state recognition encourage tribes to mimic state governance structures based on coercion and dominance. The gaming tribe's economies replicate many of the worst features of capitalism and the state's power. No matter how "green" a casino may propose to be, as a capitalist endeavor, it relies on exploiting the land and people. The decision to have gaming or to apply for federal recognition, however, are often decisions between continued poverty, lack of health care, or other struggles and being more deeply included in the racist, sexist, anti-Indigenous, and anti-Black, class-exploitive system of the colonial state. This decision and its successes should not be viewed as a "redemption" or as having righted historical wrongs but as a creative means of survival under a dominant colonial nation-state that in the near past actively vowed to exterminate Indians and continues to erase Indigenous human–land relationships. These creative forms of survival and demands for sovereignty and land back through recognition run parallel to the dynamic reforms to the logics of conquest made by the state that function as a liberal incorporation strategy. Jaskiran Dhillon explains that continuing and maintaining a colonial mode of existence through a reformed system is nonetheless premised on Native erasure.[28] And yet, to survive, it is necessary that tribes creatively resist, including by using the colonizer's tools that unfortunately further incorporate tribes into racist state structures that negate the continuation of Indigenous ways of life not premised on domination or domestication.

## Land Acknowledgments

A growing practice of universities, social justice organizations, nonprofits, and government officials in the United States is the acknowledgment of the land's Indigenous peoples. Many universities encourage presenters at public events to acknowledge which tribe's territory they are on. Land acknowledgments are an increasing form of what Coulthard calls "the politics of recognition." They are largely symbolic and provide the appearance of addressing colonial history. For example, at the University of California, Riverside, where I received my PhD, speakers are encouraged to acknowledge that they and their audience are gathered on the land of the Cahuilla, Tongva, Luiseño, and Serrano. Common rhetorical approaches to acknowledgment involve honoring, thanking, and respecting Native peoples and their lands. As I wrote elsewhere with Tongva scholar Wallace Cleaves, "we have experienced this increase in the acknowledgment of traditional territories all while our own tribal nation remains landless and formally unrecognized by the U.S."[29] Land acknowledgments do not provide a form of redress for dispossession and in many instances are what Indigenous education scholar Eve Tuck and ethnic studies scholar K. Wayne Yang have called "settler moves to innocence"—actions that alleviate guilt without direct action. They state, "There is a long and bumbled history of non-Indigenous peoples making moves to alleviate the impacts of colonization," for example, the adoption of decolonizing discourse and its tropes, such as the phrase "decolonize your mind." Tuck and Yang argue that enacting these tropes is "a series of moves to innocence, which problematically attempt to reconcile settler guilt and complicity, and rescue settler futurity."[30]

For Native education scholars Theresa Stewart-Ambo and K. Wayne

## CHAPTER FIVE

Yang, there are differences between Indigenous and settler recognition practices. They write that Indigenous communities have "sustained practices and protocols of recognizing, acknowledging, announcing, welcoming, and inviting each other as well as non-Indigenous people since time immemorial." Settler land acknowledgments "represent a broad spectrum of political intentions, from explicitly naming Indigenous sovereignty, and thus the limits of settler sovereignty, to assimilating Indigenous lands and peoples into the multicultural (neo)liberal nation-state." With their increase in use by non-Natives, land acknowledgments are becoming rote and performative. They also become less like Indigenous protocols, which provide a form of nondominance through mutual recognition meant to form relations and obligations. According to Stewart-Ambo and Yang, land acknowledgments are sometimes "conveniently understood to be the action in and of itself, as if recognition is itself a decolonizing act" without the need to do the difficult work of forming nondominating relationships.[31] When this happens, the people performing the land acknowledgment continue to enact the logic of conquest that possesses Native land. They may as well say, "This *used* to be [insert tribe's name] land. We thank them for allowing us to be here, even though we never formally asked or received permission. We are unwilling to do the real work of creating relationalities." Even when members of institutions have worked hard to establish relationships with tribal communities, individuals cannot disrupt the unequal and, therefore, dominating power relations of the institution as an agent of the capitalist colonial state through acknowledgment. Furthermore, the land acknowledgment does not move beyond recognition to form obligations to the tribes that it recognizes.

## Walking after You

California Indian precolonial life was not easy. Yet, from the vantage point of today, it looks nearly idyllic. Among what makes it appear that way are the tribal presence and stewardship of the land and the tribes' thriving in their ways of life centered on nondominating relationships between human beings and the more-than-human. According to the varying tribal histories of Southern California, protocols recognizing the sacredness of life and ways to live and survive on their lands were passed down generationally, beginning at creation. Indigenous knowledges provided a high level of individual self-determination in contrast to the colonial societies we live in today based on authoritarian power maintained through violence, coercion, and hierarchy. The mission of the colonizers has variably targeted Indigenous dispossession, including a complete disruption to their nondominant relationship with the land and all of creation. In California the Spanish conquest enacted a spiritual possession, natally alienating California Indians through enslavement at the missions. These logics of domination were altered by Mexican colonialism, followed by American colonialism into the present, yet they continue to exert their power over Indigenous peoples and lands.

Most California Indians have little land to live on or on which to recuperate their precolonial protocols of nondomination. Taraaxam and Acjachemem are nearly landless. Their lands are almost completely developed, and the remnants of their sacred places and ancestral burials are constantly threatened. The undeveloped land is either private property owned by individuals, businesses, or organizations or the property of local, state, and federal governments. Moreover, there are few options for tribal nations to move toward decolonization when millions of non-Natives live on their territories, and their lands are covered with concrete, making it nearly impossible for tribes to return to a subsistence based on the local Native resources. I do not write these words, or the many examples provided in this book, to reveal damage, in what Eve Tuck calls "damage-centered research," or to think of California Indians as broken. I do not socially and historically situate California Indians, particularly Taraaxam and Acjachemem, as subjects of exploitation and domination to explain contemporary brokenness, although these histories tell us much. My research does not seek reparation or redemption. However, it does seek to explain and better understand the profound grief of loss and dispossession and think through genealogical refusals to conquest, producing possibilities and futurity based on ancestral knowledge and genealogical obligations to place. Any action for our future must be based on anticolonial organizing. If we must use the colonizer's tools, we also must acknowledge that they are a means to an end. For example, in creating a 501(c)(3) to hold title to land back, the goal is not to have land back and hold title but to use what is available in an anticolonial way to rematriate the land.

Recognition does not disrupt the hauntings of conquest. In Genga, Acjachemem and Taraaxam were removed from their villages, and the land became possessed by colonialism. The haunting of conquest lies in the seething presence of the stolen land, even if it appears that the wrongs have been righted by apologies or recognition. The haunting is made real through each generation, despite advances made to include Acjachemem and Taraaxam into colonial society. Haunting refuses to stop, just as the tribal community refuses to only exist in the past, as dispossessed incorporeal apparitions threatening to repossess the land. If federal recognition is conceded and Acjachemem and Taraaxam tribal nations had the legal ability to engage in tribal capitalism through casinos, they would remain (dis)possessed.[32]

Acjachemem and Taraaxam have a long history of refusal and resistance, from violence against the missionaries, sacred place protection, and recuperating and reinvesting in their traditional knowledges in creative ways, from their seafaring titii'atam (canoes) to their languages, which helps them better understand their lands and places, sacred histories, and ceremonial cycles. The resurgence of Acjachemem and Taraaxam political thought and the recuperation of what Glen Coulthard calls "grounded normativity" is slowed by their lack of land. Coulthard defines "grounded normativity" as "the modalities of Indigenous land-connected practices and longstanding experiential knowledge that inform and structure our ethical engagements with the world and our relationships with human and nonhuman others over time."[33] Land, according to Coulthard, has three interrelated meanings: "land-as-a-resource central to our material survival; land-as-identity, as constitutive of who we are as a people; and land-as-relationship." These three interconnected meanings are all at play within grounded normativity.

Turning again to Coulthard, I quote him at length to help think through the ways Taraaxam and Acjachemem already work to recuperate their Indigenous intellectual traditions and what more is needed:

> Without such a massive transformation in the political economy of contemporary settler-colonialism, any efforts to rebuild our nations will remain parasitic on capitalism, and thus on the perpetual exploitation of our lands and labor. Consider, for example, an approach to resurgence that would see

Indigenous people begin to reconnect with their lands and land-based practices on either an individual or small-scale collective basis. This could take the form of "walking the land" in an effort to refamiliarize ourselves with the landscape and places that give our histories, languages, and cultures shape and content; to revitalizing and engaging in land-based harvesting practices like hunting, fishing, and gathering, and/or cultural production activities like hide-tanning and carving, all of which also serve to assert our sovereign presence on our territories in ways that can be profoundly educational and empowering; to the reoccupation of sacred places for the purpose of relearning and practicing our ceremonial activities.[34]

Southern California Indians from both recognized and unrecognized tribes are already doing many of the things Coulthard suggests.

I want to highlight the elders and strong leaders within the Acjachemem and Taraaxam communities who do their best to perpetuate their cultures and teach others within and outside the community from their traditional knowledge base. The women leaders, craftspersons, and those who pull water for the ti'aat, the traditional sewn plank canoes of the Taraaxam, actively assert our sovereign presence. The ti'aat is made possible through collaboration with other Native and non-Native peoples, including Pacific Islanders, through what Kēhaulani Vaughn calls "trans-Indigenous recognitions." These recognitions are made between Native peoples outside the state and assist in regenerating "social and political futures for Indigenous communities and are thus invaluable in combatting settler colonial institutions."[35] Furthermore, tribal members are relearning how to craft canoes, houses, and toys out of tule. The Chia Café Collective is increasing knowledge about Southern California traditional foods, such as acorns, and how to harvest, process, and cook them. The California Indian basket weavers keep the traditions of gathering, processing, weaving, storytelling, and (re)forming kinship with one another. The singers are responsible for learning the songs, creating new ones, and working collectively to dance and rattle or clap for the people, especially when they sing for the deceased. The Mother Earth Clan dedicates their families to learning and passing their heritage to their children. Tribal members work to protect white sage and ask that people grow sage rather than foraging or gathering. Individuals use their skills and

*140*  CHAPTER FIVE

education to help one another become more connected to the land, water, and the stars.

Individuals and organizations work with museums like the Blas Aguilar Adobe and Acjachemen Cultural Center in San Juan Capistrano and the Autry Museum of the American West in Los Angeles. Artists use their craft to ensure their stories are told in creative mediums. Storytellers teach everyone who will listen about their cultures. Children walk the land and visit their sacred places with their families to feel their ancestors' presence. Women are increasingly receiving their traditional facial tattoos. Volunteer leaders of land conservancies dedicate their time to the cause of rematriating land within a dominant capitalist system. Tribes and tribal members organize to protect sacred places and the burials of their ancestors from being desecrated by development. Taraaxam, Acjachemem, and their families reconnect with their traditional intelligence systems and the earth in many ways.

The amount of dedication from tribal members in Southern California should be written about in a separate book, documenting how culture persists despite imperialism's overwhelming and seething dominance. I have provided only a few examples of how California Indians engage in their cultures. Resurgence requires land, and as Mishuana Goeman argues, "the geographies foundational to Native communities have not disappeared but are waiting to be (re)mapped and 'grasped.'"[36] To perpetuate culture and empower their communities, tribes without land desperately need to rematriate place. One of those places available to the Taraaxam and Acjachemem is the shared ancestral village and sacred site of Genga—one of the last coastal open spaces in Orange County—which can be integrated into a lived reality. Genga would provide the tribes with the opportunity to refamiliarize themselves with the land and learn from its power. Rematriating Genga outside the boundaries of heteropatriarchy into a rite relationship would change the future for the Taraaxam and the Acjachemem, and the land could provide the healing that no other source can offer. The people can heal the land, and simultaneously, the land can heal the people. We must feel the land again, seeing it as a relation, enabling us to imagine a new society.[37] We must feel our way to the future through a present informed by our ancestors from the past.

# CONCLUSION
## The Afterlife of Native Alienation

The acts of violence I write about—targeted against land, bodies, and souls—are part of a long history on a global scale that necessitates specificity in language and critical evaluations of the foundational logics of conquest that produces our modern world. The violence of conquest against Indigenous bodies, lands, and souls has not been fully or adequately theorized, making any approach to solutions, even my own, inadequate until a common language is developed to analyze conquest as an ongoing alienation from the earth.

In previous scholarship, I suggested that those who live on Taraaxam and Acjachemem land can become kuuyam ("guests" in Taraaxam) of the tribe, but more importantly of the land.[1] The concept of kuuyam is anticolonial in that it is the beginning of creating relations outside the structures of dominance. Kuuyam also allows non-Indians the opportunity to learn from Native cultural values and the power of the land without also seizing Native identities and shifting their race.[2] Despite my desire to provide concrete solutions and accommodate those who want them, I refuse to end with a well-developed solution. My discussion of land back and rematriation in previous chapters argues that the way toward futurity is through kinship. More concisely, the glimpses of solutions I provide include reinvestment in love, kinship, and the future of the people of the earth.

What I want readers to take away from *Native Alienation* are not the glimpses at solutions I provide. I want readers to understand that the complex historical dimensions of violence to the body, physiology, spirituality, ontology, and kinships (including place, land, territory, and water) are beyond a language of description—despite the thousands of pages of writing that numerous scholars have produced to understand it better. I have named conquest operating through a logic of *spiritual possession* requiring *Native alienation*, but this is only my attempt to use language to explain and theorize the forms of gratuitous terror, including slavery and its afterlife, that haunt the present and our futures. A language that can explain the gratuitous

## 142  CONCLUSION

violence of terror beyond the body on an ontological level is a challenge. How can you explain a loss of self? How can we express the survival of people when their very survival means losing their past, heritage, and worlds? Some of the language we can learn from has been written by Black studies scholars, including Saidiya Hartman, Hortense Spillers, Orlando Patterson, and many others, who have deeply reflected on slavery beyond labor and property. Yet, despite the loss of self, 'Anaangere 'Ekwaa Woon—We are still here. I hope that the term *Native alienation* is useful to scholars from diverse fields to explain the loss of kinship to place and the heritage of our ancestors.

Indigenous survival is always in confrontation with modernity. Scholars can argue that Native peoples have made great advances to be included in colonial society (yes, they have), but as João Costa Vargas and Moon-Kie Jung remind us, "Constant terror does not require constant violation."[3] California Indians can be successful as individuals in the colonial system, but their social existence and kinship with land can be invaded at any moment. As Glen Coulthard has argued and as I discussed at length in chapter 5, inclusion is the disintegration of Native ways of life and sovereignty—a Native alienation. Inclusion is the ascendency of state power over Indian lives, intertwining them with the racialized economic, political, and military authority of the state and away from the cultural institutions of their ancestors.[4] Inclusion is ultimately a disappearance into whiteness. Yet, people must survive in the existing world, not the one they want. Indian gaming and tribes seeking federal recognition are not engaged in these activities to be included by the state but to better survive, even if that survival is Native alienation. These are also refusals.

Native scholars have increasingly used Gerald Vizenor's notion of survivance to explain Native existence outside of victimhood, "an active sense of presence, of native stories, not a mere reaction, or a survivable name. Native survivance stories are renunciations of dominance, tragedy and victimry."[5] Throughout this book, I retrofit the archive to tell stories of California Indians' historical, genealogical, and cultural resistance. Through these stories, I highlighted Native refusals to the structures of soul possession, enslavement, genocide, and land dispossession. Furthermore, tribes have worked to reclaim culture and land. Said differently, "We are not a conquered people."[6] Yet California Indians remain victims of gratuitous violence, which has not

CONCLUSION    *143*

been fully or satisfactorily analyzed within the scholarship. There remains a tendency and discursive impulse to write about California Indian histories of missionization as benevolent, disavowing enslavement or highlighting survivance over continued dominance. I am afraid that the move toward a scholarship centering on survivance can erase the apocalypse and its afterlife (chapter 3)—insisting that Indian people have been capable of successfully maintaining the worlds of their ancestors through a continuous presence. Moreover, how can we heal when the crimes against us continue to be covered up or, worse, celebrated (chapter 4)? This book explicitly focuses on the colonial imaginary while simultaneously displaying Native resistance and refusal.

Survivance can erase continual colonial dispossession(s) that have intended to alienate Indigenous people from land and the heritage of their ancestors. And it can disappear those who did not survive. Survivance shifts our focus away from the predatory logic of conquest to an emphasis on the advances (or agency) of Native peoples within a reality that alienates all of us from the power of the earth and sky. Survivance can also make tribes who have not been as successful at resistance (and have succumbed to dominance, historical absence, and sentiments of victimry) to be viewed as less than those with positive, effective stories of Native liberty.[7] Tribes without federal recognition, for example, can be viewed by society and other Natives as less than tribes with. Their authenticity is continually questioned due to their lack of recognition by the colonizer. Their redemption is often viewed as available through recognition, which incorporates tribes into the structures of white supremacy (chapter 5). Some California Indian tribal nations had nearly everything violently taken from them through conquest—their populations, their lands, their names for themselves, their languages, their labor power, their sovereignty and bodily sovereignty, their ceremonial traditions, and any claims respected by the colonizers—even to protect the burials of their dead.

The logic of conquest worked to alienate Native peoples from their lands as kin. As Dakota activist John Trudell theorizes through his poetry featured in the song "ALie Nation" by the electronic music group The Halluci Nation, nothing is sacred in the colonial world except violence—not even the colonizers themselves. The history and the logic of conquest, as Trudell contends, is alienation from the earth. The human beings, he explains, know that everything is related, and they see the natural world as having spirit. He states that the alienation ("Alie Nation") mines our spirits and exploits the earth and sky.[8] In his poetry, Trudell underscores the incommensurability between a worldview that values the earth as a sacred relationship and a worldview in which the earth is exploitable. This incommensurability shapes our modern world.

The exploitation of the earth is easily transferred through violence and trauma to human bodies and their souls (sold), making nothing sacred except exploitation, transforming human beings into humans (without relation to the earth) and all of creation into material to be dominated and possessed. The exploitive logic deployed against the land, bodies, and souls, Trudell argues, is the alienation of human beings from the earth—"The ALie Nation," which he compares to the "Halluci Nation," the people the colonizer cannot see. Furthermore, he says, we have been named Indians, Native Americans, hostiles, pagans, and militants—many names—but we are human beings. As California Indians, our names for ourselves translate to a variation of "the people," or "the people of" a specific place. Our DNA, Trudell emphasizes, is of earth and sky, past and present. We are not distinct from the earth or the more-than-human. And even though our worlds have been colonized, we are a continuation.[9] As I wrote in chapter 2, this hallucination disposes of California Indians by producing an imaginary that erases our presence, renames us, and rewrites our histories. Yet we continuously resist erasure, as each chapter in this book displays. Chapter 4 highlights the resistance to the canonization of Junípero Serra in 2015. We are a hallucination and a haunting—the ghosts that remind the humans that there are ways to live other than through exploitation. While I have focused on California, Trudell's argument is global—all the lands are Indian Country, just as all the earth is Indigenous. The enclosure is neither the reservation nor the prison. At this moment in history, the enclosure is the earth—our collective, industrial reservation. Everyone's DNA is of earth and sky—the earth's metals, liquids, and minerals. Everything on this planet is made up of the same thing: the universe's building blocks. The Halluci Nation, as Trudell writes, are the people who maintain Indigenous knowledge.

It is not a coincidence that Orlando Patterson, in his seminal work on enslavement, and John Trudell, philosophizing on relationships with the

CONCLUSION  *145*

earth, rely on the term *alienation* to explain how human beings are forcibly separated from their humanity. Patterson's use of "natal alienation" describes the separation of the enslaved from their kinship. Patterson states that African chattel slaves in the American South (and elsewhere) had informal relationships with one another. Still, these relationships were not formally recognized, and they could, at any moment, be separated from their informal kinship connections without consent. The principal difference between white servants and Black slaves, according to Patterson, was the view that the Black slave "did not belong to the same community of Christian, civilized Europeans. The focus of this 'we-they' distinction was at first religious, later racial." Although this focus changed, "there was really a fusion of race" with "religion and nationality in a generalized conception of 'us'—white, English, free—and 'them'—black, heathen, slave." Quoting Winthrop D. Jordan, Patterson explains, "to be Christian was to be civilized rather than barbarous."[10] The us/them binary began as Christian/non-Christian and only later became racialized conceptions of humanity. In chapter 2 I wrote about the civilized/barbarous dichotomy at the Indian boarding schools, which in the twentieth century continued the logic of conquest, alienating Native peoples from their human–land relationships.

Indigenous people's inhumanity as non-Christians (including those who were racialized as Black) was the distinction that differentiated servants from slaves. Servants could maintain kinship networks formally recognized, while Indigenous people's kinships formed through "savagery" would not be. As Patterson argues, natal alienation is "loss of native status, of deracination. It was the alienation of the slave from all formal, legally enforceable ties of 'blood' and from any attachment to groups or localities other than those chosen for him by the master, that gave the relation of slavery its peculiar value to the master. The slave was the ultimate human tool, as imprintable and as disposable as the master wished."[11] Building on Patterson's natal alienation, I argued in chapter 1 that Indigenous people's relationships with land were simultaneously alienated. This argument has historical evidence in the experience of California Indians and African peoples—and Patterson does include "localities" in his evaluation of natal alienation even if he does not specify human–land relationships. Indigenous peoples were made Black through slavery, and through this racialized transformation their

## 146  CONCLUSION

indigeneity (relationality to place) was alienated. This was similar to how California's Indigenous peoples were racialized through the mission slave regime, purposefully removing them from their villages to ones controlled by the missionaries and the soldiers. Toypurina's marriage that preexisted her baptism was not formally recognized by church or state (chapter 1). She was separated from her kinship by the Spanish because of her "wickedness," and the colonizer did not respect her informal relations.

Trudell theorizes that we all have Indigenous origins. The differentiation of Indigenous from non-Indigenous is the relationship the Indigenous maintain with the earth—a view that the land and everything on it has spirit. A Native spiritual conception of humanity relies on relationality, reciprocity, and respectful cooperation between human beings and the rest of creation.[12] The Indigenous view of the land conflicts with "the Christian doctrine of creation," as Vine Deloria Jr. explains, and the Christian "idea that man receives domination over the rest of creation." Deloria quotes Protestant theologian Harvey Cox, who explains the Christian domination of man over the earth: "Just after creation man is given the crucial responsibility of naming the animals. He is their master and commander. It is his task to subdue the earth." Domination is not a subtle feature of Christianity but is foundational to its theological worldview. "It is this attitude," as Deloria clarifies, that propels and justifies "Western peoples in their economic exploitation of the earth."[13] The natural world is unimportant in Christian doctrine compared to the post-judgment world of eternal life. The colonizers attempted to convert non-Christian Indigenous peoples not only to a belief in Christ but to their fundamental worldview that values the exploitation of the earth. The colonizers sought to alienate Indigenous people from their relationships into a predator mentality where the earth and the more-than-human could be dominated and no longer held sacred. In chapter 3, I considered the Wanáw Waníicha/Kahoo' Paxaayt/Santa Ana River to show how the predator logic of conquest has devastated (destroyed and caused extreme grief) the environment and the people who attempt to maintain a healthy relationship with it beyond the logics of conquest. Today, the worldview that justifies the domination of the earth is mostly expressed in secular terms. Capitalism has become the dominant worldview over religion, even for those of faith. No matter how "green" capitalism becomes, it will always be based on the exploitation of the earth for profit.

CONCLUSION *147*

*Native Alienation* focused on California Indians, specifically Taraaxam and Acjachemem histories, and the afterlife of the mission system, which used a clear logic of alienating California Indians from their kinship. The Spanish era was followed by Mexican and United States colonialism, in which the devastation to the environment and the development of hypercapitalism further alienated us from the power of the land. It was also during the American period, the late nineteenth and early twentieth centuries, when the history of Spanish colonialism and missionization was romanticized, creating a hallucination I call the Spanish imaginary, a story of benevolence that erases the violence of enslavement. The canonization of the founder of the mission slave regime, Junípero Serra, further reified the Spanish imaginary in 2015. My ancestor María Dolores was born in the village of Yaanga before the "spiritual conquest" of California, as Serra called it (preface). The land of her birth has been radically transformed and devastated so that today, there remains no trace of an Indian village that had existed there since time immemorial. Downtown Los Angeles, where Yaanga remains despite its erasure, is the center of one of the world's most populous megacities. The settling of Los Angeles began in 1781 as a multiculturalist project. María Dolores's husband, José Carlos Rosas, whose racial background was mixed Black, Indian, and White, was among the first settlers. The world María Dolores was born into was extinguished through the gratuitous terror of spiritual conquest, including invasion, slavery, land dispossession, and environmental devastation—this is Native alienation. The opposite of dispossession is not possession; it is increased relationality and kinship. Today, Native alienation continues in the lived experience of California Indians. However, they also creatively resist the aftermath of the spiritual conquest of their lands by integrating Native worldviews into the worlds they live in. My responsibility is to tell our stories, theorize our futurity, and organize with my relatives for land back and the difficult work of rematriating our homelands.

What is your responsibility for disrupting alienation in the place you live?

Íyo'toróvim Yaraarkokre 'Eyoo'ooxono

*We, the Caretakers, Remember Our Land*

# NOTES

### Preface

1. Palóu and Bolton, *Historical Memoirs*, 2:324.

2. Engelhardt, *Franciscans in California*, 266–67.

3. Serra to Bucareli, Mexico City, May 21, 1773, in Serra and Tibesar, *Writings of Junípero Serra*, 1:361.

4. Palóu and Bolton, *Historical Memoirs*, 3:218; Junípero Serra as quoted by Engelhardt, *San Gabriel Mission*, 11.

5. Palóu and Bolton, *Historical Memoirs*, 2:326.

6. Palóu and Bolton, *Historical Memoirs*, 2:326.

7. Engelhardt, *San Gabriel Mission*, 7.

8. Palóu and Bolton, *Historical Memoirs*, 3:328.

9. As quoted in Engelhardt, *San Gabriel Mission*, 13.

10. Serra to Rafael Verger, Monterey, California, August 8, 1772, in Serra and Tibesar, *Writings of Junípero Serra*, 1:361. For the term "scenes of subjection," see Hartman, *Scenes of Subjection*.

11. Castillo, "Gender Status Decline," 72.

12. Castañeda, "Sexual Violence," 15.

13. I borrow the term "gratuitous violence" from Black scholars explaining antiblackness; see, for example, Vargas, *Denial of Antiblackness*. Felipe de Neve as quoted in Castañeda, "Sexual Violence," 23.

14. Castañeda, "Sexual Violence," 17.

15. Junípero Serra as quoted by Engelhardt, *San Gabriel Mission*, 24.

16. ECPP, "Maria Dolores."

17. Macias, "In the Name of Spanish Colonization," 190.

18. ECPP, "Joseph Carlos Rosas & Maria Dolores."

19. ECPP, "Severiana Josefa [Rosas]"; ECPP, "Seraphina Antonia Rosas"; ECPP, "Jose Domingo [Rosas]"; ECPP, "Jose Domingo."

20. ECPP, "Jose Antonio Romero & Serafina Rosas."

21. ECPP, "Dorothea Romero."

22. For this book, I primarily use the endonym Taraaxam to refer to the Indigenous people who today use the endonyms Tongva, Tongvetam, and Kizh. Individuals will be identified using the name they prefer.

23. To read more about how DNA does not provide conclusive evidence if someone qualifies as an American Indian, see TallBear, *Native American DNA*. TallBear shows how DNA testing helps determine biological relatives but cannot prove one's tribal membership in a colonial legal category.

## Introduction

1. Akins and Bauer, *We Are the Land*, 2.

2. Boscana, *Chinigchinich*, 326–27; Boscana and Harrington, *A New Original Version*, 56.

3. Boscana, *Chinigchinich*, 326–27.

4. Boscana as quoted in Engelhardt, *Missions and Missionaries*, 241; Boscana, *Chinigchinich*, 238.

5. Guest as quoted in Costo and Costo, *Missions of California*, 187.

6. Sandos, "Between Crucifix and Lance," 206.

7. Guest, "Indian Policy, 207.

8. Junípero Serra to Fernando Rivera y Moncada, Monterey, January 7, 1780, in Serra and Tibesar, *Writings of Junípero Serra*, 3:411.

9. Engelhardt, *Missions and Missionaries*, 264, emphasis added.

10. The Holy See, "Catechism: Article 1 Sacramentals," accessed May 17, 2024, https://www.vatican.va/content/catechism/en/part_two/section_two/chapter_four/article_1.html.

11. David Crary, "Exorcism: Increasingly Frequent, Including after US Protests," APNews.com, October 31, 2020, https://apnews.com/article/portland-san-francisco-oregon-cff13a56cd41997553ea3e9a8fc21384.

12. Ed Langlois, "Archbishop Leads Rosary, Exorcism to Bring Peace to Portland," CruxNow.com, October 19, 2020, https://cruxnow.com/church-in-the-usa/2020/10/archbishop-leads-rosary-exorcism-to-bring-peace-to-portland/.

13. Rachel Elbaum, "Portland Protestors Tear Down Statues of Abraham Lincoln, Theodore Roosevelt," NBCNews.com, October 12, 2020, https://www.nbcnews.com/news/us-news/portland-protesters-tear-down-statues-abraham-lincoln-theodore-roosevelt-n1242913.

14. Theodore Roosevelt as quoted in Elizabeth Cook Lynn, "Teddy Roosevelt Wanted Indian People to Disappear," *Native Sun News Today*, September 18, 2018, https://indianz.com/News/2018/09/18/elizabeth-cooklynn-teddy-roosevelt-wante.asp.

15. Crary, "Exorcism."

16. Arvin, *Possessing Polynesians*, 15; Wolfe, "Settler Colonialism."

17. Arvin, *Possessing Polynesians*, 16, 19.

18. Nichols, *Theft Is Property!*, 4–13, 8; Holm, Pearson, and Chavis, "Peoplehood"; Deloria, *God Is Red*.

19. Hartman, *Scenes of Subjection*, 80.

20. Agamben, *Highest Poverty*, xiii.

21. Serra to Fray Juan Andrés, San Diego, July 3, 1769, and February 10, 1770, in Serra and Tibesar, *Writings of Junípero Serra*, 1:xxxix, 153.

22. Catholic News Service, "Archbishop Cordileone Plans Exorcism at Church Where Serra Statue Was Toppled," CruxNow.com, October 14, 2020, https://cruxnow.com/church-in-the-usa/2020/10/archbishop-cordileone-plans-exorcism-at-church-where-serra-statue-was-toppled/.

23. Catholic News Service.

24. Amber Lee, "Protestors Use Rocks to Chip Away at Junipero Serra Statue in San Rafael," KTVU.com, October 13, 2020, https://www.ktvu.com/news/protestors-use-rocks-to-chip-away-at-junipero-serra-statue-in-san-rafael.

25. Google Dictionary, "Possession," accessed November 6, 2020.

26. Billingslea, "Possession, Dispossession, and Haunting."

27. Rodríguez, "White Supremacy," 1.

28. Horsman, *Race and Manifest Destiny*, 2.

29. Omi and Winant, *Racial Formation in the United States*, 3–13.

30. Miranda, *Bad Indians*, 202.

31. Gordon, *Ghostly Matters*, 8; Tuck and Ree, "Glossary of Haunting," 642.

32. Butler, *Precarious Life*, 33.

33. Tuck and Ree, "Glossary of Haunting."

34. Goldberg, *Racial State*, 145.

35. Simpson, *Mohawk Interruptus*, 2, 3.

36. Bancroft, *Works of Hubert Howe Bancroft*, iii.

37. Geiger, *Life and Times*, 208.

38. Akins and Bauer, *We Are the Land*, 68.

39. Blackwell, *Chicana Power!*, 2.

40. Miranda, "Extermination of the Joyas," 256.

41. King, *Truth about Stories*, 2.

42. Miranda, "Extermination of the Joyas," 255.

43. Manriquez, "There Are Other Ways," 41.

44. Harvey, "What's Past Is Prologue," 220.

45. Wolfe, "Settler Colonialism."

46. Speed, "Structures of Settler Colonialism," 784, 785; Kelley, "Rest of Us," 268.

47. King, "New World Grammars," 79.

48. Spillers, "Mama's Baby," 68.

49. Serra and Tibesar, *Writings of Junípero Serra*, 4:125.

50. Hartman, *Lose Your Mother*, 74.

51. Simpson, *As We Have Always Done*.

52. Scholars who have used the term *slavery* to describe missionary control over Native peoples have not critically engaged with how their studies differ from those who disavow slavery at the missions. The argument used by those who disavow slavery has been centered on the fact that the priests did not buy and sell Native people. For examples of scholarship that use slavery in their assessment of the missions but

NOTES TO PAGES 17–28

do not argue how their work contradicts the disavowal, see Pfaelzer, *California*;
Castillo, *Cross of Thorns*; Miranda, *Bad Indians*; Reséndez, *Other Slavery*.

53. Hackel, *Children of Coyote*, 29.

54. Pérez, *Decolonial Imaginary*, 5.

55. Costo and Costo, *Missions of California*, x, 9; Shipek, "Saints or Oppressors," 42.

56. Google Dictionary, "Disruption," accessed November 10, 2020.

57. Sandos in *Contested Eden*, 222.

58. Hass, *Conquests and Historical Identities*, 2.

59. Google Dictionary, "Secularization" and "Secular," accessed November 11, 2020.

60. Patterson, *Slavery and Social Death*.

61. Goldberg and Champagne, "Ramona Redeemed?"

ONE   Slavery and Disavowal

1. Judicial proceedings against the accused Taraaxam leaders of the uprising against the fathers and the escort of the San Gabriel Mission on the night of October 25, 1785, Provincias Internas 120, Expediente 2, Archivo General de la Nación, Mexico City.

2. Temple, "Toypurina the Witch"; Hackel, "Sources of Rebellion." Temple's dramatization continues to be republished. As recently as 2023, in an otherwise important manuscript, Temple's misuse of the archive to tell the history of Toypurina is repeated. Pfaelzer, *California*.

3. Hackel, "Sources of Rebellion"; Vaughn, "Sovereign Embodiment: Native Hawaiian Expressions of Kuleana in the Diaspora"; Alvitre, "Revolts, Resistance, and Restitutions."

4. For the term *retrofit*, see Blackwell, *Chicana Power!*

5. Trask, *From a Native Daughter*, 167.

6. Reséndez, *Other Slavery*.

7. Fanon, *Wretched of the Earth*, 51; Forbes, *Columbus and Other Cannibals*, 25.

8. Trask, *From a Native Daughter*, 59.

9. Beebe and Senkewicz, "Revolt at Mission San Gabriel," 16.

10. Fanon, *Wretched of the Earth*, 6.

11. Beebe and Senkewicz, "Revolt at Mission San Gabriel," 22.

12. ECPP, "Nereo Joaquin"; ECPP, "Regina Josefa"; ECPP, "Manuel Montero & Regina"; ECPP, "Cesario Antonio Montero."

13. Simpson, *As We Have Always Done*, 43.

14. Hartman, *Lose Your Mother*.

15. Davis and Kelley, *Meaning of Freedom*; Davis, Barat, and West, *Freedom Is a Constant Struggle*.

16. Smith, *Decolonizing Methodologies*, 28.

17. Hackel, "Land, Labor, and Production," 122; Phillips, *Vineyards and Vaqueros*, 324–29; Castillo, "Indian Account of the Decline," 393.

18. Patterson, *Slavery and Social Death*.

19. Patterson, *Slavery and Social Death*, 72.

20. Hong, *Death beyond Disavowal*, 27. For an example of the Spanish imaginary narrating a colonial benevolence, see Engelhardt, *Missions and Missionaries*.

21. Madley, "California's First Mass Incarceration System," 14–15.

22. Sandos, *Converting California*, 107, 108.

23. Lightfoot, *Indians, Missionaries, and Merchants*, 66–67.

24. Sánchez, *Telling Identities*, 82, 83.

25. Shoup and Milliken, *Inigo of Rancho Posolmi*, 82–85.

26. Hackel, *Children of Coyote*, 281; Cook, *Conflict between the California Indian*, 96.

27. Duggan, "Beyond Slavery," 238.

28. Haas, *Conquests and Historical Identities*, 38; Tinker, *Missionary Conquest*, 51; Rawls, *Indians of California*, 5.

29. Lake, *Colonial Rosary*, 65.

30. Bancroft, *Works of Hubert Howe Bancroft*, iii.

31. Akins and Bauer, *We Are the Land*, 74, 67.

32. Patterson, *Slavery and Social Death*, 13, 21.

33. Powerlessness does not mean that the slave does not retain agency to refuse, resist, or rebel.

34. Hartman, *Lose Your Mother*, 16

35. La Perouse, *Monterey in 1786*, 219.

36. Beilharz, *Felipe De Neve*, 52.

37. Fr. Antonio de la Concepcíon [Horra] to Viceroy, July 12, 1798, in Beebe and Senkewicz, *Lands of Promise and Despair*, 272.

38. Estevan Tapis to Lasuén, Mission Santa Barbara, October 30, 1800, as cited in Guest, "Inquiry into the Role of Discipline," 32.

39. Heizer, "Impact of Colonization."

40. Lasuén as quoted in Heizer, "Impact of Colonization."

41. Hong, *Death beyond Disavowal*, 102.

42. Patterson, *Slavery and Social Death*, 6.

43. Jackson and Castillo, *Indians, Franciscans, and Spanish Colonization*, 79–80.

44. Champagne and Goldberg, *Coalition of Lineages*, 58.

45. Guest, "Cultural Perspectives," 40; Stewart-Ambo and Stewart, "From Tovaangar to the University of California, Los Angeles," 134.

46. Heizer, *Indians of Los Angeles County*, 14; Reid and Ellis, *Indians of Los Angeles County*, 67.

NOTES TO PAGES 38–48

47. Coulthard, "Place against Empire"; Deloria, *God Is Red*, 62.

48. Hartman, *Lose Your Mother*.

49. Deloria, *God Is Red*.

50. Hartman, *Lose Your Mother*, 16.

51. Hartman, *Lose Your Mother*, 80.

52. Including Captain Beechey (Beechey, *An Account of a Visit to California*) and Lieutenant George Peard (Gough, "Views of Lieutenant George Peard").

53. Engelhardt, *Missions and Missionaries*, 264.

54. Cook, *Conflict between the California Indian*, 90.

55. Reid and Ellis, *Indians of Los Angeles County*, 58.

56. Reid and Ellis, *Indians of Los Angeles County*, 58.

57. The Spanish replaced California Indian names through baptism. Patterson, *Slavery and Social Death*, 12; Hackel, "Land, Labor, and Production," 123.

58. Miranda, *Bad Indians*, 202.

59. Waziyatawin, *What Does Justice Look Like?*, 51. On the psychological impacts of colonialism and American Indian psychology, see Duran, *Transforming the Soul Wound*; Duran and Duran, *Native American Postcolonial Psychology*; Duran et al., "Healing the American Indian Soul Would"; and Duran, Firehammer, and Gonzalez, "Liberation Psychology."

60. Asisara in Mora-Torres, *Californio Voices*, 123–25.

61. Mora-Torres, *Californio Voices*, 125.

62. Castillo, "Cultural Chauvinism," 77.

63. Reid, "Medics of the Soul and the Body," 20, 93, 101–2, Father José Viñals as quoted on 87.

64. Hackel, "Sources of Rebellion," 644.

65. Solares, summarized in Laird, *Encounter with an Angry God*, 18.

66. Asisara in Mora-Torres, *Californio Voices*, 95, 127.

67. Librado in Miranda, *Bad Indians*, 23–24.

68. Harris, "Of Blackness and Indigeneity," 222.

69. Hartman, "Belly of the World," 168–69.

70. Sexton, "Veil of Slavery," 583–97.

71. Kelley, "Foreword," xvi.

72. King, *Black Shoals*; De Azurara, Beazley, and Prestage, *Chronicle of the Discovery*, iii, xi.

73. Deloria, *God Is Red*, 111.

74. Vallejo García-Hevia, *La Segunda Carolina*.

75. De Azurara, Beazley, and Prestage, *Chronicle of the Discovery*.

76. Tac and Haas, *Pablo Tac*, 12, 9.

77. As quoted in Adiele, *The Popes*.

78. Adiele, *The Popes*, 355.

NOTES TO PAGES 48–57    *155*

79. Adiele, *The Popes*, 363.

80. Hanke, *Spanish Struggle for Justice*.

81. Parry and Keith, *New Iberian World*, 290.

82. Parry and Keith, *New Iberian World*, 290.

## TWO  Hallucinations of the Spanish Imaginary

1. Savage, *Provincial State Papers*.

2. Savage, *Provincial State Papers*.

3. Mission San Juan Capistrano was first founded in 1775 but was abandoned later that year when Mission San Diego was attacked, burned, and one of the priests was killed by the Kumeyaay. The second founding was on November 1, 1776.

4. ECPP, "Leonardo and Maria Margarita"; ECPP, "Maria Margarita."

5. Savage, *Provincial State Papers*.

6. Serra and Tibesar, *Writings of Junípero Serra*, 3:452, n120.

7. Serra and Tibesar, *Writings of Junípero Serra*, April 6, 1778, 3:177.

8. The four Indians condemned to death were given clemency by the governor. Serra was grateful they had received baptism while imprisoned.

9. Serra and Tibesar, *Writings of Junípero Serra*, April 22, 1778, 3:191.

10. The webpage for Mission San Juan Capistrano, for example, boasts that the mission receives three hundred thousand visitors a year.

11. Lorimer, *Resurrecting the Past*, 76.

12. The Mission Inn Hotel and Spa has undergone numerous name changes over the years. It began as the Glenwood Cottages and later became the Glenwood Mission Inn. Owners dropped Glenwood from the name in the 1930s. In 1992 new owners Duane and Kelly Roberts renamed the property the Mission Inn Hotel and Spa. See Lech and Johnson, *Riverside's Mission Inn*, 8; "The Mission Inn Hotel & Spa," Historic Hotels of America, accessed May 17, 2024, https://www.historic hotels.org/us/hotels-resorts/the-mission-inn-hotel-and-spa/history.php. For ease of reference, I refer to it as the Mission Inn.

13. Peter D'Errico, "Luci Tapahonso, Boarding Schools, and the Smithsonian," *Indian Country Today*, September 12, 2018.

14. The original (1903) name of the school was Sherman Institute; in 1973 it was renamed Sherman Indian High School. For simplicity I refer to the school by its common name, Sherman Indian Boarding School, or Sherman.

15. Miranda, "Teaching on Stolen Ground," 181.

16. See chapter 2, "The Fantasy Heritage," in McWilliams, *North from Mexico*, 15–25.

17. McWilliams, *Southern California Country*, 35, 29.

18. Weber, *Spanish Frontier in North America*, 343.

156   NOTES TO PAGES 58–64

19. Pérez, *Decolonial Imaginary*, 5–6; Kropp, *California Vieja*, 1; Deverell, *Whitewashed Adobe*, 49–90.

20. Lorimer, *Resurrecting the Past*, 76.

21. Lefebvre, *Production of Space*, 92.

22. The homes built by Southern California Indians were primarily constructed of willow and tule, such as those created by the Tongva, Acjachemen, and Cahuilla. Sepulveda, "Our Sacred Waters"; Deloria, *God Is Red*.

23. Tac and Haas, *Pablo Tac*, 28.

24. Castillo, "Gender Status Decline."

25. For an overview of Spanish and Mexican construction in California, see Weber, *Spanish Frontier*, 343; and, generally, Lightfoot, *Indians, Missionaries, and Merchants*.

26. Weber, *Spanish Frontier*, 343.

27. Goodman, "Spring Rancheria," 44. Architectural styles popular with American builders in Riverside included Victorian Stick (in vogue from 1860 through about 1890); Queen Anne, Eastlake, and Victorian Shingle (1880–1900); Prairie (1898–1920); American Colonial Revival (1895–1925); American Foursquare (1898–1908); Craftsman (1900–1925); Classical Revival (1900–1950); and English/Tudor Revival (popular in the 1920s and 1930s). City of Riverside, California, "Riverside's Architectural Heritage."

28. Kropp, *California Vieja*, 5.

29. Gonzales, "Riverside, Tourism, and the Indian." See, e.g., Lummis, *Flowers of Our Lost Romance*. Lummis published many pieces about Spanish California, including his book *The Spanish Pioneers and the California Missions* and numerous magazine and newspaper articles.

30. Gonzales, "Riverside, Tourism, and the Indian."

31. "History of the Landmarks Program," California State Parks, accessed May 17, 2024, https://ohp.parks.ca.gov/?page_id=21748. Charles Fletcher Lummis was Landmarks Club president; Frank A. Miller was vice president, and Arthur Benton was secretary. "Landmarks Club Forces Review Notable Work: Worthy Labors," *Los Angeles Times*, December 3, 1916.

32. *Sacramento Daily Union*, December 10, 1895.

33. *Los Angeles Herald*, November 18, 1896.

34. Hodgen, *Master of the Mission Inn*.

35. *Los Angeles Herald*, February 26, 1896.

36. Serra and Tibesar, *Writings of Junípero Serra*, 3:359.

37. Vaughn, "Locating Absence."

38. McGroarty, *Mission Play*.

39. "Ramona: The History of a Classic," Ramona Bowl Amphitheatre, May 17, 2024, https://theramonabowl.com/all-about-ramona.

NOTES TO PAGES 64–71    *157*

40. Suzanne Hurt, "Riverside: Raincross Symbol Endures in Many Ways," *Press-Enterprise*, April 25, 2014, http://www.pe.com/2014/04/25/riverside-raincross-symbol-endures-in-many-ways/.

41. Klotz, *The Mission Inn*, 19; Lech and Johnson, *Riverside's Mission Inn*, 26.

42. Benton, "California Mission and Its Influence," 36.

43. Hodgen, *Master of the Mission Inn*, 121.

44. *Los Angeles Herald*, November 30, 1902, 5.

45. For an in-depth analysis of Frank Miller's political campaign to move the school from Perris to Riverside, see Gonzales, "Riverside, Tourism, and the Indian."

46. Rawls, "California Mission."

47. Frank Miller to Henry Huntington, January 23, 1899, quoted in Gonzales, "Riverside, Tourism, and the Indian." On Jackson's goals in writing the novel, see Christopher Reynolds, "On the Trail of 'Ramona' in California," *Los Angeles Times*, January 11, 2009, http://www.latimes.com/travel/la-trw-ramona11-2009jan11-story.html.

48. Whalen, *Native Students at Work*, 3.

49. "Sherman Indian High School Beginning to the Present," Sherman Indian Museum, accessed May 17, 2024, http://www.shermanindianmuseum.org/sherman_hist.htm.

50. Whalen, *Native Students at Work*, 3.

51. *San Bernardino Sun*, February 25, 1903, 5.

52. *Official Report of the Nineteenth Annual Conference of Charities and Correction* (1892), 46–59, as reprinted in Pratt, "Advantages of Mingling Indians with Whites."

53. *Studies at Large of the United States*, 26:1014, as quoted in Churchill, *Kill the Indian*, 16.

54. Waziyatawin, *What Does Justice Look Like?*, 53. For example, see Smith, *Conquest*; and Waziyatawin.

55. *Studies at Large of the United States*, 27:635, as quoted in Churchill, *Kill the Indian*, 17.

56. Chavez, *Indigenous Artists, Ingenuity, and Resistance*.

57. *Los Angeles Herald*, July 27, 1902.

58. Bahr, *Students of Sherman Indian School*; Paxton, "Learning Gender."

59. Vaughn, "Locating Absence," 155; Castillo, "Gender Status Decline."

60. Whalen, *Native Students at Work*, 4.

61. Whalen, *Native Students at Work*, 5, 30.

62. *Los Angeles Herald*, August 12, 1919.

63. *Los Angeles Herald*, February 11, 1903; Whalen, *Native Students at Work*, 4.

64. Frank A. Miller, Letter to Harwood Hall, April 25, 1903, Sherman Indian Museum Collection, https://calisphere.org/item/ark:/86086/n2xd12tf/.

158   NOTES TO PAGES 72–80

65. *San Bernardino Sun*, February 25, 1903, 5.

66. David Starr Jordan to Frank Miller, February 14, 1905, in *Sunset: The Pacific Monthly* 28 (June–July 1912): 239.

67. Schneider et al., "More than Missions," 65, 61, 67–74, emphasis added. See also Gutfreund, "Standing Up to Sugar Cubes."

68. Kropp, *California Vieja*, 3. See, e.g., Hackel, *Junípero Serra*, 242, which calls Serra "California's founding father."

69. Laura Bride Powers, "Fra Junipero Serra Is Entitled to Honors," *San Francisco Call*, September 12, 1904; Hackel, *Junípero Serra*, xiii; Costo and Costo, *Missions of California*.

70. Savage, *Standing Soldiers, Kneeling Slaves*. See also Gary Shapiro, "The Meaning of Our Confederate 'Monuments,'" *New York Times*, May 15, 2017.

71. Gomez, *Manifest Destinies*, 17.

72. "Riverside Citywide Design Guide."

73. Hurt, "Riverside."

74. "History of Riverside," City of Riverside, accessed May 17, 2024, https://www.riversideca.gov/visiting-aboutriv.asp.

THREE   Apocalyptic Colonialism

1. The tribe spells their name with the letter *n*—Acjachemen. In the language of Chamteela, the closer pronunciation is with a letter *m*—Acjachemem, pronounced: ah-HASH-ah-mem.

2. Juaneño Band of Mission Indians, Acjachemen Nation, "Resolution Calling for the Repudiation of the Doctrine of Discovery and Opposing the Canonization of Junipero Serra," San Juan Capistrano, California, September 6, 2015.

3. Juaneño Band of Mission Indians, Acjachemen Nation, press release for "Resolution Calling for the Repudiation of the Doctrine of Discovery and Opposing the Canonization of Junipero Serra," San Juan Capistrano, California, September 6, 2015.

4. Dum Diversas, 1452, and Romanus Pontifex, 1455, in Steven Newcomb, "The Vatican's Rhetorical Strategy: Serra Was a Man of His Time," *Indian Country Today Media Network*, April 28, 2015, http://indiancountrytodaymedianetwork.com/2015/04/28/vaticans-rhetorical-strategy-serra-was-man-his-time.

5. Serra and Tibesar, *Writings of Junípero Serra*, 2:297, 1:295.

6. Juaneño Band of Mission Indians, Acjachemen Nation, "Resolution."

7. Savage, *Provincial State Papers*; Rowntree, "Drought during California's Mission Period"; Fritts and Gordon, "Reconstructed Annual Precipitation."

8. Miranda, *Bad Indians*, 76, 2, 202, 16; Fanon, *Black Skin, White Masks*, 90; Forbes, *Indian in America's Past*, 75–76.

NOTES TO PAGES 80–91     159

9. Here I refer to the Gospel of Matthew 7:15–16: "Beware of false prophets who come to you disguised as sheep but underneath are ravenous wolves. You will be able to tell them by their fruits." Forbes, *Columbus and Other Cannibals*.

10. Gross, *Anishinaabe Ways of Knowing*, 33; Simpson and Weiner, *Oxford English Dictionary*, 386.

11. "Eschatology, n.," def. a, *Oxford English Dictionary*; "Nicene Creed," United States Conference of Catholic Bishops, accessed May 17, 2024, https://www.usccb .org/beliefs-and-teachings/what-we-believe.

12. A few notable exceptions that center a man of color but follow many of the same tropes include Denzel Washington in *The Book of Eli* and Will Smith in *I Am Legend*.

13. Stark, "All These Things He Saw," 78.

14. Stark, "All These Things He Saw," 72.

15. McCarthy, *The Road*, 2, 29, 40, 192, 231, 236, 306–7, 163; Stark, "All These Things He Saw," 75.

16. Lindsay, *Murder State*, 152–53. Cutcha Risling Baldy writes about the TV show *The Walking Dead* in a similar way in her blog (Baldy, "On Telling Native People to Just 'Get Over It'").

17. Derrida, *Psyche*, 402, 400.

18. Zamora, *Writing the Apocalypse*, 147; Miranda, "'Saying the Padre Had Grabbed Her,'" 95.

19. Hyde and Elliot, *Yumáyk Yumáyk*, 1197; Elliot, "Dictionary of Rincón Luiseño," 104.

20. Fireman and Servin, "Miguel Costansó."

21. Costansó, Teggart, Carpio, *Portola Expedition of 1769–1770*.

22. The watershed of the Santa Ana River is only approximately 150 square miles smaller than Rhode Island and Delaware combined to give context on scale.

23. Crespi and Bolton, *Fray Juan Crespi*, 141.

24. *Santa Ana Register*, January 8, 1908.

25. Liboiron, *Pollution Is Colonialism*, 6–7.

26. Sepulveda, "Our Sacred Waters."

27. The population living within the Santa Ana River watershed is approximately four million more than the combined populations of Rhode Island and Delaware.

28. Associated Press, "Engineers Raise Risk Level for Southern California's Prado Dam," ABC10.com, May 17, 2019, https://www.abc10.com/article/news /local/california/engineers-raise-risk-level-for-southern-california-dam/103-2cda 862e-c1f8-40ed-8ae9-609ad19b7fe1.

29. US Army Corps of Engineers, "Prado Dam," accessed May 17, 2024, https:// resreg.spl.usace.army.mil/pages/prdo.php.

30. *Los Angeles Herald*, 1884, December 1889, March 1895.

160    NOTES TO PAGES 91–100

31. *San Francisco Call*, 1906.

32. "Santa Ana Flood," *Los Angeles Herald*, 1910.

33. "Rain Swells," *Los Angeles Herald*, 1916; "Flee before Floods," *Los Angeles Herald*, 1916.

34. "Flee before Floods," *Los Angeles Herald*, 1916; "32-Year Rain Record," *Los Angeles Herald*, 1921; "Gray Describes Experience," *Coronado Eagle and Journal*, 1938.

35. City of Santa Ana, "Santa Ana River Vision Plan" (2006).

36. City of Santa Ana, "Santa Ana River Vision Plan."

## FOUR  Canonization Fodder

1. Lexis-Olivier Ray, "'This Is the Beginning of Healing': Descendants of Tongva, Chumash, and Tataviam Tribes Organized the Toppling of Junípero Serra Statue in the Birthplace of LA.," LA Taco, June 22, 2020, https://www.lataco.com /serra-statue-chumash-tongva/; Carolina A. Maranda, "At Los Angeles Toppling of Junipero Serra Statue, Activists Want Full Story Told," *Los Angeles Times*, June 20, 2020, https://www.latimes.com/entertainment-arts/story/2020-06-20/statue -junipero-serra-monument-protest-activists-take-down-los-angeles.

2. Alejandra Molina, "We Have a Story to Tell: Indigenous Scholars, Activists Speak Up amid Toppling of Serra Statues," Religion News Service, July 7, 2020, https://religionnews.com/2020/07/07/we-have-a-story-to-tell-indigenous -scholars-activists-speak-up-amid-toppling-of-serra-statues/.

3. Ray, "This Is the Beginning."

4. Miranda, "Canonization Fodder."

5. Nanette Deetz, "Indigenous Nations v. Junipero Serra: AIM Takes Serra to Court," *Indian Country Today Media Network*, September 21, 2015, http://indian countrytodaymedianetwork.com/2015/09/21/indigenous-nations-v-junipero -serra-aim-takes-serra-court-161802.

6. Deetz, "Indigenous Nations v. Junipero Serra."

7. Deetz, "Indigenous Nations v. Junipero Serra."

8. Jim Yardley and William Neuman, "In Bolivia, Pope Francis Apologizes for Church's 'Grave Sins,'" *New York Times*, July 10, 2015, http://www.nytimes .com/2015/07/10/world/americas/pope-francis-bolivia-catholic-church-apology .html.

9. Yardley and Neuman, "In Bolivia, Pope Francis Apologizes."

10. Yardley and Neuman, "In Bolivia, Pope Francis Apologizes."

11. Miranda, "Canonization Fodder."

12. Shane Croucher, "How Rich Is the Vatican? So Wealthy It Can Stumble across Millions of Euros Just 'Tucked Away,'" *International Business Times*,

December 5, 2015, http://www.ibtimes.co.uk/how-rich-vatican-so-wealthy-it
-can-stumble-across-millions-euros-just-tucked-away-1478219.

13. "Roman Catholics: The Vatican's Wealth," *Time Magazine*, February 26, 1965,
http://content.time.com/time/magazine/article/0,9171,833509,00.html.

14. Miranda, "Canonization Fodder."

15. Yardley and Neuman, "In Bolivia, Pope Francis Apologizes."

16. Abigail James, "First U.S. Hispanic Saint: Pope Francis to Canonize Junipero
Serra during U.S. Visit," Catholic Online, September 23, 2015, http://www.catholic
.org/news/international/americas/story.php?id=59917.

17. Hackel quoted in Meridith McGraw, "Why Pope Francis' Canonization of
Junipero Serra Is So Controversial," ABCNews.go.com, September 23, 2015, http://
abcnews.go.com/US/pope-francis-canonization-junipero-serra-controversial/story
?id=33961080.

18. Abigail, "First U.S. Hispanic Saint."

19. Deepa Bharath, "Inspirational Leader or Indigenous Oppressor? The Pros
and Cons of Pope Francis Making Junipero Serra a Saint," *Orange County Register*,
September 23, 2015, http://www.ocregister.com/articles/serra-683756-native
-church.html.

20. Omi and Winant, *Racial Formation in the United States*, 3–13.

21. Forbes, "Hispanic Spin."

22. Forbes, "Hispanic Spin."

23. Rodríguez, *Suspended Apocalypse*, 196.

24. Churchill, *Little Matter of Genocide*. "'Cultural Genocide': by which is
meant the destruction of the specific character of the targeted group(s) through
economic perpetuation; prohibition or curtailment of its language; suppression of
its religious, social, or political practices; forced dislocation, expulsion or disper-
sal of its members, forced transfer or removal of its children, or any other means"
(433).

25. Newcomb, "The Vatican's Rhetorical Strategy."

26. Abigail, "First U.S. Hispanic Saint."

27. "Holy Mass and Canonization of Blessed Fr. Junípero Serra, Homily of His
Holiness Pope Francis," National Shrine of the Immaculate Conception, Washington, DC, Wednesday, September 23, 2015.

28. Tim Gaynor, "Sainthood for Founder of California Missions Angers Native
American Groups," *Al Jazeera America*, May 28, 2015, http://america.aljazeera
.com/articles/2015/5/28/sainthood-for-california-missions-founder-angers-native
-american-groups.html; "Holy Mass and Canonization."

29. Boscana, *Chinigchinich*, 335, 286.

30. Granville and Hough, *Spain's California Patriots*, 2.

31. Wittenburg, "Three Generations."

162   NOTES TO PAGES 107–119

32. Engelhardt, *Missions and Missionaries*.

33. Marion Parks, "Instructions for the Recruital of Soldiers and Settlers for California—Expedition of 1781: Teodoro de Croix to Captain Fernando de Rivera y Moncada," *Annual Publication of the Historical Society of Southern California* 15, no. 1 (1931): 189–203, as quoted in Wittenburg, "Three Generations."

34. Wittenburg, "Three Generations."

35. Castañeda, "Hispanas and Hispanos."

36. Serra and Tibesar, *Writings of Junípero Serra*, 1:295, 299.

37. Serra and Tibesar, *Writings of Junípero Serra*, 1:311.

38. Castañeda, "Engendering the History," 232, 234; Castillo, "Gender Status Decline," 68.

39. Russell Chandler and Louis Sahagun, "Church Wronged Indians, Pope Says: Pontiff Admits 'Mistakes' but . . . ," *Los Angeles Times*, September 15, 1987.

40. Francis J. Weber, "Junípero Serra: Hero of Evangelization," *Knights of Columbus*, April 1, 2015, http://www.kofc.org/un/en/columbia/detail/junipero-serra-hero-evangelization.html.

41. Mendoza quoted in Bharath, "Inspirational Leader or Indigenous Oppressor?"

42. Serra and Tibesar, *Writings of Junípero Serra*, 1:299–301.

43. Christine Grabowski, "Serra-gate: The Fabrication of a Saint," *Indian Country Today Media Network*, September 16, 2015.

44. Grabowski, "Serra-gate."

45. Serra and Tibesar, *Writings of Junípero Serra*, 3:413.

46. Ricky Young, "Just Days until Father Serra Becomes Saint Junípero," *San Diego Union-Tribune*, September 19, 2015, http://www.sandiegouniontribune.com/news/2015/sep/19/saint-junipero/.

47. Castillo, "Gender Status Decline," 69; Serra and Tibesar, *Writings of Junípero Serra*, 1:299.

48. Walk for the Ancestors, "About," accessed January 30, 2024, http://walkfortheancestors.org/about/.

49. Walk for the Ancestors, "About."

50. Walk for the Ancestors, "About."

51. Fred Swegles "On a Mission: Woman, Son Walking 800 Miles to All 21 California Landmarks to Protest Serra Canonization," *Orange County Register*, November 3, 2015, http://www.ocregister.com/articles/mission-690284-native-ancestors.html.

52. Walk for the Ancestors, "San Juan Capistrano," accessed January 30, 2024, http://walkfortheancestors.org/2015/11/san-juan-capistrano/.

53. Walk for the Ancestors, "San Juan Capistrano."

54. Walk for the Ancestors, "San Juan Capistrano."

55. Walk for the Ancestors, "San Juan Capistrano."

NOTES TO PAGES 123–135 *163*

FIVE  Ramona Redeemed?

1. Letter from Sacred Places Institute of Indigenous Peoples to California Coastal Conservancy, May 4, 2022, https://scc.ca.gov/webmaster/ftp/pdf/sccbb /2022/2205/20220505Board08_Banning_Ranch_Ex3_Add1.pdf.

2. Dina Gilio-Whitaker, "Sacred Site Endangered by Development in Southern California to Be Considered at Public Hearing," *ICT News*, May 11, 2016, https:// indiancountrytoday.com/archive/sacred-site-endangered-by-development -in-southern-california-to-be-considered-at-public-hearing.

3. California Coastal Commission, "Appendix E(1)."

4. "The Mesa on Bolsa Chica: A Place of Knowledge," Acjachemen Tongva Land Conservancy, accessed May 17, 2024, https://www.atlandconservancy.com.

5. Newsom, "Executive Order N-15-19."

6. Maya Yang, "California Plan Would Give $100m to Indigenous Leaders to Buy Ancestral Lands," *The Guardian*, March 18, 2022, https://www.theguardian .com/us-news/2022/mar/18/california-indigenous-tribes-purchase-land.

7. Jackson, *Ramona*.

8. Goldberg and Champagne, "Ramona Redeemed?"

9. Letter, November 8, 1883, in Jackson and Mathes, *Indian Reform Letters*.

10. Jackson, *Glimpses of California*, 76–77; letter, January 1, 1884, in Jackson and Mathes, *Indian Reform Letters*.

11. Goldberg and Champagne, "Ramona Redeemed?," 43.

12. Goldberg and Champagne, "Ramona Redeemed?," 44.

13. Lindsay, *Murder State*; Madley, *American Genocide*.

14. Goldberg and Champagne, "Ramona Redeemed?," 60.

15. Serra and Tibesar, *Writings of Junípero Serra*, 3:99.

16. Coulthard, *Red Skin, White Masks*, 31.

17. Goldberg and Champagne, "Ramona Redeemed?," 45.

18. Fenelon, "Indian Gaming," 381–82.

19. Cattelino, "Fungibility," 190.

20. Goldberg and Champagne, "Ramona Redeemed?," 46.

21. Goldberg and Champagne, "Ramona Redeemed?," 48.

22. Champagne, "Tribal Capitalism and Native Capitalists."

23. Goldberg and Champagne, "Ramona Redeemed?," 48.

24. As quoted in Coulthard, *Red Skin, White Masks*, 36.

25. As quoted in Coulthard, *Red Skin, White Masks*, 35.

26. Coulthard, *Red Skin, White Masks*, 60, 155.

27. Coulthard, *Red Skin, White Masks*, 158–59.

28. Dhillon, *Prairie Rising*, 66–68.

29. Wallace Cleaves and Charles Sepulveda, "Native Land Acknowledgments

164    NOTES TO PAGES 135–146

Are Not the Same as Land," Bloomberg.com, August 12, 2021, https://www
.bloomberg.com/news/articles/2021-08-12/native-land-stewardship-needs-to
-follow-acknowledgment.

30. Tuck and Yang, "Decolonization Is Not a Metaphor," 3.

31. Stewart-Ambo and Yang, "Beyond Land Acknowledgment," 24, 31.

32. On haunting, see Tuck and Ree, "Glossary of Haunting"; and Gordon, *Ghostly Matters*.

33. Coulthard, *Red Skin, White Masks*, 13.

34. Coulthard, *Red Skin, White Masks*, 171.

35. Vaughn, "Sovereign Embodiment: Native Hawaiians and Expressions of Diasporic Kuleana," 227.

36. Goeman, *Mark My Words*, 205.

37. Million, *Therapeutic Nations*, 30–31.

## Conclusion

1. Sepulveda, "Our Sacred Waters."

2. Sturm, *Becoming Indian*.

3. Vargas and Jung, *Antiblackness*, 4.

4. Coulthard, *Red Skin White Masks*.

5. Vizenor, *Manifest Manners*, vii.

6. The Halluci Nation, "The Virus (feat. Saul Williams and Chippewa Travelers)," *We Are the Halluci Nation*, 2016.

7. Vizenor, *Native Liberty*, 56.

8. The Halluci Nation, "ALie Nation (feat. John Trudell, Lido Pimienta, Tanya Tagaq, and Northern Voice)," *We Are the Halluci Nation* (2016).

9. The Halluci Nation, "We Are the Halluci Nation (feat. John Trudell and Northern Voice)," *We Are the Halluci Nation* (2016).

10. Patterson, *Slavery and Social Death*, 7.

11. Patterson, *Slavery and Social Death*, 7.

12. Patterson, *Slavery and Social Death*, 81.

13. Deloria, *God Is Red*, 81.

# BIBLIOGRAPHY

Adiele, Pius Onyemechi. *The Popes, the Church and the Transatlantic Enslavement of Black Africans, 1418–1839*. New York: Georg Olms Verlag, 2017.

Agamben, Giorgio. *The Highest Poverty: Monastic Rules and Form-of-Life*. Redwood City: Stanford University Press, 2020.

Akins, Damon B., and William J. Bauer Jr. *We Are the Land: A History of Native California*. Berkeley: University of California Press, 2021.

Alvitre, Weshoyot. "Revolts, Resistance, and Restitutions: 238 Years of Tongva Survival, Today." Presented at the 63rd Annual Western History Association Conference, October 27, 2023.

Arvin, Maile. *Possessing Polynesians: The Science of Settler Colonial Whiteness in Hawaii and Oceania*. Durham, NC: Duke University Press, 2019.

Bahr, Diana Meyers. *The Students of Sherman Indian School: Education and Native Identity Since 1892*. Norman: University of Oklahoma Press, 2014.

Baldy, Cutcha Risling. "On Telling Native People to Just 'Get Over It,' or Why I Teach about 'The Walking Dead' in My Native Studies Class." *Sometimes Writer—Blogger Cutcha Risling Baldy* (blog). December 11, 2013. http://www .cutcharislingbaldy.com/blog/on-telling-native-people-to-just-get-over-it-or -why-i-teach-about-the-walking-dead-in-my-native-studies-classes-spoiler-alert.

———. *We Are Dancing for You: Native Feminisms and the Revitalization of Women's Coming-of-Age Ceremonies*. Seattle: University of Washington Press, 2018.

Bancroft, Hubert H. *The Works of Hubert Howe Bancroft*. Vol. 18, *History of California*, vol. 1, *1542–1800*. San Francisco: A. L. Bancroft, 1884.

Beebe, Rose Marie, and Robert M. Senkewicz. *Lands of Promise and Despair: Chronicles of Early California, 1535–1846*. Berkeley: Heyday, 2001.

———. "Revolt at Mission San Gabriel, October 25, 1785: Judicial Proceedings and Related Documents." *Journal of the California Mission Studies Association* 24, no. 2 (2007): 15–29.

Beechey, Frederick William. *An Account of a Visit to California, 1826–27*. San Francisco: Grabhorn, 1941.

Beilharz, Edwin A. *Felipe De Neve: First Governor of California*. San Francisco: California Historical Society, 1971.

Benton, Arthur B. "California Mission and Its Influence upon Pacific Coast Architecture." *Architect and Engineer of California* 24, no. 1 (February 1911): 35–75.

Billingslea, Sierra. "Possession, Dispossession, and Haunting: Epistemic Trauma and Resistance in Eden Robinson's Monkey Beach." *Public Philosophy Journal* 2, no. 2 (Fall 2019): 1–9.

## BIBLIOGRAPHY

Blackwell, Maylei. *Chicana Power! Contested Histories of Feminism in the Chicano Movement.* Austin: University of Texas Press, 2011.

Boscana, Gerónimo. *Chinigchinich: A Historical Account of the Origin, Customs, and Traditions of the Indians at the Missionary Establishment of St. Juan Capistrano, Alta California Called the Acagchemem Nation.* New York: Wiley and Putnam, 1846.

Boscana, Gerónimo, and John Peabody Harrington. *A New Original Version of Boscana's Historical Account of the San Juan Capistrano Indians of Southern California.* New York: Argonaut, 1966.

Butler, Judith. *Precarious Life: The Powers of Mourning and Violence.* New York: Verso, 2006.

California Coastal Commission. "Appendix E(1): Letters of Concern and Opposition." Staff Report W14d, Application no. 5-15-2097, Newport Banning Ranch, LLC, December 16, 2015. https://documents.coastal.ca.gov/reports/2016/9 /w14d-9-2016-a8.pdf.

Castañeda, Antonia I. "Engendering the History of Alta California, 1769–1848: Gender, Sexuality, and the Family." *California History* 76, no. 2–3 (1997): 230–49.

———. "Hispanas and Hispanos in a Mestizo Society." *OAH Magazine of History* 14, no. 4 (2000): 29–33.

———. "Sexual Violence in the Politics and Policies of Conquest." In *Sexual Violence in Conflict Zones: From the Ancient World to the Era of Human Rights*, edited by Elizabeth D. Heineman, 39–55. Philadelphia: University of Pennsylvania Press, 2011.

Castillo, Edward D. "Cultural Chauvinism Offered to Justify Serra Canonization." In *The Missions of California: A Legacy of Genocide*, edited by Rupert Costo and Jeannette Henry Costo, 67–80. San Francisco: Indian Historian Press, 1987.

———. "Gender Status Decline, Resistance, and Accommodation among Female Neophytes in the Missions of California: A San Gabriel Case Study." *American Indian Culture and Research Journal* 18, no. 1 (1994): 67–93. https://doi.org /10.17953.

———. "An Indian Account of the Decline and Collapse of Mexico's Hegemony over the Missionized Indians of California." *American Indian Quarterly* 13, no. 4 (1989): 391–408.

Castillo, Elias. *A Cross of Thorns: The Enslavement of California's Indians by the Spanish Missions.* Fresno: Craven Street, 2017.

Cattelino, Jessica R. "Fungibility: Florida Seminole Casino Dividends and the Fiscal Politics of Indigeneity." *American Anthropologist* 111, no. 2 (2009): 190–200. https://doi.org/10.1111/j.1548-1433.2009.01112.x.

Champagne, Duane. "Tribal Capitalism and Native Capitalists: Multiple Pathways of Native Economy." In *Native Pathways: American Indian Culture and Economic Development in the Twentieth Century*, edited by Colleen M. O'Neil and Brian C. Hosmer, 308–29. Boulder: University Press of Colorado, 2004.

Champagne, Duane, and Carole Goldberg. *A Coalition of Lineages: The Fernandeño Tataviam Band of Mission Indians*. Tucson: University of Arizona Press, 2021.

Chavez, Yve. "Indigenous Artists, Ingenuity, and Resistance at the California Missions after 1769." PhD diss., University of California, Los Angeles, 2017.

Churchill, Ward. *Kill the Indian, Save the Man: The Genocidal Impact of American Indian Residential Schools*. San Francisco: City Lights, 2004.

———. *A Little Matter of Genocide: Holocaust and Denial in the Americas, 1492 to the Present*. San Francisco: City Lights, 1997.

City of Riverside, California. "Riverside's Architectural Heritage." In *Riverside Citywide Design Guide*. Accessed March 20, 2016. https://www.riversideca.gov /historic/guidelines.asp.

Cook, Sherburne F. *The Conflict between the California Indian and White Civilization*. Berkeley: University of California Press, 1976.

Costansó, Miguel, Frederick John Teggart, and Manuel Carpio. *The Portola Expedition of 1769–1770: Diary of Miguel Costansó*. Berkeley: University of California, 1911.

Costo, Rupert, and Jeannette Henry Costo, eds. *The Missions of California: A Legacy of Genocide*. San Francisco: Indian Historian Press, 1987.

Coulthard, Glen. "Place against Empire: Understanding Indigenous Anti-Colonialism." *Affinities: A Journal of Radical Theory, Culture and Action* 4, no. 2 (2010): 79–83.

———. *Red Skin, White Masks: Rejecting the Colonial Politics of Recognition*. Minneapolis: University of Minnesota Press, 2014.

Crespi, Juan, and Herbert Eugene Bolton. *Fray Juan Crespi: Missionary Explorer on the Pacific Coast, 1769–1774*. Berkeley: University of California Press, 1927.

Davis, Angela Y., Frank Barat, and Cornel West. *Freedom Is a Constant Struggle: Ferguson, Palestine, and the Foundations of a Movement*. Chicago: Haymarket, 2016.

Davis, Angela Y., and Robin D. G. Kelley. *The Meaning of Freedom: And Other Difficult Dialogues*. San Francisco: City Lights, 2012.

De Azurara, Gomes Eanes, Raymond C. Beazley, and Edgar Prestage. *Chronicle of the Discovery and Conquest of Guinea*. Vol. 2. Farnham, England: Ashgate, 2010.

Deloria, Vine, Jr. *God Is Red: A Native View of Religion*. Golden, CO: Fulcrum, 2003.

Derrida, Jacques. *Psyche: Inventions of the Other*. Edited by Peggy Kamuf and Elizabeth Rottenberg. Stanford: Stanford University Press, 2007.

BIBLIOGRAPHY

Deverell, William F. *Whitewashed Adobe: The Rise of Los Angeles and the Remaking of Its Mexican Past*. Berkeley: University of California Press, 2004.

Dhillon, Jaskiran. *Prairie Rising: Indigenous Youth, Decolonization, and the Politics of Intervention*. Toronto: University of Toronto Press, 2017.

Duggan, Marie Christine. "Beyond Slavery: The Institutional Status of Mission Indians." In *Franciscans and American Indians in Pan-Borderlands Perspective: Adaptation, Negotiation, and Resistance*, edited by Jeffrey Burns and Timothy Johnson, 237–50. Oceanside, CA: American Academy of Franciscan History, 2017.

Duran, Eduardo. *Transforming the Soul Wound: A Theoretical/Clinical Approach to American Indian Psychology*. Meerut, India: Archana, 1990.

Duran, Eduardo, and Bonnie Duran. *Native American Postcolonial Psychology*. Albany: State University of New York Press, 1995.

Duran, Eduardo, Bonnie Duran, Maria Yellow Horse Brave Heart, and Susan Yellow Horse-Davis. "Healing the American Indian Soul Wound." In *Intergenerational Handbook of Multigenerational Legacies of Trauma*, edited by Yael Dannieli, 341–53. New York: Plenum, 1998.

Duran, Eduardo, Judith Firehammer, and John Gonzalez. "Liberation Psychology as the Path toward Healing Cultural Soul Wounds." *Journal of Counseling and Development* 86, no. 3 (2008): 288–95.

Early California Population Project Database (ECPP). Edition 1.1. University of California, Riverside, and Henry E. Huntington Library, 2022.

"Cesario Antonio Montero." https://ecpp.ucr.edu/ecpp/app/user/view/records/baptismal/42848?defaultTab=baptism.

"Dorothea Romero." https://ecpp.ucr.edu/ecpp/app/user/view/records/baptismal/13479?defaultTab=baptism.

"Jose Antonio Romero & Serafina Rosas." https://ecpp.ucr.edu/ecpp/app/user/view/records/marriage/9083?defaultTab=groom.

"Jose Domingo." https://ecpp.ucr.edu/ecpp/app/user/view/records/death/22501.

"Jose Domingo [Rosas]." https://ecpp.ucr.edu/ecpp/app/user/view/records/baptismal/38523?defaultTab=baptism.

"Joseph Carlos Rosas & Maria Dolores." https://ecpp.ucr.edu/ecpp/app/user/view/records/marriage/1611?defaultTab=groom.

"Leonardo and Maria Margarita." https://ecpp.ucr.edu/ecpp/app/user/view/records/marriage/8250?defaultTab=groom.

"Manuel Montero & Regina." https://ecpp.ucr.edu/ecpp/app/user/view/records/marriage/5373?defaultTab=groom.

"Maria Dolores." https://ecpp.ucr.edu/ecpp/app/user/view/records/baptismal/8770?defaultTab=baptism.

"Maria Margarita." https://ecpp.ucr.edu/ecpp/app/user/view/records/baptismal/36551?defaultTab=baptism.

"Nereo Joaquin." https://ecpp.ucr.edu/ecpp/app/user/view/records/baptismal/9222?defaultTab=baptism.

"Regina Josefa." https://ecpp.ucr.edu/ecpp/app/user/view/records/baptismal/8902?defaultTab=baptism.

"Seraphina Antonia Rosas." https://ecpp.ucr.edu/ecpp/app/user/view/records/baptismal/9149?defaultTab=baptism.

"Severiana Josefa [Rosas]." https://ecpp.ucr.edu/ecpp/app/user/view/records/baptismal/8881?defaultTab=baptism.

Elliot, Eric Bryant. "Dictionary of Rincón Luiseño." PhD diss., University of California San Diego, 2013.

Engelhardt, Zephyrin. *The Franciscans in California*. Harbor Springs, MI: Holy Childhood Indian School, 1897.

———. *The Missions and Missionaries of California*. San Francisco: James H. Barry, 1915.

———. *San Gabriel Mission and the Beginnings of Los Angeles*. San Gabriel, CA: Mission San Gabriel, 1927.

Fanon, Frantz. *Black Skin, White Masks*. New York: Grove, 2008.

———. *The Wretched of the Earth*. New York: Grove, 2005.

Fenelon, James V. "Indian Gaming: Traditional Perspectives and Cultural Sovereignty." *American Behavioral Scientist* 50, no. 3 (2006): 381–409.

Fireman, Janet R., and Manuel P. Servin. "Miguel Costansó: California's Forgotten Founder." *California Historical Society Quarterly* 49, no. 1 (1970): 3–19.

Forbes, Jack D. *Columbus and Other Cannibals: The Wetiko Disease of Exploitation, Imperialism, and Terrorism*. New York: Seven Stories, 2008.

———. "The Hispanic Spin: Party Politics and Governmental Manipulation of Ethnic Identity." *Latin American Perspectives* 19 (1992): 59–78.

———. *The Indian in America's Past*. Englewood Cliffs, NJ: Prentice-Hall, 1964.

Fritts, Harold C., and Geoffrey A. Gordon. "Reconstructed Annual Precipitation for California." In *Climate from Tree Rings*, edited by M. K. Hughes, P. M. Kelley, J. R. Pilcher, and V. C. LeMarche Jr. Cambridge, MA: Cambridge University Press, 1982.

Geiger, Maynard J. *The Life and Times of Fray Junípero Serra, O.F.M.* Washington, DC: Academy of American Franciscan History, 1959.

Goeman, Mishuana. *Mark My Words: Native Women Mapping Our Nations*. Minneapolis: University of Minnesota Press, 2013.

Goldberg, Carol, and Duane Champagne. "Ramona Redeemed? The Rise of Tribal Political Power in California." *Wičazo Ša Review* 17, no. 1 (2002): 43–63.

Goldberg, David Theo. *The Racial State*. Hoboken, NJ: Wiley-Blackwell, 2001.

BIBLIOGRAPHY

Gomez, Laura E. *Manifest Destinies: The Making of the Mexican American Race.* New York: NYU Press, 2007.

Gonzales, Nathan. "Riverside, Tourism, and the Indian: Frank A. Miller and the Creation of Sherman Institute." *Southern California Quarterly* 84, no. 3 (2002): 193–222.

Goodman, John David. "Spring Rancheria: Archaeological Investigations of a Transient Cahuilla Village in Early Riverside, California." MS thesis, University of California, Riverside, 1993.

Gordon, Avery F. *Ghostly Matters: Haunting and the Sociological Imagination.* Minneapolis: University of Minnesota Press, 2008.

Gough, Barry M. "The Views of Lieutenant George Peard, R.N., on Alta California, 1826 and 1827." *Southern California Quarterly* 56, no. 3 (1974): 213–32.

Granville, W., and N. C. Hough. *Spain's California Patriots in Its 1779–1783 War with England.* Laguna Hills, CA: Society of Hispanic Historical and Ancestral Research, 1998.

Gross, Lawrence William. *Anishinaabe Ways of Knowing and Being.* Burlington, VT: Ashgate, 2014.

Guest, Florian F. "The Indian Policy under Fermín Francisco de Lasuén, California's Second Father President." *California Historical Society Quarterly* 45, no. 3 (1966): 195–224.

Guest, Francis F. "Cultural Perspectives on California Mission Life." *Southern California Quarterly* 65, no. 1 (1983): 1–65.

———. "An Inquiry into the Role of Discipline in California Mission Life." *Southern California Quarterly* 71, no. 1 (1989): 1–68. https://doi.org/10.2307/41171346.

Gutfreund, Zevi. "Standing Up to Sugar Cubes: The Contest over Ethnic Identity in California's Fourth-Grade Mission Curriculum." *Southern California Quarterly* 92, no. 2 (Summer 2010): 161–97.

Haas, Lisbeth. *Conquests and Historical Identities in California, 1769–1936.* Berkeley: University of California Press, 1995.

Hackel, Steven W. *Children of Coyote, Missionaries of Saint Francis: Indian-Spanish Relations in Colonial California, 1769–1850.* Chapel Hill: University of North Carolina Press, 2005.

———. *Junípero Serra: California's Founding Father.* New York: Hill and Wang, 2013.

———. "Land, Labor, and Production: The Colonial Economy of Spanish and Mexican California." In *Contested Eden: California before the Gold Rush*, edited by Ramón A. Gutiérrez and Richard Orsi, 111–46. Berkeley: University of California Press, 1998.

———. "Sources of Rebellion: Indian Testimony and the Mission San Gabriel

Uprising of 1785." *Ethnohistory* 50, no. 4 (Fall 2003): 643–69. https://doi.org /10.1215/00141801-50-4-643.

Hanke, Lewis. *The Spanish Struggle for Justice in the Conquest of America*. Philadelphia: University of Pennsylvania Press, 1949.

Harris, Cheryl I. "Of Blackness and Indigeneity: Comments on Jodi A. Byrd's 'Weather with You: Settler Colonialism, Antiblackness, and the Grounded Relationalities of Resistance.'" *Journal of the Critical Ethnic Studies Association* 5, no. 1–2 (2019): 215–28. https://doi.org/10.5749/jcritethnstud.5.1-2.0215.

Hartman, Saidiya. "The Belly of the World: A Note on Black Women's Labors." *Souls: A Critical Journal of Black Politics, Culture and Society* 18, no. 1 (2016), 166–73. http://dx.doi.org/10.1080/10999949.2016.1162596.

———. *Lose Your Mother: A Journey along the Atlantic Slave Route*. New York: Farrar, Straus and Giroux, 2008.

———. *Scenes of Subjection: Terror, Slavery, and Self-Making in Nineteenth-Century America*. New York: Oxford University Press, 1997.

Harvey, Sandra. "What's Past Is Prologue." In *Otherwise Worlds: Against Settler Colonialism and Anti-Blackness*, edited by Tiffany Lethabo King, Jenell Navarro, and Andrea Smith, 218–35. Durham, NC: Duke University Press, 2020.

Heizer, Robert. "Impact of Colonization on the Native California Societies." *Journal of San Diego History* 24, no. 1 (Winter 1978): 1–68.

Heizer, Robert E. *The Indians of Los Angeles County: Hugo Reid's Letters of 1852*. Los Angeles: Southwest Museum, 1968.

Hodgen, Maurice. *Master of the Mission Inn: Frank A. Miller, a Life*. North Charleston, SC: Ashburton, 2013.

Holm, Tom, J. Diane Pearson, and Ben Chavis. "Peoplehood: A Model for the Extension of Sovereignty in American Indian Studies." *Wičazo Ša Review* 18, no. 1 (2003): 7–24.

Hong, Grace Kyungwon. *Death beyond Disavowal: The Impossible Politics of Difference*. Minneapolis: University of Minnesota Press, 2015.

Horsman, Reginald. *Race and Manifest Destiny: The Origins of American Racial Anglo-Saxonism*. Cambridge, MA: Harvard University Press, 1981.

Hyde, Villiana Calac, and Eric Elliot. *Yumáyk Yumáyk: Long Ago*. Berkeley: University of California Press, 1994.

Jackson, Helen Hunt. *Glimpses of California and the Missions*. Boston: Little, Brown, 1902.

———. *Ramona*. Boston: Little, Brown, 1884.

Jackson, Helen Hunt, and Valerie Sherer Mathes. *The Indian Reform Letters of Helen Hunt Jackson, 1879–1885*. Norman: University of Oklahoma Press, 1998.

Jackson, Robert H., and Edward D. Castillo. *Indians, Franciscans, and Spanish*

*Colonization: The Impact of the Mission System on California Indians*. Albuquerque: University of New Mexico Press, 1995.

Kelley, Robin D. G. "Foreword." In *Black Marxism: The Making of the Black Radical Tradition*, by Cedric J. Robinson. Chapel Hill: University of North Carolina Press, 2020.

———. "The Rest of Us: Rethinking Settler and Native." *American Quarterly* 69, no. 2 (June 2017): 268.

King, Thomas. *The Truth about Stories: A Native Narrative*. Minneapolis: University of Minnesota Press, 2008.

King, Tiffany Lethabo. *The Black Shoals: Offshore Formations of Black and Native Studies*. Durham, NC: Duke University Press, 2019.

———. "New World Grammars: The 'Unthought' Black Discourses of Conquest." In *Otherwise Worlds: Against Settler Colonialism and Anti-Blackness*, edited by Tiffany Lethabo King, Jenell Navarro, and Andrea Smith, 77–93. Durham, NC: Duke University Press, 2020.

Klotz, Esther. *The Mission Inn, Its History and Artifacts*. Riverside, CA: Rubidoux, 1981.

Kropp, Phoebe S. *California Vieja: Culture and Memory in a Modern American Place*. Berkeley: University of California Press, 2006.

Laird, Carobeth, ed. *Encounter with an Angry God: Recollections of My Life with John Peabody Harrington*. Banning, CA: Malki Museum Press, 1975.

Lake, Alison. *Colonial Rosary: The Spanish and Indian Missions of California*. Athens, OH: Swallow Press, 2006.

La Perouse, Jean Francois de Galaup. *Monterey in 1786: Life in a California Mission, The Journals of Jean Francois de La Perouse*. Berkeley: Heyday, 1989.

Lech, Steve, and Kim Jarrell Johnson. *Riverside's Mission Inn*. Mount Pleasant, SC: Arcadia, 2006.

Lefebvre, Henri. *The Production of Space*. Oxford, England: Blackwell, 1991.

Liboiron, Max. *Pollution Is Colonialism*. Durham, NC: Duke University Press, 2021.

Lightfoot, Kent. *Indians, Missionaries, and Merchants: The Legacy of Colonial Encounters on the California Frontiers*. Berkeley: University of California Press, 2005.

Lindsay, Brenden C. *Murder State: California's Native American Genocide, 1846–1873*. Lincoln: University of Nebraska Press, 2012.

Lorimer, Michelle M. *Resurrecting the Past: The California Mission Myth*. Pechanga, CA: Great Oak, 2016.

Lummis, Charles Fletcher. *Flowers of Our Lost Romance: A History of Old California*. Boston: Houghton Mifflin, 1929.

———. *The Spanish Pioneers and the California Missions*. Chicago: A. C. McClurg, 1893.

Macias, John. "In the Name of Spanish Colonization: Formulating Race and Identity in a Southern California Mission, 1769–1803." *Southern California Quarterly* 103, no. 2 (Summer 2021): 155–97. https://doi.org/10.1525/scq.2021.103.2.155.

Madley, Benjamin. *An American Genocide: The United States and the California Indian Catastrophe, 1846–1873.* New Haven, CT: Yale University Press, 2016.

———. "California's First Mass Incarceration System: Franciscan Missions, California Indians, and Penal Servitude, 1769–1836." *Pacific Historical Review* 88, no. 1 (2019): 14–47. https://doi.org/10.1525/phr.2019.88.1.14.

Manriquez, L. Frank. "There Are Other Ways of Getting Tradition." *Museum Anthropology* 24, nos. 2/3 (2001): 41.

McCarthy, Cormac. *The Road.* London: Picador, 2010.

McGroarty, John Steven. *The Mission Play: A Pageant Play in Three Acts.* California: n.p., 1939.

McWilliams, Carey. *North from Mexico: The Spanish Speaking People of the United States,* 3rd ed. Santa Barbara: Praeger, 2016.

———. *Southern California Country: An Island on the Land.* New York: Duell, Sloan and Pearce, 1946.

Million, Dian. *Therapeutic Nations: Healing in an Age of Indigenous Human Rights.* Tucson: University of Arizona Press, 2013.

Miranda, Deborah A. *Bad Indians: A Tribal Memoir.* Berkeley: Heyday, 2013.

———. "Canonization Fodder: California Indians and the Sainthood of Junípero Serra." *Bad Indians Blog,* September 20, 2015. http://badndns.blogspot.com/2015/09/canonization-fodder-california-indians.html.

———. "Extermination of the Joyas: Gendercide in Spanish California." *GLQ* 16, no. 1–2 (2010): 253–84.

———. "'Saying the Padre Had Grabbed Her': Rape Is the Weapon, Story Is the Cure." *Intertexts* 14, no. 2 (2010).

———. "Teaching on Stolen Ground." In *Placing the Academy: Essays on Landscape, Work, and Identity,* edited by Jennifer Sinor and Rona Kaufman, 169–87. Logan: Utah State University Press, 2007.

Mora Torres, Gregorio, ed. *Californio Voices: The Oral Memories of Jose Maria Amador and Lorenzo Asisara.* Denton: University of North Texas Press, 2005.

Newsom, Gavin. "Executive Order N-15-19." Executive Department, State of California, June 18, 2019. https://www.gov.ca.gov/wp-content/uploads/2019/06/6.18.19-Executive-Order.pdf.

Nichols, Robert. *Theft Is Property! Dispossession and Critical Theory.* Durham, NC: Duke University Press, 2020.

Omi, Michael, and Howard Winant. *Racial Formation in the United States: From the 1960s to the 1990s.* New York: Routledge, 1994.

*174* BIBLIOGRAPHY

Palóu, Francisco, and Herbert Eugene Bolton. *Historical Memoirs of New California*. Berkeley: University of California Press, 1926.

Parry, John H., and Robert G. Keith. *New Iberian World: A Documentary History of the Discovery and Settlement of Latin America to the Early 17th Century*. New York: Times, 1984.

Patterson, Orlando. *Slavery and Social Death: A Comparative Study*. Cambridge, MA: Harvard University Press, 1982.

Paxton, Katrina A. "Learning Gender: Female Students at the Sherman Institute, 1907–1925." In *Boarding School Blues: Revisiting American Indian Educational Experiences*, edited by Clifford E. Trafzer, Jean A. Keller, and Lorene Sisquoc, 174–86. Lincoln: University of Nebraska Press, 2006.

Pérez, Emma. *The Decolonial Imaginary: Writing Chicanas into History*. Bloomington: Indiana University Press, 1999.

Pfaelzer, Jean. *California: A Slave State*. New Haven, CT: Yale University Press, 2023.

Phillips, George Harwood. *Vineyards and Vaqueros: Indian Labor and the Economic Expansion of Southern California, 1771–1877*. Norman, OK: Arthur H. Clark, 2010.

Pratt, Richard H. "The Advantages of Mingling Indians with Whites." In *Americanizing the American Indians: Writings by the "Friends of the Indian," 1880–1900*, edited by Francis Paul Prucha, 260–71. Cambridge, MA: Harvard University Press, 1973.

Rawls, James J. "The California Mission as Symbol and Myth." *California History* 71, no. 3 (Fall 1992): 342–61.

———. *Indians of California: The Changing Image*. Norman: University of Oklahoma Press, 1984.

Reid, Anne Marie. "Medics of the Soul and the Body: Sickness and Death in Alta California, 1769–1850." PhD diss., University of Southern California, 2013.

Reid, Hugo, and Arthur M. Ellis. *The Indians of Los Angeles County*. Los Angeles: Private Printing, 1926.

Reséndez, Andrés. *The Other Slavery: The Uncovered Story of Indian Enslavement in America*. Boston: Houghton Mifflin Harcourt, 2016.

Rodríguez, Dylan. *Suspended Apocalypse: White Supremacy, Genocide, and the Filipino Condition*. Minneapolis: University of Minnesota Press, 2010.

———. "White Supremacy." In *The Wiley-Blackwell Encyclopedia of Social Theory*, edited by Bryan S. Turner, Kyung-sup Chang, Cynthia F. Epstein, Peter Kivisto, J. Michael Ryan, and William Outhwaite. West Sussex, UK: Wiley-Blackwell, 2017.

Rowntree, Lester B. "Drought during California's Mission Period, 1769–1834." *Journal of California and Great Basin Anthropology* 7, no. 1 (1985): 7–20.

Sánchez, Rosaura. *Telling Identities: The Californio Testimonies*. Minneapolis: University of Minnesota Press, 1995.

Sandos, James A. "Between Crucifix and Lance: Indian-White Relations in California, 1769–1848." In *Contested Eden: California before the Gold Rush*, edited by Ramón A. Gutiérrez and Richard Orsi, 196–229. Berkeley: University of California Press, 1998.

——. *Converting California: Indians and Franciscans in the Missions*. New Haven, CT: Yale University Press, 2004.

Savage, Kirk. *Standing Soldiers, Kneeling Slaves: Race, War, and Monument in Nineteenth-Century America*. Princeton, NJ: Princeton University Press, 1997.

Savage, Thomas. *Provincial State Papers, 1767–1822*. Vol. 2, 1778–1780. Hubert Howe Bancroft Collection, Bancroft Library, University of California, Berkeley.

Schneider, Khal, Dale Allender, Margarita Berta-Ávila, Rose Borunda, Gregg Castro, Amy Murray, and Jenna Porter. "More than Missions: Native Californians and Allies Changing the Story of California History." *Journal of American Indian Education* 58, no. 3 (2019): 58–77.

Sepulveda, Charles. "Our Sacred Waters: Theorizing *Kuuyam* as a Decolonial Possibility." *Decolonization: Indigeneity, Education, Society* 7, no. 1 (2018): 40–58.

Serra, Junípero, and Antonine Tibesar. *Writings of Junípero Serra*. Washington, DC: Academy of American Franciscan History, 1955.

Sexton, Jared. "The Veil of Slavery." *Critical Sociology* 42, no. 4–5 (2016): 583–97.

Shipek, Florence Connolly. "Saints or Oppressors: The Franciscan Missionaries of California." In *The Missions of California: A Legacy of Genocide*, edited by Rupert Costo and Jeannette Henry Costo, 29–48. San Francisco: Indian Historian Press, 1987.

Shoup, Laurence H., and Randall T. Milliken. *Inigo of Rancho Posolmi: The Life and Times of a Mission Indian*. Ballena Press, 1999.

Simpson, Audra. *Mohawk Interruptus: Political Life across the Borders of Settler States*. Durham, NC: Duke University Press, 2014.

Simpson, John A., and Edmund S. C. Weiner. *The Oxford English Dictionary*. Oxford, England: Clarendon, 1989.

Simpson, Leanne Betasamosake. *As We Have Always Done: Indigenous Freedom through Radical Resistance*. Minneapolis: University of Minnesota Press, 2021.

Smith, Andrea. *Conquest: Sexual Violence and American Indian Genocide*. Cambridge, MA: South End, 2005.

Smith, Linda Tuhiwai. *Decolonizing Methodologies: Research and Indigenous Peoples*. New York: St. Martin's, 1999.

Speed, Shannon. "Structures of Settler Colonialism in Abya Yala." *American Quarterly* 69, no. 4 (2017): 783–90.

Spillers, Hortense. "Mama's Baby, Papa's Maybe: An American Grammar Book." *Diacritics* 17, no. 2 (1987): 65–81.

Stark, Hannah. "'All These Things He Saw and Did Not See': Witnessing the End of the World in Cormac McCarthy's 'The Road.'" *Critical Survey* 25, no. 2 (2013): 71–84. https://www.jstor.org/stable/42751035.

Stewart-Ambo, Theresa, and Kelly Leah Stewart. "From Tovaangar to the University of California, Los Angeles." *American Indian Culture and Research Journal* 46, no. 2 (2023): 125–50.

Stewart-Ambo, Theresa, and K. Wayne Yang. "Beyond Land Acknowledgment in Settler Institutions." *Social Text* 39, no.1 (2021): 21–46.

Sturm, Circe. *Becoming Indian: The Struggle over Cherokee Identity in the Twenty-First Century*. Santa Fe: School for Advanced Research Press, 2011.

Tac, Pablo, and Lisbeth Haas. *Pablo Tac, Indigenous Scholar: Writing on Luiseño Language and Colonial History, C. 1840*. Berkeley: University of California Press, 2011.

TallBear, Kim. *Native American DNA: Tribal Belonging and the False Promise of Genetic Science*. Minneapolis: University of Minnesota Press, 2013.

Temple, Thomas Workman, II. "Toypurina the Witch and the Indian Uprising at San Gabriel." *Masterkey* 32, no. 5 (1958): 136–52.

Tinker, George E. *Missionary Conquest: The Gospel and Native American Cultural Genocide*. Minneapolis: Fortress Press, 1993.

Trask, Haunani-Kay. *From a Native Daughter: Colonialism and Sovereignty in Hawaiʻi*. Honolulu: University of Hawaiʻi Press, 1999.

Tuck, Eve, and Christine Ree. "A Glossary of Haunting." In *Handbook of Autoethnography*, edited by Stacy Holman Jones, Tony E. Adams, and Carolyn Ellis, 639–58. Walnut Creek, CA: Left Coast, 2013.

Tuck, Eve, and K. Wayne Yang. "Decolonization Is Not a Metaphor." *Decolonization: Indigeneity, Education, and Society* 1, no. 1 (2012): 1–40.

Vallejo García-Hevia, José María. *La Segunda Carolina: el Nuevo código de leyes de las Indias: sus juntas recopiladoras, sus secretarios y el Real Consejo (1776–1820)*. Spain: Boletín Oficial del Estado, 2016.

Vargas, João H. Costa. *The Denial of Antiblackness: Multiracial Redemption and Black Suffering*. Minneapolis: University of Minnesota Press, 2018.

Vargas, João H. Costa, and Moon-Kie Jung, eds. *Antiblackness*. Durham, NC: Duke University Press, 2021.

Vaughn, Chelsea. "Locating Absence: The Forgotten Presence of *Monjerios* in the Alta California Missions." *Southern California Quarterly* 93, no. 2 (Summer, 2011): 141–74.

Vaughn, Kēhaulani. "Sovereign Embodiment: Native Hawaiian Expressions of Kuleana in the Diaspora." PhD diss., University of California Riverside, 2017.

―――. "Sovereign Embodiment: Native Hawaiians and Expressions of Diasporic Kuleana." *Hūlili Journal* 11 (2019): 227–45.

Vizenor, Gerald Robert. *Manifest Manners: Narratives on Postindian Survivance.* Lincoln: University of Nebraska Press, 1999.

―――. *Native Liberty: Natural Reason and Cultural Survivance.* Lincoln: University of Nebraska Press, 2009.

Waziyatawin. *What Does Justice Look Like? The Struggle for Liberation in Dakota Homeland.* Saint Paul, MN: Living Justice Press, 2008.

Whalen, Kevin. *Native Students at Work: American Indian Labor and Sherman Institute's Outing Program, 1900–1945.* Seattle: University of Washington Press, 2018.

Wittenburg, Mary Joanne. "Three Generations of the Sepulveda Family in Southern California." *Southern California Quarterly* 73, no. 3 (1991): 197–250.

Wolfe, Patrick. "Settler Colonialism and the Elimination of the Native." *Journal of Genocide Research* 8, no. 4 (2006): 387–409.

Zamora, Lois Parkinson. *Writing the Apocalypse: Historical Vision in Contemporary U.S. and Latin American Fiction.* Cambridge, England: Cambridge University Press, 1989.

# INDEX

Page numbers in *italics* indicate illustrations.

Acjachemem: building materials, 59; environmental devastation of, 80, 89; and Genga, 121–24; rematriation of land, 123, 126, 137; resistance of, 2–3, 25, 51–55, 68, 77–79; and Walk for the Ancestors, 114–19. *See also* Boscana, Father Gerónimo; Genga; Juaneño Band of Mission Indians; Santa Ana River; Wanáw Waníicha

Acjachemen Cultural Center, 140

Acjachemen Tongva Land Conservancy, 124–25

activism: condemnation of, 6–8; against memorial statues, 5–6, 95–96; of John Trudell, 143–44

Adams, Mechelle Lawrence, 101

Adiele, Pius Onyemechi, 48

Agamben, Giorgio, 7

*ahíichu*, 83–84

Akins, Damon B.: *We Are the Land*, 1, 32

Alexander VI (pope), 47–48

Alfred, Taiaiake, 132–34

*Al Jazeera America*, 104

Amaugenga, 52

American Indian: and apocalypse, 80; DNA and genealogy, xix, 149n23; gaming, 131; Indigenous worldview, 38; as political term, xviii; psychology, 154n59; US government legal designation, xviii

American Indian Movement, 97, 118

American Indian Religious Freedom Act, 133

antiblackness: "gratuitous violence," 149n13

apocalypse: *ahíichu*, 83–84; definition of, 81; Jacques Derrida, 83; enslavement, 126, 143; erasure of, 143; Cormac McCarthy, 21, 82–83; post-, 82–84; and spiritual conquest of California, 21, 80

architectural styles, 20–21; Americans in Riverside, 60, 156n27; as capitalist product, 58; Mexicans in California, 60; Mission Revival, 51, 56–57, 62, *65*, 73–75; Spanish Colonial Revival, 56, 59–60, 64, 73

Army Corps of Engineers, 90, 92

Arvin, Maile, 6–7

Asisara, Lorenzo, 42, 44

'Axachme, 52

*Bad Indians* (Miranda), 1, 79

Bancroft, Hubert Howe: early California history, 11; enslavement of Indians, 32–34

baptism, 16, 130; cesareans and, 43; debate about consent, 39–40; Indian slaves, 8, 36, 78; loss of freedom, 8, 41; name changes, 121, 154n57; records of, xvi–xvii, 122; and saving, 3, 7; Junípero Serra on, 54, 111, 155n8; of Toypurina, 27, 146. *See also* neophytes; *razón*

Bartolomea, Victoria, 38, 127

Bauer, William J., Jr., 1, 32

Belardes, Matias, 77, 123

Benton, Arthur, 61–62, 64, 156n31

180    INDEX

blacksmith, 69, *70*

Black studies, 20, 28; radical tradition, 17; scholarship, 142; theories and methods, 14–15, 29–30, 45

Blackwell, Maylei, 13

Blas Aguilar Adobe Museum, 140

blasphemy, 2–3, 6, 9, 11

Boscana, Father Gerónimo: baptism, 3; giving last rites, 2–4; writing about Mission San Juan Capistrano, 5, 43, 105

Bureau of Indian Affairs (BIA), 66–68

Calderon, Jessa, 95–96

California grizzly bear: trap, 87, 89

California Native American Heritage Commission, 121

California State Coastal Conservancy, 122

*California v. Cabazon Band of Mission Indians*, 131, 133

Carriquiry, Guzman, 101

Castañeda, Antonia I., xiv, 107–9

Castillo, Edward D., 109, 113

Catholicism, 2: baptism, 30, 43; Catechism, 4; Communion, 2, 100; evangelism, 99; involvement in colonialism, 3, 21, 41, 47, 80, 98; wealth and banking, 99–100

cesarean sections, baptism and, 43

Champagne, Duane: on casinos, 130–31, 134; Mission San Fernando, 37; on "the Ramona story," 21, 127–30

*Chichiinavroʼam* (Spanish people), xi, xii

childbirth: Lorenzo Asisara, 42, 44; death of mother, 43; María Solares, 44

Christian: biblical narratives, 82; binary with non-Christian, 7, 10, 41, 46–48, 78, 145; education, 67–68;

family life, 107–8; marriage, 28; redemption and stolen land, 127; and Spanish architecture, 56; Spanish colonial practices, 9, 47, 58, 60; Spanish patriarchal system, 89, 109; violence with Indians, 54; women and settlement, 106–9. *See also* baptism; Geiger, Maynard J.; Toypurina

Christianity: apocalypse and, 81; baptism and "indelible mark," 4, 53; conversion to, 30, 49, 68, 106–7; and domination, 33, 146; Native resistance to, 2–6, 55; spiritual faith, 99; Sunday as day of prayer, 114; theological perspective, 84, 126, 146. See also *razón*; *sin razón*

Churchill, Ward, 161n24

*chuuʼar* (arrow), xi–xii, 53, 106

Civil War, US, 74

Cleaves, Wallace, 135

colonialism: psychological impacts of, 41–42, 80, 84, 154n59

Confederacy, 74

*congregación*, 37–38, 40

conquest: secularization, 20; spiritual possession, 20. *See also* settler colonialism

Cordileone, Archbishop Salvatore: exorcism by, 6, 8; on Serra, 8–9

Coronni: married Qchàinoque, 121–22; remarried Cuenànauvit, 122

Costanoan, 44, 79

Costansó, Miguel: journal with Portolá expedition, 85, 87

Costo, Jeannette: *Missions of California*, 1, 18

Costo, Rupert: *Missions of California*, 1, 18

Coulthard, Glen: "grounded

normativity," 138; on recognition, 131–35, 139

Crespí, Father Juan; journal with Portolá expedition, 85, 87; influence on pueblos, 107. *See also* Santa Ana River

Culiacán, 107

Dakota scholars and activists, 41, 67, 143; and Abraham Lincoln statue, 5

D'Arcy, Angela Mooney, 97

Davis, Angela Y., 28

Dawes Act (1887), 67

Deetz, Nanette, 97

Deloria, Vine, Jr., 38–39, 46, 146

Derrida, Jacques, on apocalypse, 83

Deverell, William F., 58

Dhillon, Jaskiran, 135

DNA, 144; and blood quantum, xix, 149n23. *See also* tribal membership

Doctrine of Discovery, 8; conquest and slavery, 29, 49, 78, 98; demands to rescind, 77, 115

doctrine of patriarchy, 109. *See also* heteropatriarchy

Dolores, María: baptism, xvii; birth, xvi; marriage with José Carlos Rosas, xvii, 107, 147

Duran, Eduardo: on "soul wounds" of conquest, 10, 41, 79–80

Early California Population Project Database (ECPP), xv; baptismal records, xvi. *See also* Hackel, Steven

Engelhardt, Zephyrin, xiii; on "indelible mark" of Christianity, 4

enslavement: and alienation, 17; Catholic Church, 113; and chattel slavery, 29–30, 32, 34; conquest of California, 14–15, 21, 29, 126; disavowal of,

29, 33, 76, 143, 151n52; in discourse of US Black history, 20, 29; and land dispossession, 29, 126; Native experiences in missions, 29; Pueblo Revolt of 1680, 25; resistance to, 13, 93, 142; sexual violence, 20, 28; social death, 45; and the Spanish imaginary, 12, 19, 47–48, 58, 147; spiritual conquest, 45–46, 49, 104, 137. *See also* Patterson, Orlando; slavery

eschatology, 81–82

Fages, Pedro: as governor of California, 26; and punishment of Indians, 26; removal from command, 110–11; and soldiers' sexual violence against Native women, xiii, 110

Fairbanks, Corine, 97, 118. *See also* American Indian Movement

Fanon, Frantz: on colonialism and resistance, 26, 80; influence on Glen Coulthard, 131–32

flood: Miguel Costansó on, 85; Father Juan Crespí on, 87; Flood Control Act, 90; flooding, 91–93; seasonal, *86. See also* Santa Ana River

Forbes, Jack D., 80; on Gospel of Matthew, 159n9; on political construct of Hispanic identity, 102–3

Foucault, Michel: Emma Pérez's arguments based on work of, 17

Francis (pope): canonization of Junípero Serra, 95–98, 101, 103–5; demands to rescind Doctrine of Discovery, 77, 96; empty apology, 98; shifting of blame to military, 105, 107, 110

Franciscan order, 7

Fuerte (town), 107

# 182 INDEX

Gabrieleño, xviii, 28, 123
Gabrielino, xviii, 16, 95
Geiger, Maynard J., 12
Genga, 121–26, 140; haunting of, 138
Glenwood Mission Inn, 20, 56–57, 61, 64, 65, 155n12
Goeman, Mishuana, 140
Goldberg, Carole: on casinos, 130–31, 134; on Mission San Fernando, 37; on "the Ramona story," 21, 127–30
Gomez, Laura E., 74
Gordon, Avery, 10
Grabowski, Christine, 111–12
Gross, Lawrence, 80–81
Guest, Father Francis, 3, 8, 37

Hackel, Steven: on canonization of Junípero Serra, 101, 104, 112; on conquest, 17; critiques of historical accounts, 23; on enslavement, 32. *See also* Early California Population Project Database (ECPP); Toypurina
Harris, Cheryl, 45
Hartman, Saidiya, 15, 142; on kinship, 28; on racialized sexuality, 45; on slavery, 16, 38–39; on violence, 33, 39
Harvey, Sandra, 14
Hass, Lisbeth, 19
Haudenosaunee, 11
*hechizera* (witch), 27. *See also* Toypurina
Heidegger, Martin: on the past, 83
Heizer, Robert, 36
heteropatriarchy, 20, 27, 52, 107–8, 113, 134; and rematriating Genga, 140; at Sherman Indian Boarding School, 69
Hispanic people: conversions of Indians, 105; heritage of Riverside, 75; Junípero Serra as first Hispanic saint, 100–103; term, 103; and white supremacy, 104

Hittell, Theodore, 33–34
Hoaglin, Dean, 9
Hodgen, Maurice, 64
Holland, Caroline Ward, 113–14, 119
Holme, Garnet, 64
Horra, Padre Antonio de la Concepcion, 34
Horsman, Reginald, 9
Hotuukgna (village), 87
Hyde, Villiana, 83

incarceration, 30. *See also* enslavement
Indian: agency, 7–9, 25, 143, 153n33; survivance, 11, 142–43. *See also* Native alienation; neophytes; non-Christian
Indian Bill of Rights, 112
Indian boarding schools, 145; Bureau of Indian Affairs, 66–67; comparison with missions, 65; enrollment in, 68; Mission Inn, 56; Native resistance to, 68. *See also* Sherman Indian Boarding School
*Indian Country Today*, 97, 111
Indian Gaming Regulatory Act, 131, 133

Jackson, Helen Hunt: influence on California Indians, 127–28, 157n47. See also *Ramona*
Jayme, Father Luís, 114, 117
*jayuntes* (male dormitory), 62, 68
Jordan, David Starr: on Mission Inn, 72
José, Nicolás, 23–27, 36. *See also* Taraaxam; Toypurina
Juaneño Band of Mission Indians (Acjachemen Nation), 21, 77, 123
Jung, Moon-Kie, 142

Kahoo' Paxaayt, 84–85; alienation of, 92; environmental devastation of,

79, 87, 89, 146; and Genga, 122. *See also* Crespí, Father Juan; Taraaxam
Kānaka Maoli scholar, 6
Kelley, Robin D. G., 14–15
King, Thomas, 13
King, Tiffany, 15
kinship: and alienation, 27–28, 56; and freedom, 133; Indigenous futurity, 119, 139, 141; rematriation of land, 53, 55, 123, 126; role of missions and, 38; Junípero Serra and, 107; severed, 36–37, 39, 52. *See also* slavery; Toypurina
Kizh, xviii, 149n22. *See also* Taraaxam
Kropp, Phoebe S., 57, 60
Kumeyaay, 25, 55, 114, 117
*kuuyam* (guests), xi–xii, 141

land acknowledgments, 135–36
Landmarks Club, 61–62, 64, 156n31
La Pérouse, Jean François Galaup de, 34
Lasuén, Father Fermín de, 34, 36, 54
"Leather Jackets" (Soldados de Cuera), 106
Leo X (pope), 48
Liboiron, Max, on pollution as violence, 89
Lightfoot, Kent, 31
Los Alamos (town), 107
Los Angeles: Basin, xi; County, 80; military defense of, 106–7; Olvera Street, 73; Pacific Electric Railway, 71, 91; slave market, 83; statue of Junípero Serra, 95–96; Yaanga, 147; Yabit, xvi. *See also* Acjachemen Tongva Land Conservancy; José, Nicolás; Tongva: Tongva Taraxat Paxaavxa Land Conservancy; Toypurina
*Los Angeles Herald*, 62, 64, 68, 71–72, 91–92

Luiseño-Cahuilla, 47, 52, 83–84, 127, 135. *See also* Serrano

Macias, John, xv
Madley, Benjamin, 30
Manifest Destiny, 8, 46, 61, 72
maniisar, 38
"man of his time," 77–78, 104, 110
Manriquez, L. Frank, 14
McCarthy, Cormac: *The Road*, 21, 82–83
McGroarty, John Steven, 64
McKinley, President William, 66
McWilliams, Carey, 57
Miller, Frank A., 61–62, 64; integrating the Sherman School and Mission Inn, 69–72; relocating the Perris Indian School, 64–66, 157n45; and the Spanish imaginary, 71, 73–76. *See also* Mission Inn Hotel and Spa
Millikin, Randall, 32
Miranda, Deborah A.: *Bad Indians*, 1, 79; on canonization of Junípero Serra, 96; on "genealogy of violence," 79–80, 83; on Indigenous reading, 13; on intergenerational trauma, 41
Mission Carmel, 64, 106
Mission Inn Hotel and Spa, 155n12. *See also* Glenwood Mission Inn
missions: bells, 55, 64, 73–75, 117; comparisons with Middle Passage, 39–40, 48; heteropatriarchal logic, 69
Mission San Antonio de Padua, 106
Mission San Borja, 52
Mission San Buenaventura, xiii
Mission San Carlos Borroméo de Carmelo, 34
Mission San Diego, 53–54, 112, 114, 117, 155n3
Mission San Fernando, 37, 95

184 INDEX

Mission San Francisco, 6, 106; presidio, 105

Mission San Gabriel, xi–xvii, 64; Native resistance, 53, 68; punishment of women and children, 40, 42–43; *Ramona*, 127; uprising of 1785, 23–28, 45, 152n1. *See also* Toypurina

Mission San Juan Capistrano, *63*, 68, 79, 155n3; burial of Qchàinoque, 121–22; erasure of Indians, 101–2; Landmarks Club, 62; Pánhe, 52; rebellion against, 51–54, 77; tourist destination, 55; Walk for the Ancestors, 114–19. *See also* Acjachemem; Acjachemen

Mission San Luis Obispo, 27, 106, 111

Mission Santa Barbara, 19, 60, 106; presidio, 105

Mission Santa Clara, 106

*Missions of California* (Costo and Costo), 1, 18

Mission Ventura, 106

Moccasin John, 87–88

Mohawk, 11, 132

*monjeríos* (women's dormitory/prison), 20, 40–44, 68, 89, 97; labeled as "guest rooms," 62

Monterey: Portolá's failed mission to locate, 85; presidio at, 105; recall of Pedro Fages at, 110; trail to, 108

Monterey Bay, 34

Morales, Anthony, 123

nanaawme'ar (fighters), xi, xiii

natal alienation, 36–38, 145

Native alienation: and canonization of Junípero Serra, 96, 101, 103; definition of, 22, 38, 52; and discourse of conquest, 38, 141–42; environmental devastation as, 84, 93, 147; social

death as, 39; survivors and, 83, 96. *See also monjeríos*; slavery; spiritual possession

Native American Graves Protection and Repatriation Act, 133

Navarro, Galindo, 23–24

neophytes (converts to Christianity), 16, 39; abuse of, 40–42; alcaldes and, 103; baptisms, 39–40; Communion, 2; fugitivism, 54; marriage, xvii. *See also* non-Christian; punishment; Toypurina

Neve y Padilla, Governor Felipe de, xiv, 34, 106–7

Newcomb, Steven, 78, 103

*News from Native California*, 96

Newsom, Gavin, 124–26

New Spain, 4, 108, 112

Nicholas V (pope), 47

Nichols, Robert, 6

non-Christian, xviii, 37, 46, 145–46; deemed evil and criminal by church and state, 7, 9–10. *See also* Christian; Christianity; neophytes; *sin razón*

Nuñez, Jacque, 114, 117–18

Omi, Michael, on racial formation, 102

Orange County: Anaheim, 85, *88*; flood basin, 92; flood plain, 90–91; flood zone, 89; land values, 93; last coastal open spaces, 121, 140; Pánhe, 52; Prado Dam, 90. *See also* Santa Ana River

Ortega, José Francisco de, 51

Palóu, Father Francisco, xi, 106

Pamó Indians, 54

Pánhe (village), 51–52

patriarchy. *See* doctrine of patriarchy; heteropatriarchy

Patterson, Orlando, 15, 142–45;

INDEX  *185*

disavowing slavery, 30, 33, 41, 142; natal alienation, 36

Payómkawichum, 25, 52, 55, 83

Pérez, Emma, 17, 57

Perris Indian School, 65–66

Perry, Joyce Stanfield, 123

*poblador* (settler), xvi

Portolá, Gaspar de, 12, 85

powerlessness, 33, 45, 69, 153n33

Prado Dam, 87, 90, 92

Pratt, Richard Henry, 67

presidios, 25, 31, 105–7

Public Law 280 (US), 129

Pueblo Revolt of 1680, 25

punishment: *azotes* (lashes), 35; capital, 79; floggings, 34, 41–42; by priests, 3–4; public, 36; for refusing Christian hegemony, 3–4; Junípero Serra views on, 111–12; shackles, 4, 35, 42; spiritual, 4, 35; for uprisings, 26. *See also* "man of his time"

Raincross Hotel, 75

*Ramona* (novel, Helen Hunt Jackson), 127–28; analysis of, by Champagne and Goldberg, 21, 127–30; influence on tourism, 66; popularity of, 66; theater performance, 64. *See also* Jackson, Helen Hunt

Rawls, James J., 32

*razón*, xvii, xviii, 27, 105

Reconstruction, 74

redemption, 126–27, 130

Redondo, María Candelaria de, 107

Red River Métis, 89

*reducción*, 37, 121

Ree, Christine, 11

Reglamento of 1779, 106–7

Reid, Anne Marie, 43

Reid, Hugo, 37–38, 40, 127

Reséndez, Andrés, 25

responsibility: and conquest, 3, 26, 48; relationality with land, 1, 7, 24, 28, 39, 52; and Junípero Serra, 110, 112; State of California, 126; and Tovaangar, 27, 38

Risling Baldy, Cutcha, 1, 159n16

Rivera y Moncada, Captain Fernando Xavier de, 106

Riverside, CA: architecture, 60, 75, 156, 156n27; city symbol, 64; Helen Hunt Jackson, 66; Pacific Electric Railway, 71, 91; Perris Indian School, 64–66, 157n45. *See also* Miller, Frank A.; Mission Inn Hotel and Spa; Santa Ana River; Sherman Indian Boarding School; Spanish imaginary

Rizzo-Martinez, Martin, xv

*Road, The* (novel, McCarthy), 21, 82

Robinson, Cedric, 45

Rodríguez, Dylan, 103

Roosevelt, Theodore, 5, 71

Rosario, Mexico, xvi, 107

Rosas, José Carlos, 103–9, 147; marriage with María Dolores, xvii, 107, 147

Rubios, Juan López de Palacios, 48

Sacred Places Institute for Indigenous Peoples (SPI), 122–23

Salazar, Alan, 95–96

Samala Chumash, 44

*San Bernardino Sun*, 71

Sánchez, Rosaura, 31–32

San Diego Presidio, xvii, 51, 106, 117

Sandos, James A., 3, 19, 30–32, 34

Sandoval, Adelia, 114–15, 117–18

*San Francisco Call*, 91

Santa Ana River, *88*; Miguel Costansó on, 85, 87; Father Juan Crespí on, 87; and environmental devastation through colonialism, 21, 80, 88–89; flood plain, 90–92; Mainstem

186 INDEX

Santa Ana River (*continued*)
  Project, 92; Prado Dam, 87, 90; Vision Plan, 92; watershed, *86*, 159n22, 159n27. *See also* flood; Kahoo' Paxaayt; Wanáw Waníicha
Sepúlveda, Francisco Xavier, 107–9
Serra, Father Junípero: canonization of, 10, 77, 96, 98, 101, 117; entombed, 114; Father Serra Park, 95; National Statuary Hall, 74; Native refusal to acknowledge as a saint, 93, 118; resolution passed by the Acjachemen Nation, 79; "spiritual conquest," 2, 77, 105, 112–13, 130; statue toppled, *10*, 95
Serrano, 16, 135. *See also* Luiseño-Cahuilla
settler colonialism, 6, 138; and enslavement, 14; role of families, 107–9; use of the term "conquest," 15. *See also* conquest
Sexton, Jared, 45
sexually transmitted infections, 62; syphilis, 44
sexual violence, xiii–xiv, 45, 79; erasure from history, 62; "gratuitous violence," 149n13; Mission San Gabriel, xiii; Mission Santa Cruz, 44; mock trial against Serra, 97–98; *monjerío*, 20, 40, 62; and vulnerability of Native child laborers, 69. *See also* Castañeda, Antonia I.; Miranda, Deborah A.
Shawnee-Lenape, 78
*shaxaat* (willow), xi. *See also* willow
Sherman, James S., 66
Sherman Indian Boarding School, 20, 56–57, 61, 67–73. *See also* Mission Inn Hotel and Spa
Sherman Indian High School, 64,

155n14. *See also* Sherman Indian Boarding School
Sherman Institute, 72, 155n14. *See also* Sherman Indian Boarding School
*shi'iiy* (tule), xi
Shiishongna, xviii
Shoshone, xviii
Shoup, Laurence, 32
Simpson, Audra, 11
Simpson, Leanne, 17, 28
Sinaloa, Mexico, xvi, 107
*sin razón*, xviii, 35. *See also* Christianity; *razón*
slavery: chattel, 29–30, 32, 34; comparisons with enslaved Black communities, 31, 33–34; debates about, 20; Doctrine of Discovery, 29, 49, 78, 98; Saidiya Hartman on, 16, 38–39; Portugal's history in west Africa, 46–48; scholars' use of term, 29–30; and settler colonialism, 14; and severed kinship, 28, 49; and spiritual conquest, 17, 28. *See also* enslavement
Smith, Linda Tuhiwai, 29
Solares, María, 44
Spanish imaginary, 12, 17, 49, 58; and architecture, 20, 56–57, 61; of colonial benevolence, 147, 153n20; and debates about enslavement, 20; as hallucination, 55; Helen Hunt Jackson and, 21, 128; Frank A. Miller and, 71, 73–76; and mislabeling of monjeríos, 62; scholarship about, 18, 56; Junípero Serra and, 114, 147; in theater, 62, 64. *See also* Glenwood Mission Inn; *monjeríos*; Sherman Indian Boarding School
Spanish military: *congregación*, 37–38, 40; disagreements with the church, 98, 104; killing tomyaar, xi–xiii;

logic of spiritual possession, 49, 80; rape and sexual violence against Indian women and children, xi–xiv, 44, 110; *reducción*, 37, 121

Spanish missionaries, 2, 4, 46, 48; canonization of, 74; genocide committed by, 104; kidnapping committed by, 47–48, 55, 68; and metaphorical cannibalism, 80–83; mission studies' disavowal of Indian enslavement, 29; violence against, 138. *See also* baptism; enslavement; *monjeríos*; "spiritual conquest"

Spanish priests, 59, 66, 104; benevolent portrayal of, 66; Franciscan, 8, 60; kidnapping committed by, 47–48, 55, 68; local parish, 60. *See also* enslavement; *Ramona*

Speed, Shannon, 14–15

Spillers, Hortense, 15–16, 142

"spiritual conquest," 80, 147; alienation from ancestral heritage, 105; and the canonization of Junípero Serra, xiv, xviii, 7–8, 77, 112–13; enslavement and, 17, 28; haunting of, 11; Indian resistance to, 62; logic of, 46; meaning of redemption and, 130

spiritual possession, xiii, xviii, 55; as enslavement, 68, 137; logic of, 7–9, 49, 80, 93, 127, 141. *See also* baptism

Stark, Hannah, 81–82

Stewart-Ambo, Theresa, 135–36

stockade, xi, 7

structures of possession, xv

Taboada, Father Luis Gil y, 44

Tac, Pablo, 47, 83

TallBear, Kim, 149n23. *See also* DNA

Tapis, Father Estevan, 34

Taraaxam, xviii, xix, 38, 131, 149n22;

building materials, xi, 59; against colonialism, 23, 25–28, 38, 45, 68, 152n1; environmental devastation of, 80, 89; haunting, 138; rematriation of land, 123, 126, 137; sovereignty, 109, 121–25, 138–39; Spanish military, xii–xiv; Yaanga, 107. *See also* Acjachemen Tongva Land Conservancy; Boscana, Father Gerónimo; Genga; Kahoo' Paxaayt; *kuuyam*; Santa Ana River; Tongva: Tongva Taraxat Paxaavxa Land Conservancy

Taxaat, xi. *See also* Bartolomea, Victoria; Toypurina

Temple, Thomas Workman, II: history of Toypurina, as flawed, 23, 152n2

tomyaar (village chief), 38; murder by Spanish soldiers, xi–xiii

Tongva, 122–23, 135, 149n22; Acjachemen Tongva Land Conservancy, 124–25; American Indian Movement, 97; scholars, 14, 24, 95, 135; Tongva Taraxat Paxaavxa Land Conservancy, 125

Tongvetam, 149n22

Tovaangar: background, xi; as homeland, 26–27; and kinship and responsibility, 38; Taraaxam history, xviii, 28

Toypurina: banishment from Tovaangar, 26; baptism and marriage with Manuel Montero, 27–28, 146; led Taraaxam uprising with Nicolás José, 23–27, 36, 49; Temple's flawed history, 152n2

Trask, Haunani-Kay, 25

tribal membership, 149; Certificate of Degree of Indian Blood, 129

Trudell, John, 143–44, 146

Trust for Public Land, 122, 125

188   INDEX

Tuck, Eve, 11, 135, 137
tule, xi, 59, 139, 156n22

unfree labor, 30. *See also* enslavement; slavery
University of California, Riverside: and land acknowledgment, 135

Vargas, João Costa, 142, 149n13
Vaughn, Kēhaulani, 139
Ventereño Chumash, 95
Vizenor, Gerald, 142

Walk for the Ancestors, 21, *116*
Wanáw Waníicha, 84–85; and alienation, 92; and environmental devastation, 79, 88, 90, 146; and Genga,

122. *See also* Crespí, Father Juan; Kahoo' Paxaayt; Santa Ana River; Taraaxam
Waziyatawin (Dakota scholar), 41, 67
*We Are the Land* (Akins), 1, 32
Weber, Francis J., 110–12
Whalen, Kevin, 66, 69
willow, xi, 59, 85, 87, 156n22
Winant, Howard, 102
Wittenburg, Mary, 106
Wolfe, Patrick, 6, 15

Yaanga (Los Angeles), xvi, xviii, 107, 147
Yabit (village), xvi. *See also* Yaanga
Yang, K. Wayne : on land acknowledgments, 135–36

Indigenous Confluences

CHARLOTTE COTÉ AND COLL THRUSH  *Series Editors*

Indigenous Confluences publishes innovative works that use decolonizing perspectives and transnational approaches to explore the experiences of Indigenous peoples across North America, with a special emphasis on the Pacific Coast.

*Native Alienation: Spiritual Conquest and the Violence of California Missions*, by Charles A. Sepulveda

*Refusing Settler Domesticity: Native Women's Labor and Resistance in the Bay Area Outing Program*, by Caitlin Keliiaa

*Unrecognized in California: Federal Acknowledgment and the San Luis Rey Band of Mission Indians*, by Olivia M. Chilcote

*Alaska Native Resilience: Voices from World War II*, by Holly Miowak Guise

*Settler Cannabis: From Gold Rush to Green Rush in Indigenous Northern California*, by Kaitlin Reed

*A Drum in One Hand, a Sockeye in the Other: Stories of Indigenous Food Sovereignty from the Northwest Coast*, by Charlotte Coté

*A Chemehuevi Song: The Resilience of a Southern Paiute Tribe*, by Clifford E. Trafzer

*Education at the Edge of Empire: Negotiating Pueblo Identity in New Mexico's Indian Boarding Schools*, by John R. Gram

*Indian Blood: HIV and Colonial Trauma in San Francisco's Two-Spirit Community*, by Andrew J. Jolivette

*Native Students at Work: American Indian Labor and Sherman Institute's Outing Program, 1900–1945*, by Kevin Whalen

*California through Native Eyes: Reclaiming History*, by William J. Bauer Jr.

*Unlikely Alliances: Native Nations and White Communities Join to Defend Rural Lands*, by Zoltán Grossman

*Dismembered: Native Disenrollment and the Battle for Human Rights*, by David E. Wilkins and Shelly Hulse Wilkins

*Network Sovereignty: Building the Internet across Indian Country*, by Marisa Elena Duarte

*Chinook Resilience: Heritage and Cultural Revitalization on the Lower Columbia River*, by Jon Daehnke

*Power in the Telling: Grand Ronde, Warm Springs, and Intertribal Relations in the Casino Era*, by Brook Colley

*We Are Dancing for You: Native Feminisms and the Revitalization of Women's Coming-of-Age Ceremonies*, by Cutcha Risling Baldy

www.ingramcontent.com/pod-product-compliance
Lightning Source LLC
Chambersburg PA
CBHW022305211224
19295CB00001B/3